Frontispiece

MAJOR-GENERAL HUGH ELLES, C.B., D.S.O.
From a portrait by Sir William Orpen, A.R.A.

THE
TANK CORPS

BY
MAJOR CLOUGH WILLIAMS-ELLIS, M.C.
AND
A. WILLIAMS-ELLIS

WITH AN INTRODUCTION BY
MAJOR-GENERAL H. J. ELLES, C.B., D.S.O.

TO THE TANK CORPS

THE authors are aware that, despite their endeavours, the present book must, inevitably, contain certain inaccuracies.

Of many omissions they are fully conscious. The very scope of the subject, and the strict physical limitations of the book, have made necessary a drastic compression.

Most reluctantly they had to put aside or cut out the accounts of many brilliant individual achievements, many that would have added lustre to these annals.

Even the glorious and fatal action by which Captain Richard Wain won the Victoria Cross in the battle of Cambrai has found no place in the narrative.

Perceiving that not one-half of the deeds of gallantry could be recorded, the authors chose only those whose story chanced to illustrate a particular phase of the fighting, or of which a first-hand account was available.

The full tale of such actions—at least of those that were rewarded by decorations—may be found in the Tank Corps *Book of Honours*.

September 26, 1919.   *14 Queen Anne's Gate, S.W. 1*

INTRODUCTION

My dear Williams-Ellis,

You ask me for a foreword to your history, and invite me, too, to agree to, criticise, or even refute the conclusions of your Epilogue.

The first task I undertake with pleasure, though I feel it would be more justly and more skilfully done either by one of the pioneers who sowed that we might reap, or by the rare thinker who in our own time has contributed so much to keep us on the lines of clear understanding and progress.

As to the second task I must decline a direct reply, and for many reasons I can no more than touch generally upon the questions you have dealt with in so interesting a way. I find them, however, not yet sufficiently remote in time, either to be clear themselves, or to be distinctly placed in a picture itself still obscure.

. . . .

Of the early days of the Tanks, and of the early struggles, difficulties and hopes of the pioneers, I have no first-hand knowledge—to comment at any length upon them would be out of place. They do, however, represent a remarkable effort of persistent and courageous faith, of determination to succeed in the face of lukewarmness and even scepticism, of the overcoming of many practical difficulties. Above all, they present a great clearness of vision on the part of three men in particular—Swinton, Stern and d'Eyncourt.

It is remarkable that one of the first official papers on the tactical use of Tanks, written by General Swinton early in 1915, should have been almost literally translated into action on August 8, 1918.

To General Swinton, too, is due the implanting into all ranks of the fundamental idea of the Tank as a weapon for saving the lives of infantry. This idea was indeed the foundation of the moral of the Tank Corps, for it spread from the fighting personnel to the depots and workshops, and even to the factories.

More than anything else, it was this sentiment which kept men ploughing through the mud of 1917, in the dark days when often the chance of reaching an objective had fallen to ten per cent.; which kept workshops in full swing all round the clock on ten and eleven hour shifts for weeks and, once, for months on end; which, finally, secured from the factories an intensive and remarkable output.

Sir Albert Stern brought to his labours a whole-hearted energy and enthusiasm unsurpassed. But more practical than this alone, he ensured initial production by a contempt for routine and material difficulties and a resilience to rebuff as fortunate as they were courageous.

To Sir Eustace d'Eyncourt, the only member of the original Committee still officially connected with us, a great debt is due. We have been fortunate to have had at our disposal an engineer of his wide practical experience, who devoted much of his scanty leisure to our guidance both in policy and in detail, whose sagacious counsels have more than once checked the impetuosity of some of his associates.

. . . .

Before passing to the aspects of Tank history with which I have been directly concerned, I wish to make reference to two organisations vital to the Tank Corps in the field. For if that represented the point of the spear, they combined to form a most solid and dependable shaft.

The first of these two was the Training Organisations set up in England to produce the men; second, the manufactories which produced the machines.

The task of the Training Centre and the cadet schools was particularly onerous. The organisation of any new instructional centre in the haste and pressure of the times was no easy task—its work was often thankless and subject to much ill-informed and light-hearted criticism.

The Training Centre of the Tank Corps had additional difficulties. There was no guidance as to training—the entire system had to be thought out from the beginning, and continually modified by the experience of the battlefield—instructors had not only to be found but trained—esprit de corps and discipline had to be built up; and all this against time.

It may perhaps be a compensation to the many officers and men who lived laborious days, and were not rewarded by seeing the results of their work in the field, to know that " France " has never been under any illusion as to the great thoroughness of their work.

. . . .

The work carried through in the munitions factories, and the ingenuity and solid labour that backed the efforts of the soldier in the field, are perhaps not yet fully appreciated by the fighting men. In France one might hear of sporadic unrest, but till one met with it, one realised nothing of the genuine faithful grind at production of objects of whose destination the worker often knew nothing, of the blind patience under duress of shortage, and of crowded accommodation; of hope deferred.

The Tank Corps was fortunate indeed in having established at an early date close relations with its workers, and more fortunate still at a critical time in being able to declare a substantial dividend on the capital of wealth, labour and brains entrusted to it by its section of industrial Britain.

Once touch was obtained with the worker himself, the interest taken by J. Bull in the factory, in T. Atkins in the field, was more than fully proved, not only by the demand for copies of accounts of Tank actions, but by the steadily increased output that was maintained.

The thing is only natural. Put a man or a woman to turn out bolts from a machine for eight hours a day, and you will get a certain result. Tell her or him that the bolts will go into a Tank that will fight probably in six weeks' time; that the Tank will save lives and slay Huns; that yesterday Tanks did so-and-so; that last week No. 10567, made in Birmingham, and commanded by Sergeant Jones of Cardiff, rounded up five machine-guns . . . you will get quite a different result; moreover, it is John Bull's right and due to be told these things.

We had not got quite a complete result in this direction, but we were getting near it, and perhaps our co-operation of the back and the front was as nearly a microcosm of an ideal national co-operation in war as has been achieved. We aimed at Team Work.

. . . .

You who have coped in a short compass with the whole story of Tanks can well realise the difficulties of dealing concisely, even by comment, with the kaleidoscopic events of two and a half crowded years—with the questions of organisation, training, personnel, design, supply, fighting, reorganisation, workshops, experiments, salvage, transportation, maintenance.

I shall attempt no more than to supplement your admirably drawn narrative as to one or two points which appear to me to be of major importance or interest.

. . . .

The employment of Tanks in the field was one long conflict between policy and expediency. Policy seemed always to demand that we should wait until all was prepared, until sufficient masses of machines should be ready to use in one great attack that would break the German defensive system. Expediency necessitated the employment of all available forces at dates predetermined, and in localities fixed for reasons other than their suitability as Tank country. Battles are not won with Tanks alone, and in early 1917, for example, the Tank was still a comparatively untested machine. Indeed, the later issues of the Mark I. developed weaknesses in detail so alarming as to preclude anything more than a short-lived effort in battle.

Not until the Mark IV. machine was well into delivery could a guarantee as to its degree of mechanical reliability be given, and by that time the trend of the year's campaigning was unalterably fixed.

And so it was that it was our fate up to the first Cambrai battle to " chip in when we could " in conditions entirely unfavourable.

The employment of Tanks in Flanders has often been criticised, without intelligent appreciation of the fact that had they not fought in Flanders they would have probably fought nowhere. Better, therefore, that they should fight and pull less than half their weight, and still save lives, than that they should stand idle while tremendous issues were at stake.

. . . .

If employment in the field was a struggle between policy and expediency, the principles of production and design represented a direct conflict of opposing policies, resulting happily in compromise. The fighting man, conscious of the weaknesses of the earlier weapons, and visualising development which he believed to be obtainable, and knew to be necessary, and the soldier-engineer overburdened with difficulties of maintenance and cursed with the nightmare of Spares and Spares and more Spares—both cried aloud from France for rapid progress in design.

In England the other side of the picture was presented with equal force. The process of bulk production necessitates orders placed long in advance, materials were difficult to obtain, plans of track work and workshop organisation are not susceptible of change without delay, change, too, entailing irritation of factory staffs and workmen. Production once agreed to and embarked upon, a very complicated machinery is with difficulty set in motion. To stop or change this machinery results often in a loss of output which is in no way compensated by the improvements ultimately obtained.

The same problem must have occurred in many branches of war production. The best, however, is only the enemy of the good, if the good is good enough.

You have portrayed the difficulties arising from these conditions in Chapter V. The picture you draw belongs to the earlier stages, when the two sides worked rather upon regulation than upon formula. The later stages of the war saw a very full appreciation of each other's point of view and the growth of a very sturdy spirit of co-operation, which carried us over more than one difficulty to meet which special appliances or special construction were necessary.

. . . .

The Tank, as a weapon, has been threatened with several crises. Some have been averted by intelligent forecast in specification. Some have been dealt with by the improvisations of the engineers both in France and in England. Some have disappeared before a

Introduction

general improvement in design. You, I think, have touched on one crisis only—the mud crisis. The mud crisis was defeated at long last, but the swamp crisis, never. Although none of the other troubles was of long duration, any one of them, unless cured, would have caused a permanent disappearance of the arm.

Failure of rollers was succeeded by failure of sprockets. Sprockets and rollers were hardly cured when the German produced a very reliable armour-piercing bullet. This after a very short innings was defeated by the arrival of the Mark IV. Tank. The Mark IV. Tank was barely rescued from the mud of Flanders by the invention of the unditching beam, when we discovered that the Hindenburg trenches were about one foot too wide to cross without some form of help to the Tank. This difficulty was overcome, but about this time the effect of concentrated machine-gun fire upon Mark IV. Tanks must have become known to the Germans, as also their vulnerability to the ordinary field gun. The position with regard to both splash and casualties from guns firing over the sights, was becoming serious when the arrival of Mark V. Tank, with its increased handiness and speed, put an end to the splash difficulty for ever, and defeated the field gun for a good long time.

So on to the last days of the war, when we were able to look forward to 1919 with a certain knowledge that we had much in hand against any measure of opposition—short of a superior Tank—that the enemy could produce.

The idea undoubtedly exists still in the minds of certain people that the particular form of Tank which they have seen or fought with represents the latest word in design. It does not. The latest Tank produced in any bulk was the type that marched through London on July 19. It has never fought, and it represents the last word only of the elementary series of Tanks of which Mark I. was the original.

. . . .

If finality in design has by no means been approached in the war, the same may be said as regards the employment of the then existing types. This depended, after due consideration of their limitations and powers, on the training of personnel, not only of the Tank Corps, but essentially of infantry too. Lack of time, lack of opportunity, and wastage of trained personnel were the great difficulties which confronted commanders of every arm and formation in their efforts to reach even average standards of skill in only a few of the commoner phases of warfare. With the Tank Corps the additional difficulties of mechanical training were no more than balanced by freedom from the trench routine of troops employed for defence. For the infantry Tank, the training of Tank personnel alone is not sufficient. In the assault, Tanks are no more than a part of infantry, an integral part of the troupes d'assaut. *For real success, i.e., cheap success, not only must the two arms train and re-train together, but they should live together, feed together, and drink together.*

Much was attempted and much was done to supplement the lack of opportunity by demonstration, lectures, attachments. But by reason of the incomplete military education of our hastily-trained troops it was necessary to limit manœuvre and tactics on the battlefield to the simplest elements. Anything in the nature of finesse had to be avoided. Skilful use of ground and mutual fire support were things hoped for more often than achieved.

It was a question of bulk production against time, but the results obtained only prove how much more could be achieved with the same material had conditions of training been those of peace time with its long service and rigorous and plentiful supervision.

. . . .

The preceding paragraph may seem ungracious from one who has had the privilege of commanding a great force of citizen soldiers. It is nevertheless true that soldiering, like any other trade, takes time and experience to learn—that though there may be many who, being engineers, or advocates, or business men, or farmers, learn soldiering with great aptitude, the great bulk of any body of men, call them regular soldiers or citizen soldiers, require a deal of training under the best instructors, if they are to draw the full advantage from the ever-varying conditions of the battlefield.

. . . .

I have alluded above to the Tank Corps as a citizen force. It was, indeed, peculiarly so, for of the 20,000 odd souls that went to compose it, perhaps not more than two or three per cent. were professional soldiers ; and, while the General Staff officers on H.Qs. were almost without exception regulars, the whole of the Administrative and Engineering staffs with one solitary exception were drawn from various civil vocations.

Moreover, units as they came into being were built up, not on any old-time tradition of a parent regiment, but each one very much around the personality of its own commanding officer. And it has indeed been interesting to watch the development of particular idiosyncrasies of whole battalions and companies from the characters of their leaders.

Your record has faithfully set forth what has been accomplished by these troops. They are well able to sustain criticism in the light of their achievements.

. . . .

I have alluded before to the esprit de corps, founded as it was upon the sentiment of saving of life—a sentiment to which appeal has never failed. Other factors went to strengthen it. It was braced by a high standard of results demanded, by the determination to make good in spite of partial first successes. But the strongest element in it was the faith in our weapon—the machine necessary to supplement the other machines of war, in order to break the stalemate produced by the great German weapon, the machine-gun—our mobile offensive answer to the immobile defensive man-killer.

. . . .

It is indeed a curious reflection that the Germans before committing themselves to their great final offensive, should not have followed to their logical conclusion the preparations which they made for the preceding phases of the war with such meticulous forethought. In 1914, they removed from the path of their attacking infantry the prepared obstacles of permanent fortification by means of specially-constructed machines—siege cannon of unprecedented size. Later, they developed the machine-gun in bulk, and so modified the preconceived course of warfare to their own advantage for defence. It is astonishing that for their final offensive effort, they should not have equipped their men with armament for overcoming the very defence in depth supported by the very machine-guns from which they had reaped so much advantage in the previous years.

And yet we see them in March 1918 reverting after an initial attack, powerfully covered by artillery fire, to the same attempt to break through with men that had failed in 1914. Although machine-gun support was stronger, there was little help from the other arms beyond scanty artillery support and considerable frightfulness of day and night bombing and long-range bombardment. The German infantry was well, often magnificently, led, whether in Picardy or Flanders; and one could not watch the work of the strong offensive patrols without intense admiration of their skill and courage.

The Germans failed against defence in depth. The elements that were wanting were those of continuous mobility necessary to overcome such defence, against which infantry without powerful support and plentiful supply sooner or later become powerless. The Germans lacked the means to move and to supply their guns rapidly. They lacked Tanks to produce surprise or to carry forward the battle as an alternative to guns. They lacked lorries, they lacked cross-country vehicles.

With us, when the tide turned, the converse was the case, and it was at least a part reason of success against an enemy who fought bravely and often bitterly almost to the end.

. . . .

Whether you justly appraise the contribution of the Tank Corps towards the final victory is for history to declare—at some interval yet—but I am hardy enough to give you a parable in the terms of a great national pastime.

Rugby football of all games affords the closest analogy to war—

to warfare on the Western Front the parallel, without labouring the detail, is remarkable.

In the early nineties the accepted tactics of the game demanded a distribution of the team into nine forwards and six backs. The orthodox believed in forward play, and in emergency sometimes even a tenth forward would be added at the expense of one back.

At this time there occurred in the annual matches between two countries an uninterrupted series of defeats for one. As a measure of resource or despair, I do not know which, a new distribution was made in its forces. Instead of nine, eight forwards were played, one back was added—the fourth three-quarter.

The tactics were for the forwards to hold the opposing attack and for the backs to play offensively. The game is historic. For three-quarters of the match the nine forwards pressed the eight heavily, and these were very hard put to it to maintain their lines. In the last phase of the game one of the four three-quarters got away unmarked, the game was won and lost.

That was twenty-five years ago. The rules of the game remain unchanged, but the distribution of the players has been modified and the tactics of teams have developed on the lines of that historic match and beyond.

Whether the parallel of the Tank Corps to the extra three-quarter is a completely true one history will record in due season. What, however, we may claim is that the fourth three-quarter after a nervous start, in which perhaps he was sometimes out of his place, nevertheless on more than one occasion got away unmarked; that he ran straight even when he was being heavily tackled and drew the opposition for his side; that he went down well to the rushes of the German forwards; and that, finally, he more than once handled the ball in the great combined run which took his team from within its own twenty-five over the opponents' goal line.

Yours sincerely,

Hugh Elles

U.S. Club,
   July 28, 1919.

CONTENTS

CHAP.		PAGE
	INTRODUCTION	v
I.	A BRIEF ACCOUNT OF THE TANK, ITS CREW AND ITS TACTICAL FUNCTIONS, AS THEY WERE AT THE DATE OF THE ARMISTICE . . .	1
II.	THE EARLIEST TANKS—GENERAL SWINTON—ADMIRAL BACON—THE HOLT TRACTOR AND THE EVOLUTION OF THE "LAND CRUISER" .	6
III.	THE TANK CORPS IN EMBRYO	16
IV.	THE FIRST TANK BATTLES—THE ATTACK ON MORVAL, FLERS, THE QUADRILATERAL, THIEPVAL AND BEAUMONT-HAMEL	24
V.	WINTER TRAINING, EXPANSION AND READJUSTMENTS	39
VI.	THE BATTLES OF ARRAS AND BULLECOURT .	48
VII.	THE BATTLE OF MESSINES AND THE "HUSH" OPERATION	63
VIII.	THE FLANDERS CAMPAIGN—PREPARATIONS FOR THE THIRD BATTLE OF YPRES . . .	73
IX.	THE THIRD BATTLE OF YPRES	84
X.	THE FIRST BATTLE OF CAMBRAI . . .	100
XI.	THREE NEW TYPES OF TANK—THE DEPOT—CENTRAL WORKSHOPS	121
XII.	THE FRENCH TANK CORPS—AMERICAN TANKS AND BRITISH TANKS IN EGYPT	135
XIII.	SUSPENSE—THE "SAVAGE RABBITS" EPISODE—THE ENEMY'S INTENTIONS	153
XIV.	THE MARCH RETREAT	159

CONTENTS (*continued*)

CHAP.		PAGE
XV.	THE EQUILIBRIUM—MINOR ACTIONS—HAMEL—THE *BALLON D'ESSAI*	174
XVI.	WITH THE FRENCH—THE BATTLE OF MOREUIL	185
XVII.	THE BATTLE OF AMIENS, OR BATTLE OF AUGUST 8	191
XVIII.	THE GERMAN ATTITUDE—"MAN-TRAPS AND GINS"—THE BATTLE OF BAPAUME	216
XIX.	BREAKING THE DROCOURT-QUÉANT LINE—THE BATTLE OF EPEHY	228
XX.	THE SECOND BATTLE OF CAMBRAI, OR THE BATTLE OF CAMBRAI–ST. QUENTIN	243
XXI.	THE SECOND BATTLE OF LE CATEAU—THE RUNNING FIGHT	257
XXII.	THE ROUT—MORMAL FOREST—THE BATTLE OF THE SAMBRE—THE ARMISTICE	266
	EPILOGUE	273
	INDEX	285

LIST OF ILLUSTRATIONS

	Facing page
MAJOR-GENERAL HUGH ELLES, C.B., D.S.O. (*Frontispiece*)	
DIAGRAM OF MARK V. TANK	2
HOW THE UPTURNED SNOUT AND SLIDING TRACK WERE DERIVED FROM THE " BIG WHEEL " IDEA . *page*	15
THIEPVAL. THE ORIGINAL MARK I. TANK WITH ANTI-BOMB ROOF AND " TAIL "	32
FIELD CAMOUFLAGE	33
DIRECT HITS	48
BELLIED ON A TREE-STUMP AND SUBSEQUENTLY HIT .	48
A DERELICT, VALLEY OF THE SCARPE	49
A BURNING TANK	49
THE STEENBEEK VALLEY BEFORE THE BATTLE . .	82
THE SAME AFTER BOMBARDMENT	82
A FLANDERS " PILL-BOX "	83
THE " UNDITCHING BEAM " IN ACTION	83
A DEADLY SWAMP. (THE WRECKS OF SIX TANKS MAY BE COUNTED)	94
THE SALIENT	95
" CLAPHAM JUNCTION " NEAR SANCTUARY WOOD . .	95
A TANK CRUSHING DOWN THE ENEMY'S WIRE . .	116
PREPARING FOR CAMBRAI. (A TRAIN OF TANKS WITH FASCINES IN POSITION)	117
THE BAPAUME-CAMBRAI ROAD	117
GUN-CARRYING TANK TAKING UP A HOWITZER . .	124

LIST OF ILLUSTRATIONS (continued)

Facing page

A WHIPPET GOING IN	124
BERMICOURT CHÂTEAU, NEAR ST. POL. (TANK CORPS MAIN HEADQUARTERS)	125
SLEDGE-TOWING TANK TAKING UP SUPPLIES	125
THE ARMOURED CARS GOING UP	210
A TANKODROME	210
SMOKE-SCREEN AND SEMAPHORE	211
MOVING UP—BATTLE OF AMIENS	211
GERMAN ANTI-TANK GUNNERS	222
A GERMAN ANTI-TANK RIFLE	222
A CAPTURED GERMAN TANK	223
AN ANTI-TANK GUN IN A STEEL CUPOLA (YPRES)	223
THE BELLICOURT CANAL TUNNEL	248
CARRIER-PIGEON BEING RELEASED	248
INFANTRY ADVANCING BEHIND TANKS. A PRACTICE ATTACK AT BERMICOURT	249
HIS MAJESTY THE COLONEL-IN-CHIEF AND GENERAL ELLES	260
MANUFACTURE	261
THE WESTERN EDGE OF MORMAL FOREST	268
A " WIRELESS " TANK	269
MAP OF TANK OPERATIONS, AUGUST–NOVEMBER, 1918	272

THE TANK CORPS

CHAPTER I

A BRIEF ACCOUNT OF THE TANK, ITS CREW AND ITS TACTICAL FUNCTIONS, AS THEY WERE AT THE DATE OF THE ARMISTICE

I

THE secrets of the Tank Corps have been so well kept that there are few civilians who even now know anything of Tanks or their crews beyond what might be learned from photographs, or a distant view of " Egbert " or some other War Bond or Olympian Tank.

The Censorship has seen to it that the civilian has had no opportunity of making himself familiar with the tactical opportunities and problems that the use of Tanks has introduced or with the conditions under which Tank crews fight.

It is for the civilian reader that the present chapter is intended. He is to be given some idea of the oak tree before he is invited to dissect the acorn.

If he has no idea of the appearance and habits of the Tanks that fought at the Canal du Nord or that pushed back the enemy at Mormal, he cannot be expected to thrill as he should over the vicissitudes of the first converted Holt Tractor. For to one who had never seen the engine of a through express the history of " Puffing Billy " would almost certainly prove insufferably tedious.

The authors, therefore, propose to deal, very briefly, with the modern Tank before plunging the reader into the dark ages of 1914, where, to pursue our analogy, Watt's kettle-lid and the " Rocket " dwell obscurely.

II

Every detail of Tank Corps training, equipment, and tactics has been modified in view of some limitation or opportunity arising from the structure of the Tank itself. Therefore, though this book is principally concerned with the development of the Tank Corps rather than with the intricate evolution of the Tanks themselves, the reader will find it necessary to have a general idea of the construction and workings of the different types of machine.

It would indeed be as idle to describe the anatomy of a snail or a lobster without mention of its shell, as to endeavour to separate the story of the Tank Corps from that of its Tanks.

When the War ended in November 1918 there were, besides obsolete types which were still used for such work as carrying and the towing of supply sledges, three main types of Tank. First, the Mark V., which was 26 ft. long, 8 ft. 4 in. wide, weighed 27 tons, and had a horse-power of 150. The Male Tanks carried two 6-pounder guns, and one Hotchkiss gun. The Female carried five Hotchkiss machine-guns and no 6-pounder guns.

The Mark V. Star.—This Tank resembled the Mark V., except that it had a length of 32 ft. 6 in., and was designed for the transport of infantry and for the traversing of trenches too wide for the Mark V. Each had a normal speed of about five miles an hour, and was protected by armour up to five-eighths of an inch thick.

They were both so designed as to turn easily at their maximum speed, and carried attachments for use on soft ground, which increased the grip of the tracks.

Each was fought by a crew consisting of a subaltern and seven men, three drivers (two of whom normally fought the Hotchkiss guns), and three gunners.

The third type was the Whippet. The tracks were nearly as long as those of a heavy Tank, but the body had been reduced to a small cab perched at the back, rather as an urchin rides a donkey. It was armed with two machine-guns, managed by a crew of three men, and developed a speed of seven miles an hour. Whippets were designed for use as raiders and in conjunction with cavalry. In practice, however, the cavalry was seldom able to act with them. Partly in consequence of this, partly owing to the state of open warfare being of such short duration, the Whippets, though having brilliant feats to their credit (see the exploits of " Musical Box," Chapter X), remained creatures of promise rather than of achievement.

III

As a rule Male Mark V. Tanks were used against Pill-Boxes and other " strong points," while the special work of Female Tanks was to deal with hostile infantry (for example, by sitting astride and thus enfilading their trenches), and then

DIAGRAM OF A "MARK V."

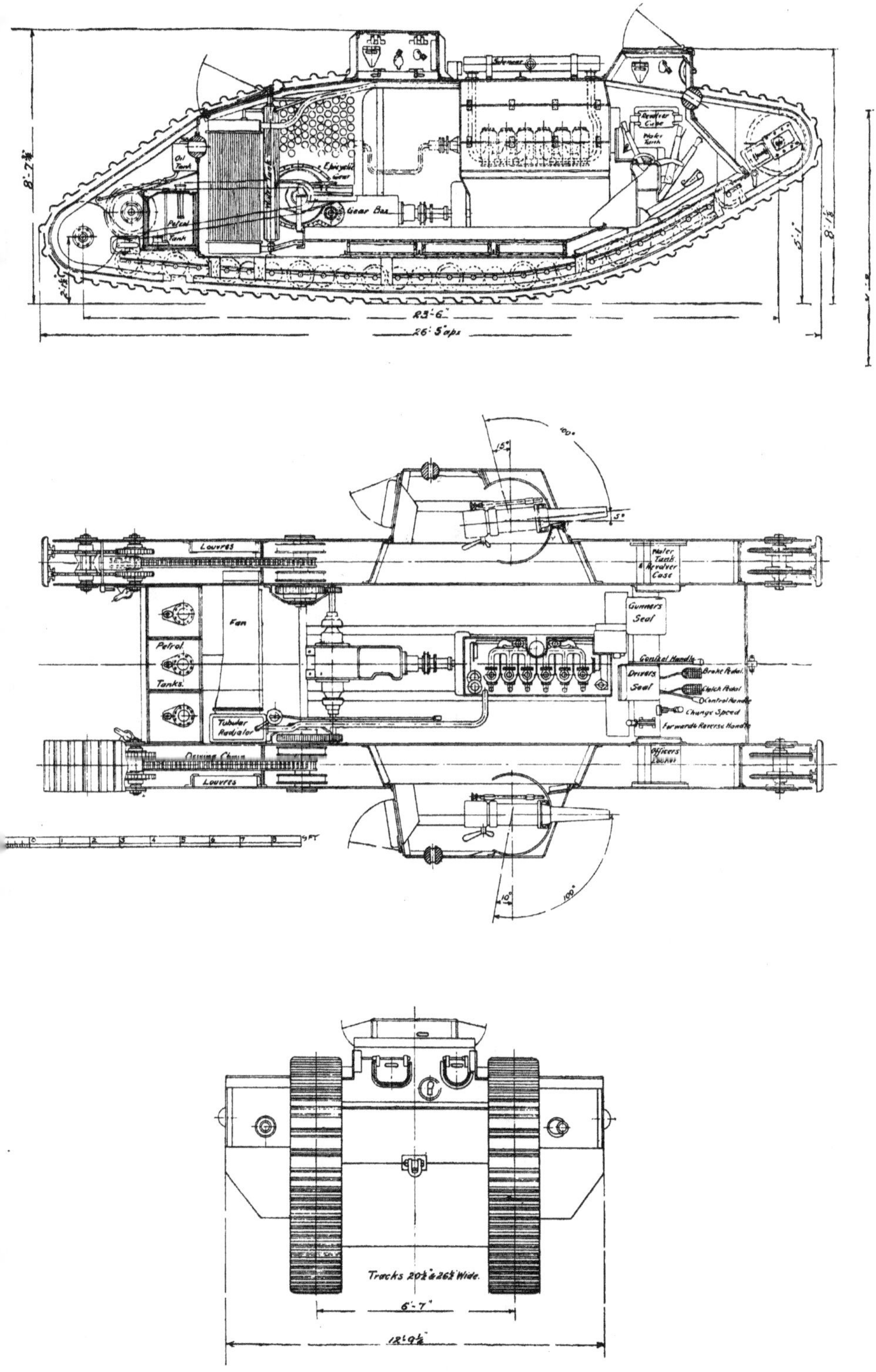

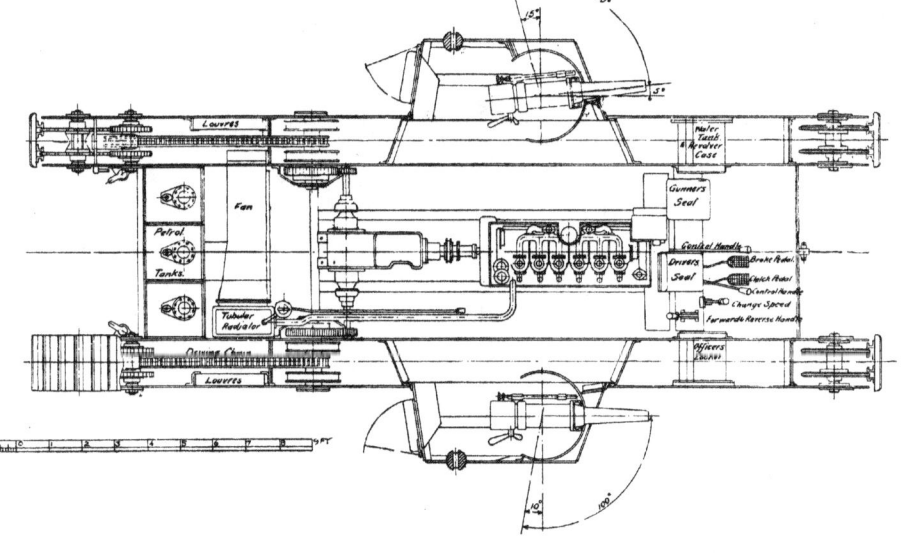

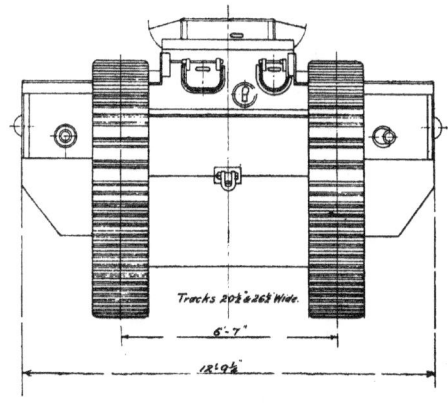

Tank Obstacles

to finish the process of flattening the enemy's wire which the Male Tanks had begun.

All three types of Tank were capable of going across country. That is to say they could, for example, follow a pack of hounds anywhere, except perhaps in the Fens.

Ditches, heavy plough, banks, walls, hedges, or fences could all be negotiated.

Tanks could also go over many obstacles—notably over wire—where the Field, even were they willing " to take a windmill in the hardour of the chase," must go round.

But as a moment's reflection will show, there must remain in every country certain features which will prove absolute barriers to the progress of Tanks.

Chief among these are canals and deep rivers (unless spanned by strong bridges), very steep railway cuttings, railway embankments, marsh, or woods in which the trees are too strong to be pushed over, and too dense-set to be steered through.

Besides these natural, or at least civilian, obstacles, there will be inevitable military obstacles in any country that has been fought over.

For example, old half-blown-in trench systems make ground " awkward," and Tanks operate at extreme disadvantage in country like that round Ypres, which was by 1917 a continuous network of water-logged shell and mine craters, with no original ground left at all.

Again, by the close of hostilities the number of anti-Tank devices employed by the Germans was very considerable. They paid the new arm the compliment of an intricate system of defence and counter-offence which included concealed Tank traps made on the model of elephant-pits, formidable double-traversed trenches, a branch of special anti-Tank artillery, heavily reinforced concrete stockades, and an elaborate system of land mines.

With so many obstacles to avoid or to negotiate, with their fate often hanging upon a prompt and accurate use of their guns, the crew inside the Tank were doomed by the conditions under which they fought to an almost incredibly limited view of the surrounding world.

When the flaps were closed (see Diagram showing interior of a Mark V. Tank), as they had to be directly the Tank came under close fire, the crew were in almost complete darkness, and had to rely upon their periscope or, alternatively, upon minute eye-holes (about the size of the capital O's used in this text) bored through the armour-plating. If the fire was at all heavy the periscope was usually quickly put out of action, and the officer and gunners had only the extremely limited view afforded by these holes.

They were thus almost entirely dependent upon their maps, the special Tank compass, and upon the information which a preliminary reconnaissance of the ground had given them.

This circumstance not only profoundly modified the training of the officers and crews, but also necessitated the organisation of what was almost a new service. This service was the "Reconnaissance" branch of the Intelligence. When the Tank Corps was ordered to take part in an attack, the Reconnaissance Staff was responsible for the preliminary survey of the proposed battle site, for a report as to where and how Tanks could best operate, and finally for a series of detailed maps and sketches. In these maps and sketches the route of every individual Tank was set forth from landmark to landmark, together with the assigned objectives of each machine and the obstacles which it was likely to encounter. These maps and sketches were compiled from aerial surveys, captured German maps and documents, information gained from local inhabitants, accounts given by prisoners, the original Ordnance survey, and from personal reconnaissance. By 1918 this system had been so developed that the infantry came to rely almost entirely upon their accompanying Tanks for direction.

This added greatly to the importance and responsibility of the work both of Tank Reconnaissance officers and of commanders.

IV

Topographical information can only be adequately conveyed to a more or less trained receiver, and it was therefore found necessary to add an elementary course on Reconnaissance to the already long list of subjects in which the members of every Tank crew must train. The crew were an assemblage of experts.

An average of about a month was spent by every soldier at the training depots and battle-practice grounds. Here each man did about ten days' course as a driver or gunner, learned revolver-shooting, signalling, and the management of carrier pigeons, and went through a gas course. In view of the probability of casualties, each man was also given a working knowledge of every other man's job. But most vital of all—the conditions under which Tank crews fought being out of the common trying and arduous—the scheme of training aimed at creating a high sense of discipline; that *esprit de corps* and that tradition of valour which teaches men to endure the unendurable.

This supreme end it achieved, as a perusal of the Tank Corps Honours List will show.

The Crews

Such, then, were the Tanks and their crews in the autumn of 1918.

In the pages which follow, the reader will see from how crude an embryo the Tank sprang, and through what hair-breadth escapes alike from official overlaying and annihilation by the enemy, it passed in the four years of which we are about to relate the history.

CHAPTER II

THE EARLIEST TANKS—GENERAL SWINTON—ADMIRAL BACON—
THE HOLT TRACTOR AND THE EVOLUTION OF THE "LAND
CRUISER"

I

THE War had only been in progress for a few weeks when the first idea of the first Tank was born almost simultaneously in the minds of General E. D. Swinton, Major Tulloch, Captain Hetherington and Mr. Diplock, and—if we are to believe rumour and their own account of the affair—of several hundreds of other gentlemen.

"Born" is perhaps not quite the appropriate word. At any rate it is to be understood, if not in a Pickwickian, at least in a Pythagorean sense.

For by 1914 the Tank had successively passed through several tentative and inconclusive incarnations.

In 1482 Leonardo da Vinci invented a kind of Tank;* a wooden "War Cart" was used by the Scottish in the fifteenth century.†

There were designs for a Tank for the Crimea, but the project of this weapon was abandoned as being barbarous Lastly, a really practical design for a kind of "Caterpillar" to be driven by steam was made in 1888. A trial machine was even constructed. But Fate decreed that all trace of design and model should be instantly lost, only apparently to be rediscovered after the modern Tank had been thought out afresh.

Why, if the Tank was constantly being invented, did it as constantly disappear? The reason appears to have been that, like the early aeroplanes, all these abortive machines had failed in one particular.

The engine was not powerful enough. The steam Tank had not in the least answered the riddle. The horse-power could, it is true, be almost indefinitely increased, but, like a kind of

---

* "I am building secure and covered chariots which are invulnerable, and when they advance with their guns into the midst of the foe even the largest enemy masses must retreat, and behind them the infantry can follow in safety and without opposition."

† It differed from an ordinary chariot in that the two little fat hollow-backed horses, which are depicted as providing the motive power, were, like the crew, enclosed within the wooden armour.

Old Man of the Sea, the engine weight would have increased proportionately and the " free " power have been no more.

Indeed, till the invention of the petrol engine the Tank was doomed to be unpractical. Its three essentials—armour-plating, guns, and ability to surmount obstacles and traverse open country—demanded a large amount of this " free " power.

Only, therefore, when an engine was produced whose proportion of power to weight was about 100 H.P. to every ten hundredweight, did the Tank become a possible and effective engine of war.

Thus, till the time was ripe the Tank had been doomed to enjoy very brief excursions into the actual, and to sojourn, long forgotten, beyond the waters of Lethe.

Does memory survive transmigration? Were General Swinton and his co-inventors aware of the Crimean Tank and the 1888 Tractor? In any case the matter is not one of great importance, for—to put it briefly—ultimately their Tank went, and the others did not.

By October 1914 Colonel Swinton and Captain Tulloch had independently worked out the details of an engine of war. Like the other early inventors, they imagined a machine that was to " arise " out of a cross between an armoured car and an agricultural tractor. It was to be slower, more formidable and far heavier than any armoured car that had yet been seen, a kind of "Land Cruiser" capable of plodding on its caterpillar feet across country right up to the enemy's gun positions. Like the other early " mobile machine-gun destroyers," it was to be strongly armed with guns and machine-guns, and so heavily steel-plated as to be impervious to shrapnel, H.-E. fragments and rifle bullets. It was to cross trenches with ease, and was to be capable either of cutting or of flattening the enemy's wire in the mere act of its progress.

By November Colonel Swinton and Captain Tulloch were in close touch with one another, and the child of their fancy descended from the clear regions of pure thought to battle its slow way forward amid the fogs and thornbrakes of actual experiment and official memoranda.

Well-informed readers will perhaps wonder why the present authors have singled out Captain Tulloch and Colonel Swinton from amid " the press of knights." Do they intend to lay the laurel on their brows? To declare that they alone invented the Tank?

The chroniclers pretend to no such judicial powers. Be theirs rather the genial rôle of the Dodo in *Alice in Wonderland*, who at the end of the Caucus-race allotted one of Alice's comfits to each of the competitors.

As far, however, as they can disentangle the complexities of the evidence, it does appear to have been through these two enthusiasts that the Tank idea first took tangible shape. The notion was in the air, perhaps it took unsubstantial form in other minds before October 1914—it seems probable that it did in Mr. Diplock's and Mr. McFee's, for example. Perhaps, too, in other minds it was later to take clearer and more practical shape.

But it does seem to have been Colonel Swinton and Captain Tulloch who, first of the band of pioneers, had the courage and the practical energy to forward a somewhat startling notion in official quarters.

For Mr. Diplock's first " Pedrail " machine, whose plans he laid before Lord Kitchener and Mr. Winston Churchill in November 1914, was a Gun Tractor, not a fighting machine. It was not till February 1915 that Mr. Diplock (in conjunction with a Committee appointed by Mr. Churchill) officially so much as contemplated the building of a " Land Cruiser."

Fortunately one of the first of the Swinton memoranda was submitted through Colonel Sir Maurice Hankey, Secretary to the Committee of Imperial Defence, who was an early and active friend to the idea of the new arm.

Difficulties, however, abounded. Many were actual, some were imaginary.

For example, it was urged that to design and build such machines would take over a year. Surely the war would be over!

Then when the counsels of those kill-joys prevailed who believed that the war would " hold," and it was decided to experiment with the " mobile machine-gun destroyers," various technical difficulties arose.

It was difficult to procure some of the essentials without elaborate manufacture and the making of special tools, and makeshift parts were, therefore, substituted. Fitted with these makeshifts, the Land Cruisers were a disappointment.

The first tests were carried out in February 1915, when Captain Tulloch's adaptation of the Holt Tractor was given a trial. It did not prove a complete failure, and much was learned from the experiment. For example, the machine was unexpectedly effective in rolling in the wire which it had been originally intended that its automatic " lobster-claw " wire-cutters should alone deal with.

In June Admiral Bacon's Forster-Daimler Tractor of 155 H.P., fitted with a self-bridging apparatus, was experimented with.

This, too, proved disappointing, in so far as the device was to fulfil the proposed functions of a Land Cruiser. It refused to cross trenches, though it proved a practical Tractor, and it was later used in "trains" of eight machines for the transport of 15-in. guns.

The position, therefore, in June 1915, as far as the War Office was concerned, was as follows : Proposals had been put forward by Colonel Swinton, Admiral Bacon, and Captain Tulloch, and submitted to the War Office; certain trials had been made, the result of which was, in the view of the authorities, to emphasise the engineering and other difficulties. It was only in June that the War Office ascertained that investigations on similar lines were being carried out by the Admiralty.

For the Admiralty, with a large land force at its disposal, had been for some time casting about for means whereby the men of that force might go into battle more in Navy fashion, that is (to misquote the "heroic Spanish Gunners") with something better than serge, "joined to their own invincible courage," between them and the enemy's bullets.

Mr. Churchill had, as early as January 1915, written a letter to the Prime Minister expressing his entire agreement with Colonel Hankey's remarks "on the subject of special mechanical devices for taking trenches."

The idea of employing a large armoured shield on wheels, or of using ordinary steam tractors on which a small bullet-proof shelter had been fitted, had been considered. Mr. Churchill interested himself personally in the scheme, and he and his expert, Major Hetherington of the R.N.A.S.—the third independent inventor—worked hard to evolve and then "push" a practical machine.

In the early spring of 1915 a Committee, called the Land Ship Committee, was appointed,* and many designs of wheel and caterpillar tractors were submitted to it. One of these designs was especially interesting not only for its astonishing appearance, but for the influence which it exerted upon the "profile" of the future Tank. The curious will find a brief account of it in the Note at the end of the chapter. It was Mr. Churchill's Committee who called in Major Wilson, Mr. Tritton, and Mr. Tennyson-d'Eyncourt as consultants, "when a design was evolved which embodied the form finally adopted for Tanks."

Thus, while the honour of the first designs and experiments belongs to the War Office, it was to the enterprise of this Admiralty Committee that most of the credit of the evolution of the Mark I. Tank was due.

It was, as we have said, apparently not until the Admiralty Committee had been at work for some time that the Director of Fortifications and Works, on behalf of the War Office,

* It appears to have been the Committee which investigated Mr. Diplock's machine, with some additional members.

ascertained that the Admiralty had designs for a Land Cruiser in hand.

The two Departments met at Wormwood Scrubs to witness the Admiralty's trials of a Killen-Straight tractor. It was a remarkable occasion, for a number of men who were destined profoundly to influence the history of the Tanks now saw a foreshadowing of such an engine for the first time.

Among them were Lord Kitchener, Mr. Lloyd George, Mr. Balfour, and Mr. McKenna. Mr. Winston Churchill was also there, but to him an armoured tractor was no novelty.

After this gathering the Tank enthusiasts of the two Departments fell upon each other's necks, swore eternal friendship, and in the middle of June formed a Joint Committee, of which Lieutenant Stern was Secretary.

Tanks—when any existed which would work—were to be a military service in the Department of the Master-General of Ordnance.

The Admiralty was to continue its work of designing, was to provide cash for experiments, and Mr. Churchill, its late First Lord, was to continue his invaluable work as a "propellant." All seemed prosperous, for the representatives of the two Services appear to have worked pretty harmoniously, and the better informed and more progressive heads of Departments on both sides showed an interested benevolence.

But unfortunately—especially at the War Office—there appear to have been a certain number of obstructionists.

One senior Officer, fearing, one supposes, to be diverted from his ideal of the official attitude by the sight of these ungodly engines, refused so much as to attend the trials. The "Competent Military Authority" (then, no doubt, poor man, sufficiently harassed) rigidly refused a single man for the new arm. Fortunately the Joint Committee was resourceful, and, after a preliminary appeal to Mrs. Pankhurst for militant suffragists,* they induced the Admiralty to turn over to them the 20th Squadron of the Armoured Car Reserve, and to increase the strength of this unit from 50 to 600 men.

By July Colonel Swinton—another of the Tank's best sources of power—had returned to France. G.H.Q. was later to be more propitious, but now the taste of those inconclusive experiments was still in its mouth, and their chief technical adviser had begun to have horrid doubts about the whole affair. "Caterpillars," he remarked, that he had lately seen "could only go at the rate of $1\frac{1}{2}$ miles an hour on roads, were very slow in turning, and nearly every bridge in the

---

* Although the appeal was necessarily tentative and unofficial, and no details of the nature of the work could be given, sixty women immediately volunteered.

country would require strengthening to carry them." "It was necessary to descend from the realms of imagination to solid fact."

Colonel Swinton explained and exhorted and expostulated.

II

Meanwhile the Joint War Office and Admiralty Committee system was too simple to last.

From August 1915 to August 1917, when the " New " Tank Committee was formed, the control and administration of Tank manufacture and design were extraordinarily tentative and shifting. Necessarily so. The home organisation had to expand very rapidly, and constantly to adapt itself to changed conditions of Tank tactics abroad and Tank manufacture at home.

Even the multiplicity of the authorities concerned seems to have been to a great extent inevitable. The Tank had, of course, initially complicated its early history by starting life in Infantry puttees and a south-wester.

At the point we have reached, its story plunges into a whirling quicksand of departments, branches, committees, and conferences, which were reorganised and rearranged—changed hats and functions with bewildering frequency. This tangle of activity Colonel Swinton throughout made it his hobby to understand and his business to co-ordinate.

The present historians, on the contrary, feel tempted to adopt the simple method of their Hebrew predecessor, who, having picked out one plum, so often blandly continues: " And the rest of the acts of the Trench Warfare Department and all that they did, are they not written in the book of the archives of the War Office?"

However, it is possible that the Hebrew historian honestly believed that the lost books of the Chronicles were really available to the inquiring reader. The present authors have no such illusion about War Office papers, and therefore propose to give at least an outline of the vicissitudes and fluctuations of early Tank control.

The chief persons of the Drama remain throughout:

The War Office: (1) In its capacity as Ordnance, and (2) in its capacity as General Staff. Later (3) as the Tank Department, War Office.

G.H.Q.: (1) In its main capacity, and as (2) The Experiments Committee.

Later, the *H.B.M.G.C.*

Finally, the Tank Corps.

The Admiralty: (1) In its capacity as the Land Ship Committee, and (2) as Squadron 20 of the R.N.A.S.

The Ministry of Munitions: (1) In its capacity as the Trench Warfare Department; (2) in its capacity as the Inventions Department. (3) Later, as the Mechanical Warfare Supply Department (really another Tank Committee). (4) Later still, as the Tank Supply Department.

The successive Main Tank Committees: (1) The Joint Naval and Military Committee (which did not survive Act I.). (2) The Tank Supply Committee, afterwards called the Advisory Committee of the Tank Supply Department, and divided into a main committee and a sub-committee. (It was this sub-committee which afterwards formed the backbone of the very active and occasionally criticised M.W.S.D., before referred to). Later, (3) after a gap, the First Tank Committee; (4) the Second reconstructed Tank Committee.

Grand Chorus of Directors General, Interdepartmental Conferences, Manufacturers, and Workshop Personnel.

III

We find that the period from August 1915 to February 1916 constitutes a kind of Act I. in the history of Tank administration and manufacture, for the 1914 and early 1915 period is too dim and legendary to serve as anything but prologue.

During the whole of the Act I. period it was the Admiralty and the Joint Land Ship Committee which played the "leads."

It was the Admiralty which defrayed the whole cost of the extensive experimental work and provided the necessary personnel, and it was by members of the Joint Committee in consultation that the Mark I. Tank, " Mother," was ultimately designed.

On September 11, two months after Colonel Swinton's visit, the Experiments Committee, G.H.Q., laid down in an excellent and far-sighted memorandum what were the qualities which they desired should be aimed at in designs for the caterpillar cruiser and what were the tactical purposes which it must serve.

By September 28 the Joint Committee had so far perfected the design of " Mother " as to have had a wooden dummy (officially described as a "mock-up") made, and on that day her counterfeit was inspected at Wembley by an Interdepartmental Conference, and approved.

Some weeks elapsed while the Joint Committee worked out the further details of their machine, and about December 3 Mr. Churchill wrote a Memorandum entitled "Variants of the Offensive," in which he paradoxically accentuated the value of defensive armour as a preservative of mobility. There was to be a new form of attack. It was to be launched at night under the guidance of searchlights. Caterpillar Tractors were to breach the enemy's line, and then turn right and left. The Infantry were to follow them closely under cover of bullet-proof shields.

On Christmas Day Sir Douglas Haig (who had lately taken over from Sir John French, and who as yet " knew not Joseph ") read the paper with interest, and pinned a pencil slip upon it, " Is anything known about the Caterpillar referred to in para. 4, page 3? "

No time was lost in finding out, and a few days later G.H.Q. sent an officer to England to inquire into the matter. This officer was Lieutenant-Colonel Hugh Elles, who was afterwards to be the first Tank General.

By the end of January 1916 the experimental machine—no pasteboard simulation, but " Mother " herself—was complete, and on February 2 the official trial was held at Hatfield, before the Army Council and a representative of G.H.Q.

" Mother " made good, and G.H.Q. asked to be supplied with a certain number of the Land Cruisers. A small Executive Tank Supply Committee with much fuller powers than the old Joint Committee, was formed under the Presidency of Lieutenant (now Colonel Sir Albert) Stern, and orders were at once given to begin manufacture.

So ended Act I.

IV

The first scene of Act II. (March to mid-August) was occupied with one of the most dramatic achievements of the War.

This was the manufacture at Lincoln of the first 150 " Land Ships " ordered by the Government, in the space of six months, and in absolute secrecy.

The public discussed the phantom Russians who travelled through England by night. It discussed the Germans who nightly signalled to each other throughout the inland counties. But it did not discuss the large water-tanks or cisterns that were being made for Petrograd, Egypt, or Mesopotamia, or some such place.

That this vital secrecy was kept for months by hundreds of people was chiefly due to the happy effect of copious and imaginative lying.

There was no mystery about these grotesque armour-plated creatures! They were not really for Mesopotamia at all. Every one knew that.

The Russian Government had ordered them. They were ridiculous things? Of course they were. It was a Russian design. Was there not even an inscription in Russian characters on them? At least they might frighten the Germans if they served no other useful purpose.

Tradition relates that when the first drawings were brought to the manager's office of the factory which had been selected for the manufacture of the "water-carriers," the manager and his staff expressed themselves as being seriously concerned for the sanity of the designers, and of those who submitted such drawings to practical men like themselves.

They were, however, let into the secret of the real part which Tanks were to play, and though still profoundly incredulous, decided, like good citizens, to carry out whatever work was asked of them. The vital necessity of secrecy having been impressed upon them, they were asked—tradition continues—what arrangements they would like made about sentries and the isolation of their workpeople. After a little consideration they answered that they would only guarantee that the secret should be kept on condition that they were given a completely free hand and not interfered with.

They proposed to have no sentries, no "isolated area" to proclaim trumpet-tongued, "Here is a secret!"

They desired merely to propound a satisfactory system of lies, to give an "alternative explanation"—to put it more delicately—and to carry out their work with a disarming publicity.

After some hesitation the authorities consented to this strange system. We shall see how, on September 15, " wisdom was justified of her children."

The factory where these curious interviews are reported to have taken place was that of Messrs. Forsters, Agricultural Implement Manufacturers of Lincoln. We almost literally beat our ploughshares into swords.

In London, changes in Tank administration were going on as usual. The trend as far as supply and manufacture were concerned was towards centralisation.

A Tank Supply Department was created at the Ministry of Munitions, and the Tank Supply Committee changed its name to "Advisory Committee of the Tank Supply Department." In August this Committee—gradually, as it were—turned into the Mechanical Warfare Supply Department before alluded to. Lieutenant (by now Colonel) Stern was at its head.

In the M.W.S.D. were now concentrated three separate functions:

They were Tank designers; they were responsible for supply; they were responsible for the final inspection of machines. The future was to show that such concentration had some drawbacks as well as many obvious advantages.

The Big Wheel

Note.—The genesis of the " large-wheeled tractor " was as follows : Trenches with a parados and parapet about 4 ft. high were being constructed by the enemy in Flanders.

The engineers consulted by the Land Ship Committee gave it as their considered opinion that if these obstacles were to be crossed, a wheel of not less than 15 ft. diameter would be necessary.

Machines with these gigantic wheels were actually ordered, but the wooden model that was knocked together as a preliminary at once convinced even its best friends that the design was fantastic, and that any machine of the kind would be little better than useless on account of its conspicuousness and vulnerability.

However, the " big wheel " idea did not utterly die, for in the upturned snout of the Mark I. Tank we have, as it were, its " toe " preserved, the track turning sharply back at about axle level, instead of mounting uselessly skyward, as would have been the case had not the old wheel idea been supplanted by that of the sliding track.

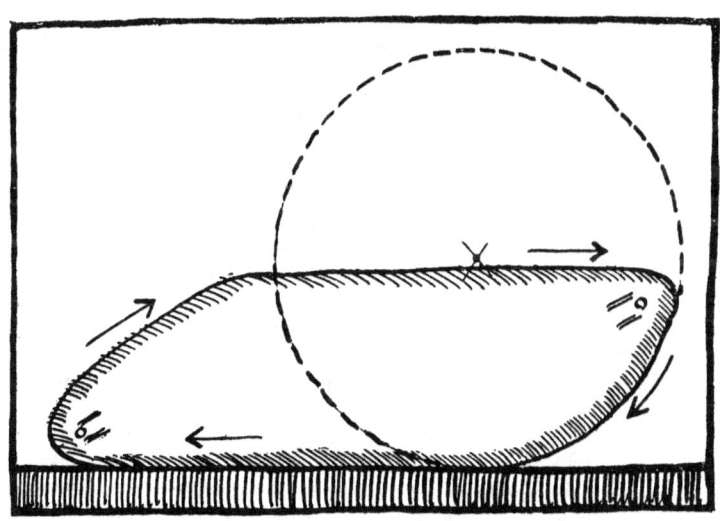

HOW THE UPTURNED SNOUT AND SLIDING TRACK WERE DERIVED FROM THE " BIG WHEEL " IDEA.

CHAPTER III

THE TANK CORPS IN EMBRYO

PART I

I

NOT till Act III. do we get the opening of the main plot of our drama. For it was only at the end of March 1916 that recruiting for the new arm began, and therefore that " The Fighting Side " first appeared.

*" At the end of March certain officer cadets with engineering experience and drawn from the 18th, 19th, and 21st Royal Fusiliers, were asked to volunteer their services for what they were given to understand was an experimental armoured car unit. (The Armoured Car Section of the Motor Machine Gun Corps.)

" Those who decided to throw in their lot with the new Service were interviewed by Colonel Swinton and Colonel Bradley, who, in the course of their examination, threw out no hints as to further details relative to the new unit. Results of these interviews were communicated on the Thursday before Easter Friday, when successful volunteers were informed that they were to be granted temporary commissions in the M.M.G.C., and were despatched the same morning to report to the M.M.G.C. Headquarters at Bisley. Upon arrival further information was received from the Adjutant that short leave would be granted for the purpose of obtaining kit, and that all officers would report their return with kit on the following Tuesday evening.

" During the week that followed Easter the two first selected Companies, *i.e.*, ' K ' and ' L,' were formed, officers being posted to one or other of the Companies."

Specially selected officers and men of the original M.M.G.C. formed the nucleus of these Companies, and the Companies

* Major Renouf.

were formed into a Battalion as further reinforcements arrived. On the Monday after Easter Bank Holiday training began, instructions being given in the use of the Vickers and Hotchkiss ·303 Machine Guns and later in the Hotchkiss 6-pounder Naval gun.

An officer who arrived in about the second batch tells how he and another man from the same regiment were sent down to Bisley after the usual brief but formidable interview with Colonel Swinton. They arrived at Brookwood Station only to be told that the ever-mysterious Motor Machine Gun Corps had left two days before for Siberia.

Tableau !

" Siberia " proved, however, to be a camp not so far from Bisley as to be beyond the radius of the station cab in which they both presently set off.

No Tanks were, of course, yet available for training, and therefore instruction was concentrated upon the use of the three guns, " each officer, N.C.O. and man being required to pass out at the examination."

> * " With the above exception, physical drill and an occasional route march, no further training of military character was imposed; thus in the early summer of 1916 practically all the personnel of the new branch of the service were efficient in the manipulation of the three guns in question. During the whole of the foregoing period no further information other than widely different rumours could be obtained by the junior personnel of the Unit as to the purposes for which they, or the experimental armoured car, would be used."

About June it became increasingly evident that if the Land Cruisers were to be fought that year, production must be accelerated.

> * " A very limited number of officers, N.C.O.'s and men, totalling about one dozen, were despatched to Lincoln and other centres, where they were employed in connection with what they later understood to be Tank production."

Meanwhile a very carefully chosen and elaborately prepared training area had been organised on Lord Iveagh's estate near Thetford, and as soon as information came that the first machines would soon be available for training, the Battalion was again moved.

* Major Renouf.

C

This time the still mystified companies found themselves in a camp more ringed about than was the palace of the Sleeping Beauty, and more zealously guarded than the Paradise of a Shah. Three rows of plantations and shelter belts guarded them from the eyes of the profane, and the intruder or the breaker of camp must pass six lines of sentries assisted by cavalry patrols.

A highroad which ran through the training ground was closed, and all inhabited farms within the area were evacuated. No civilians were allowed under any pretext to pass the guard, nor were troops allowed to leave the area except on production of special passes which were very difficult to get.

Once an aeroplane from a neighbouring aerodrome flew over, moved by a friendly spirit of inquiry. It was immediately greeted with a hail of machine-gun bullets and was obliged to depart in some haste.

For now the Tanks had to appear in their true character as fighting machines, and needed a better screen than Russian Fairy Tales. The machines had been long expected. Almost daily some one in the camp had " heard " an unfamiliar engine throb, and when this happened the entire camp would rush out to see if " they " had come.

The wildest rumours were afoot.

The car could climb trees! It could swim! It could jump like a flea!

Any one who has lived in an ordinary camp where there were no secrets and remembers what rumours flourished on the most ethereal food, can imagine their growth in a camp where there was a real mystery.

But at last, towards the beginning of June, a limited number of Mark I. machines were detrained at a special railhead within the area.* The training of the Battalion now began in earnest. Machines and men were destined to be launched in little over six weeks' time into the then newly begun Somme offensive.

Two types of Tank were detrained, " Big Willie " and " Little Willie." The Mark I. (Big Willie) was very different from the Mark V. machine described in Chapter I.

It took four men to drive it. It had an unwieldy two-wheeled tail, or to give this appendage its official name, a " Hydraulic Stabiliser." By this device it could let itself down gently over a drop of over 5 ft., and partly with the aid of it, the machine was steered.

In practice, compared with the handy Mark V., the whole steering arrangement of the Mark I. was extraordinarily clumsy and laborious. She would not turn sharply at all on rough

* Most of these Tanks were training machines, in the sense that their " armour " was boiler-plate instead of hardened steel.

ground, and had to be coaxed to any change of direction. Her engine and tracks also needed constant adjustment, the rollers being an everlasting source of trouble. Drivers and mechanics who have handled both machines, seem to regard the running of a Mark V. as child's-play after struggling with the caprices of " Mother."

" Little Willie " was used only as a training Tank, as in practice he was found to have a defective balance. His centre of gravity was misplaced, and he was, besides, too short for the work of crossing trenches.

II

But there were other than technical problems awaiting solution.

It would be difficult to over-estimate the difficulties which confronted those officers who were responsible for the preliminary training of the Heavy Section of the Machine Gun Corps; no one had ever actually fought inside a Tank, and it was, therefore, upon the spirit of prophecy alone that they must rely in their preparations. There was no manual to help them. They had, however, one very excellent official document, the secret *Notes on the Employment of Tanks*, which was issued in February 1916 (signed " E. D. S." *), which gave an extraordinarily good forecast of what the rôle of Tanks would probably be when in action.

But the paper was very short and very objective, and was more concerned with an analysis of the place of the Tanks in the orchestra of battle than with the difficulties presented by their individual score.

This was where the training of the first Tank crew fell short—almost inevitably. Their teachers had a rather hazy mental picture of the actuality of battle. They did not squarely face the essential question upon whose answer all specific training and all specific preparation depend, the question, that is, " What is it going to be like? "

Thus, though they did teach most of the essentials, they left out half a dozen subjects of which an accurate knowledge was, as we shall see, ever afterwards held to be absolutely necessary.

One of their difficulties was the shortness of the time. What must the crews know? Would physical fitness or map reading prove more important when the day came? Signalling or *esprit de corps?* Visual training or revolver drill? There was no time for everything. There were, however, obviously three

* Colonel Swinton.

or four essentials. Most of the officers and men were already first-rate engineers or mechanics, but they must be trained exactly in the strange machine they were to use. They must understand the peculiarities of Tanks, and, if possible, of their individual Tank, the monster which they had to render animate.

They must be thoroughly at home with their Vickers guns, be accurate shots with them, be able to remedy all stoppages, and to strip their weapons with speed and accuracy. Above all, crews must train together, be accustomed to work under their officer, each with his special work as brakesman, gearsman, driver or gunner, but each still part of an organic whole. They must also attain to a certain physical level, must undergo some visual training, and must know how to fire a revolver.

All this and more was achieved, for the men were picked individuals of more than ordinary intelligence, and soon became extraordinarily keen on their work.

* " If anything went wrong with the Tank, they used to look upon it not as a bore but as a pleasure to put it right. . . . We felt a terrific pride in our Company and Section, and also as a Tank crew against other crews. There was always healthy competition, and this competition carried us right out to France. . . . Besides that, Tank Commanders had the very great advantage of training their crews themselves. . . . We knew our men thoroughly."

But, as another Tank Commander wrote afterwards:

" The first Company to go out had to work at tremendous speed. The Tanks did not arrive till the last minute, and I and my crew did not have a Tank of our own the whole time we were in England . . . as our Tank went wrong the day it arrived. . . . Again we had no reconnaissance or map reading . . . no practices or lectures on the compass. . . . We had no signalling . . . and no practice in considering orders. This was a thing I very much missed when I got out to France. When you work with a Division you get very long orders, and you have to analyse these orders to discover what concerns you and what does not. . . . We had no knowledge of where to look for information that would be necessary for us as Tank Commanders, nor did we know what information we should be likely to require."

No one, in short, had sat down to imagine a Tank in action from within.

* Captain Henriques.

We had official painters in France, but alas! we had no official writers of prophetic fiction.

The history of the attack on Morval shows that this probably inevitable lack of, say, an official clairvoyant, this dependence upon methods of trial and error, though it ultimately did little to hurt the development of Tanks, did very much to prevent the Tank personnel from feeling satisfied by their début.

PART II

I

It must have been with some sense of having taken a momentous step that the authorities sanctioned the manufacture of 150 Tanks after witnessing the trials at Hatfield.

We were short of men and short of steel, and to divert steel from shells and men from the infantry was a grave decision. Our rulers were for a moment, perhaps, granted the gift of prevision. They saw that the new weapon might prove the sword that was ultimately to tip the level balance, and to break the intolerable equilibrium which had settled on the line from the Alps to the sea.

This prophetic mood did fitfully visit the authorities.

For a few months they would, as it were, have faith, and personnel would be granted and machines would be ordered.

Then perhaps for half a precious year they would relapse and backslide and revert, till Colonel Swinton, the Fighting Side, and all the other missionaries and preachers of the Tank Corps almost despaired.

But in February 1916 there was much to uphold them. The situation demanded some desperate remedy.

The balance hung deadly level. We could hold the Germans *now*, but for how long? The race for the coast had been a draw, and the First Battle of Ypres had ended open warfare on the Western Front.

> * "Quick-firing field guns and the machine-guns used defensively, proved too strong for the endurance of the attackers, who were forced to seek safety by means of their spades rather than through their rifles. Whole fronts were entrenched, and, except for a few small breaks, a man could have walked by trench, had he wished to, from Nieuport almost into Switzerland."

* From *Weekly Tank Notes*, a confidential official periodical for private circulation.

The Germans were dug in.

> *" And with the trench came wire entanglements—the horror of the attack—and the trinity of trench, machine-gun, and wire made the defence so strong that each offensive operation was brought to a standstill.
> " The problem which then confronted us was a twofold one:
> " Firstly, how could the soldier in the attack be protected against shrapnel, shell-splinters and bullets? Helmets were reintroduced, armour was tried, shields were invented, but all to no great purpose.
> " Secondly, even if bullet-proof armour could be invented, which it certainly could, how were men laden down with it going to get through the wire entanglements which protected every position?"

It was, in fact, impossible for infantry alone to attack such positions without the most extensive artillery preparation. The enemy and his trenches and his wire must be blown out of the ground. This was the accepted answer to the problem of the deadlock. But as yet we had not got the shells. We were straining every nerve to reach the solution by bombardment, but in February 1916 we had not got the necessary ammunition. Was there no other answer to the problem? Nothing that could be done meanwhile?

This was the mood in which the missionaries of the " mobile machine-gun destroyer " found the High Command. Had we had shells in February 1916 we should not have had the Tank. We must have waited another year for it, till, in fact, we had found out the defects of the hoped-for solution by bombardment.

The German, who was full fed with ammunition, felt at this early date no urging to go out and seek any such fantastic remedy. His High Command would have laughed at the idea of Tanks as Dives may have laughed at hungry Lazarus' antics over broken victuals.

II

So while our shells were making, we built Tanks. And Fate, whose taste in humour is not ours, and who knew what we did not, namely, that the Tank and prolonged artillery preparation are alternative weapons, decreed that both shells and Tanks should be ready for the Somme offensive.

It was thus upon a " substructure " of the new artillery preparation that we gaily imposed the Tank. We were to

* *W.T.N.*

take fourteen months in working out the proposition that they could never be effectively used together.

The Tanks had been designed for the sort of conditions which had prevailed at Loos. Their training grounds had been carefully modelled on the "Loos" pattern. By the time Tanks could be put into the field, a year later, our artillery superiority had completely changed the nature of the fighting.

At Beaumont-Hamel in November 1916, for example, we fired off as much ammunition as was expended in three weeks at the Battle of Loos.

On the Somme—owing to our having advanced—four miles of churned-up, shell-pitted ground had to be crossed before the front line could be reached. It had also—to state the case after the manner of the author of *Erewhon*—become the fashion, just before the day of battle, for the attacking side to blast the ground which they were about to cross to the condition of plum pudding on stir-up Sunday. This blasting process, moreover, necessarily gave the enemy several days' warning of any proposed attack.

It had also incidentally had another effect upon the industrious German. When we were bombarded our chief idea was retaliation; when the German was shelled he dug.

So it had come about that on the Somme, everywhere behind the German lines, were great electrically-lit and comfortably-warmed dug-outs, where a company or so could lie secure thirty or forty feet below ground and there wait for the bombardment to "blow over." Then they would emerge ready to welcome our infantry. Thus the system of the, say, six days' artillery preparation, though it did very much to raise our *moral* and depress that of the enemy, in time resulted in an almost complete system of enemy counter-measures, and in a state of the battle-ground which caused attackers and attacked to be almost immobile. The system, necessary as had been our adoption of it, had not solved the problem of the deadlock.

The Tank, as we have said, had been intended for use on reasonably sound ground. It was also to be a surprise weapon. Not once for the next fourteen months did we omit to give the enemy at least five days' notice of our proposed attacks, nor did we decline to co-operate with his artillery in reducing the intended battle-ground to a morass. It was, therefore, not till the First Battle of Cambrai, when we did adopt other tactics, that Tanks came by their own.

CHAPTER IV

THE FIRST TANK BATTLES—THE ATTACK ON MORVAL, FLERS, THE QUADRILATERAL, THIEPVAL AND BEAUMONT-HAMEL

I

It was not till the Somme offensive, which was launched on July 1, 1916, had been in progress for two months and a half, that it was found possible for the new arm to take its place in the fighting. We have seen how, secretly, urgently, behind a rich curtain of ingenious and circumstantial lies, the manufacture of the Tanks had been going on. How, secretly, urgently, the crews had been training for their unknown job.

Of the fifty Tanks which were destined to take part in the battle of September 15, about thirteen left England on August 15, and the rest followed at intervals and in driblets as the limited transport allowed. The last batch arrived on August 30 and, like its fellows, proceeded to the training centre at Yvrench. Here trenches had been dug and wire entanglements erected, and machine-gun and 6-pounder practice could be carried out after a fashion. But there was no staff of instructors, the ranges were too short, and the conditions for battle practice quite unlike those which prevailed on the Somme. But it had to suffice. The Tanks were wanted at once, and by September 10 "C" and "D" Companies had arrived in the forward area, their H.Q. being established at the Loop. It was thus within a week of their arrival forward that Tanks were called upon to take part in the attack.

The battle had now been in progress for nearly ten weeks. We had advanced and occupied a depth of four miles of devastated country.

Most of the men and many of the officers had not been to France before. They found themselves in a strange world. Endless lines of transport crawled over incredibly bad roads bordered by gaunt stumps of trees and by a sordid and tragic litter of dead men and horses, rags, tin cans, rotting equipment, and derelict transport.

Dilemmas

The enemy was counter-attacking over the whole of the thirty-mile front, and the sound of our guns was everywhere. At night the stream of lorries never ceased, and at some point or other in our line, far away, a star shell could always be seen sailing up from behind a rise of ground, giving some fringe of shattered wood, or ruined sugar factory, a fleeting silhouette against its cold white light.

All ranks were desperately busy, from the mechanics who had new spare engine parts to adjust, to those in command who had their own minds and those of several Major-Generals to make up. Colonel Brough had commanded when the Tanks disembarked, but had now handed over to Colonel Bradley, and he and the Army, Corps, and Divisional Commanders with whom he conferred on the 13th seem, perhaps inevitably, to have been as uncertain how to wield the new weapon as were the Tank Commanders of such details as how to fit their new camouflage covers or anti-bombing nets.

In an advance when ought a Tank to start? If it started too soon it would draw the enemy barrage; if it started too late the infantry would reach the first objective before it, and it would be of no use.

This and other similar dilemmas darkened their counsels, and it was finally decided that the Tanks' start should be so timed that they reached the first objective five minutes before the infantry, and, further, that Tanks should be used in twos and threes against strong points. No special or detailed reconnaissance work had been done, and a somewhat indigestible mass of aerial photographs was presented by the Divisional Staff to the bewildered Tank Commanders, many of whom had never seen such things before.*

Much more useful were a series of maps with routes marked out and annotated with the necessary compass bearings, and a detailed time-table with full barrage and other particulars. At least they would have been more useful had not all orders been changed in such a way at the last moment as to invalidate almost every route and hour which they showed.

Meanwhile the Tank crews and commanders had been enjoying three or four days of almost comically complete nightmare. In the first place, they had all manner of mechanical preoccupations—newly arrived spare engine parts to test, new guns to adjust, box respirators to struggle with, and an astounding amount of " battle luggage " to stow away. But worst of all, they found themselves regarded as the star variety-turn of the Western Front.

Already, before leaving Thetford, they had given a demon-

* See Plate facing p. 82. (An unannotated air photograph of badly crumped ground.)

stration before the King and several members of the Cabinet. At Yvrench they had performed before General Joffre, Sir Douglas Haig, and the greater part of the G.H.Q. Staffs,* but on reaching the Loop they found to their horror that it was to be " Roses, roses, all the way." A Tank Commander wrote bitterly :

> " It rather reminded me of Hampstead Heath. When we got there we found that the Infantry Brigades had been notified that the Tanks were to perform daily from 9 to 10 and from 2 to 3, and every officer within a large radius and an enormous number of the Staff came to inspect us. We were an object of interest to every one. This did not help on one's work."

On the 13th they were to move from the Loop to the point of assembly, and the problems of " housekeeping " became acute.

> † " The officer and each man carried two gas helmets and one pair of goggles, and in addition to their ordinary service caps, a leather ' anti-bruise ' helmet; we also had a large field dressing as well as an ordinary first-aid dressing. The usual equipment consisted of revolver, haversack, water-bottles and iron rations. There are eight people in a Tank, and as soon as they get in they naturally take off all these things, which lie about on the floor, unless you devise some method of packing all your equipment. . . . We carried, in addition to iron rations, sixteen loaves and about thirty tins of food, cheese, tea, sugar and milk. These took up a lot of room. We also had one spare drum of engine oil and one of gear oil, two small drums of grease, three water-cans and two boxes of revolver ammunition . . . four spare Vickers barrels, one spare Vickers gun, a spare barrel for the Hotchkiss and two wire-cutters. We also had three flags for signalling purposes, which unfortunately proved to have been lost when they were really wanted."

But Captain Henriques' list was, even so, not complete. Many Tanks also carried two carrier pigeons, 33,000 rounds of S.A. ammunition for their machine-guns, a lamp-signalling set, and a telephonic contrivance consisting of an instrument and one hundred yards of cable wound upon a drum. The second instrument was to be left at the " jumping-off place,"

---

* Among other Army Commanders was General Sir H. S. Rawlinson, who was later to be so good a friend to the Tanks. On this occasion, however, it is said that their performances left him completely cold and unconvinced.

† Captain Henriques.

and the Tank was to unwind the cable as it advanced, relating its experiences the while to the telephone operator or other interested person in the rear. What was to happen when the Tank began to traverse the hundred and first yard we do not know. In practice the device was not used.

But that was not all. The orders, time-tables and maps upon which the Tank Commanders depended, proved to have been issued in insufficient quantities.

> " For every three Tanks only one set of orders had been issued, and only one map supplied : consequently we had to grasp these orders before we passed them on to the other two officers."

However, at 5 p.m. on the day before the battle, these written orders were cancelled and new verbal instructions substituted. Roughly, the Tanks were to operate as follows :—

On the right with the 14th Corps, ten Tanks were to work with the Guards Division, and seven with the 6th and 56th Divisions, their objectives being Ginchy and the Quadrilateral.

On the left eight Tanks were allotted to the 3rd Corps, operating through High Wood and East of Martinpuich. The 15th Corps had seventeen Tanks attached, and the Reserve (5th) Army—fighting between Pozières and Martinpuich—had six Tanks.

With all these groups of Tanks the preliminary moving up into the first-line positions—in the pitch dark, through the mud and in and out of the shell-holes of badly crumped ground—proved most arduous, and a good many Tanks broke down in the process. One Tank Commander who struck a narrow sunken road remarks :

> " It was full of the bodies of dead Boches, and my driver did not like going along it."

For the Tanks' crews the remainder of the night passed in a final tightening of loose tracks and adjustment of the engines, and in listening to the steadily increasing crash and roar of the British bombardment.

The strain on men and officers had been tremendous. Most of them seem to have started the battle having had no sleep for over twenty-four hours.

They were desperately anxious, too, that Tanks should prove their worth, and the Mark I. machine was too capricious to give them much assurance.

To this list of discomforts must be added that most of the men had never heard guns before, and that the lying-up places were close to our batteries.

II

The morning of the 15th was fine with a thin ground mist, and at six o'clock the thunder of the British artillery rose to a final hurricane. The barrage crept forward, and our Tanks and infantry crossed the parapets.

The Germans seemed to have heard no breath of the nature of the new arm which was to be used against them, and the light haze added greatly to the looming mystery of the approaching Tanks.

Official documents that were later on captured from the enemy revealed something of the deep psychological effect that our Tanks had had on the German infantry. These significant admissions might have done more to convince our own High Command of the great potentialities of the new weapon than they actually did.

One of the best-known individual Tank exploits was that of the machine belonging to " C " Company, which helped a New Zealand and an English division in their assault upon Flers.

This was the furthest penetration achieved by any Tank that day.

This machine led its infantry, and these had their first taste of entering a village which they knew bristled with enemy machine-guns without suffering a single casualty.

The adventure had all the exhilaration of surprise, and the men, who had nerved themselves for the usual ordeal of house-to-house fighting, laughed at the astonishing anticlimax presented by their own and the Tanks' stately progress down an almost empty street.

" All dressed up and no one to fight."

It was on this occasion that the airmen's now famous message was sent back, a message whose repetition rather galled the Tank Corps in the days of ill-rewarded effort that still lay between it and its final triumphs :

> " A Tank is walking up the High Street of Flers with the British Army cheering behind."

Of two other Tanks which did particularly well, the first, a male, entered Gueudecourt, where it attacked a German Battery and destroyed a field gun; the other gave great assistance to attacking infantry which was held up by wire and machine-guns. The Tank Commander placed his machine astride the trench and enfiladed it; the Tank then travelled along behind the trench and 300 Germans surrendered and were taken prisoners.

Blooded

The following is a short summary of the returns of Tanks engaged.

The casualties among Tank personnel were insignificant, though one officer of great promise was lost:

- 49 Tanks were employed.
- 32 reached their starting-points.
- 9 pushed ahead of the infantry and caused considerable loss to the enemy.
- 9 others did not catch up the infantry but did good work in " clearing up."
- 5 became ditched.
- 9 broke down from mechanical trouble.

Of these last fourteen, some served as useful rallying-points for the infantry after they had become immobile, and several could have been extricated in time to render some service if they had not been knocked out by direct hits.

Crews who had been obliged to abandon their Tanks either got out their machine-guns and continued fighting or helped the wounded.

III

The battle had been essentially experimental. What opinion had been formed of the Tanks?

We now know what was the opinion of the German infantry. The German High Command seems in public to have ignored the new arm.

In a secret " Instruction " the Chief of the Staff of the 3rd Army Group, however, reminds units that they must " hold ground at whatever cost " and " defend every inch of ground to the last man."

" The enemy in the latest fighting have employed new engines of war as cruel as effective."

Every possible counter-measure is to be used against these " monstrous engines," which will probably be adopted on an extensive scale by the British.

To our own infantry the Tank appeared as a lusty friend, who had at last found a convenient way of dealing with the hitherto deadly partnership of wire and machine-gun—a friend, too, who had a grotesqueness of gait and appearance which was intrinsically endearing.

A wounded London Territorial said:

> " ' Old Mother Hubbard ' they called her and lots of other funny names as well. She looked like a pantomime animal or a walking ship with iron sides moving along,

very slow, apparently all on her own, and with none of her crew visible. There she was, groanin' and gruntin' along, pokin' her nose here and there, stopping now and then as if she was not sure of the road, and then going on—very slow, but over everything.

"It was her slowness that scared us as much as anything, and the way she shook her wicked old head and stopped to cough. It *was* a circus—my word! I only saw her for about ten minutes. She came humping out of the fog at one end of the line and humped into it again at the other. The last I saw of her was when she was nosing down a shell crater like a great big hippopotamus with a crowd of Tommies cheering behind."

To the British High Command the Tanks appeared as engines of war which showed considerable promise. They must overcome certain mechanical weaknesses, and tactics must be further modified to suit their peculiarities. The G.H.Q. attitude was, in short, that of men satisfied, though not enthusiastic, and was well expressed by Sir Douglas Haig in his Somme Despatch:

"Our new heavily armoured cars, known as 'Tanks,' now brought into action for the first time, successfully co-operated with the infantry, and coming as a surprise to the enemy rank and file, gave valuable help in breaking down their resistance."

The despatch goes on to mention the taking of Flers.

The delight of the British and French Press knew no bounds. The correspondents threw up their hats and set to to ransack their dictionaries for octosyllables in which to describe the new "All British" destroyer of Germans.

It was "Diplodocus Galumphant," it was a "Polychromatic Toad." It was a "flat-footed monster" which "performed the most astonishing feats of agility as it advanced, spouting flames from every side."

"It 'leant' against a wall until it fell and then crawled over the fallen débris.

"It went irresistibly through High Wood, the trees smashing like matchwood before it.

"It went up to machine-gun emplacements, 'crushed the gun under its ribs,' and passed on, spitting death at the demoralised Germans.

"It 'stamped' down a dug-out as though it were a wasps' nest.

"It crashed through broken barns and houses, 'straddled' a dug-out and fired enfilading shots down German trenches.

"It put a battery and a half of guns out of action at Flers."
Reuter added a cow-catcher to its equipment.
The French Press was enthusiastic:

> "At the precise moment when the bombardment stopped, the Germans had the surprise of seeing advance in front of the waves of assaulting troops, enormous steel monsters from which spurted a continuous fire of great violence. One would have described them as gigantic infernal machines. Their front, which was shaped like a ram, smashed down every obstacle. The heavy automobiles bounded across the overturned and uneven ground, breaking through the barbed wire and jumping the trenches. In the German ranks there was a really mad terror. A prey to panic, the soldiers of the German Emperor fell back in haste, abandoning their arms, ammunition and equipment."

And how did the Tank personnel itself view the events of the day?

Half choked with the engine fumes, boxed up for many hours without respite in the intolerable clamour and shaking of their machines, or, worse, having wrestled for hours under heavy shelling with a broken-down Tank, they were inclined to see the exasperations of the battle rather than its successes. It is indeed curious to note the difference in tone between the accounts of those who saw the Tanks dispassionately from without and those who had weltered within, between those who saw what the Tanks did and those whose view of achievement was obscured by a knowledge of what might have been.

The Tank Corps was too keen to be in the least satisfied by the measure of success which it had achieved.

Only the Press and the Germans perceived that a new "Excalibur" had been forged in England. "Out of the mouths . . ."

IV

After the battle, such of the Tanks as could go under their own power rallied, and steps were at once taken to salve as many as possible of those which had become incapacitated.

From this point, till all available Tanks had been used up and till the ground became finally impossible in mid-November, Tanks were to be constantly employed in insignificant numbers in a series of small experimental actions.

This method of fighting by twos and threes against special strong points was afterwards discarded, as it proved unsatisfactory. Several of these small actions were nevertheless very successful, and showed in miniature some special purpose which Tanks could serve, or illustrated the importance of some special Tank organisation.

For example, Thiepval showed how Tanks could be used without artillery preparation, and Beaumont-Hamel showed the importance of a good Reconnaissance Branch. These small actions were therefore important, not in themselves but because they were microcosms. In one or two unsuccessful actions it was rather the state of the ground which spoiled the battle than mistaken tactics.

For as the campaign drew on conditions became worse and worse. By the beginning of October the Army in general, and particularly the Tanks, had a foretaste of the miseries of Flanders. The general conditions of this part of the campaign are admirably described by Colonel Buchan in his *History of the War*:

> " October was one long succession of tempestuous gales and drenching rains.
>
> " To understand the difficulties which untoward weather imposed on the Allied advance, it is necessary to grasp the nature of the fifty square miles of tortured ground which three months' fighting had given them, and over which lay the communications between their fighting line and the rear. . . . Not the biggest mining camp or the vastest engineering undertaking had ever produced one tithe of the activity which existed behind each section of the battle line. There were places like Crewe, places like the outskirts of Birmingham, places like Aldershot or Salisbury Plain. . . .
>
> " There were now two No Man's Lands. One was between the front lines; the other lay between the old enemy front and the front we had won. The second was the bigger problem, for across it must be brought the supplies of a great army. . . .
>
> " The problem was hard enough in fine weather; but let the rain come and soak the churned-up soil, and the whole land became a morass. There was no *pavé*, as in Flanders, to make a firm causeway. Every road became a water-course, and in the hollows the mud was as deep as a man's thighs. . . .
>
> " The expected fine weather of October did not come. On the contrary, the month provided a record in wet, spells of drenching rain being varied by dull, misty days, so that the sodden land had no chance of drying. The carrying of the lower spurs—meant as a preliminary step

THIEPVAL. THE ORIGINAL MARK I. TANK WITH ANTI-BOMB ROOF AND "TAIL."

FIELD CAMOUFLAGE.

to a general attack—proved an operation so full of difficulties that it occupied all our efforts during the month, and with it all was not completed. The story of these weeks is one of minor operations, local actions with strictly limited objectives undertaken by only a few battalions. In the face of every conceivable difficulty we moved gradually up the intervening slopes."

Such was the setting of this batch of experimental actions. The first of them took place on September 25, when two small parties of Tanks were employed in two distinct actions; the first with the 3rd Corps, and the second on September 25 and 26 with the 15th Corps near Gueudecourt.

The first was a failure. Only two Tanks had been allotted; one was ditched on the way to the starting-point, and the other machine was caught in the enemy barrage and knocked out.

Very different is the story of the Tanks operating with the 15th Corps at Gird Trench near Gueudecourt, when with the help of a low-flying aeroplane 1500 yards of trench and 370 prisoners were taken by one Tank at a cost to us of five casualties.

The story is told in the Somme Despatch :

"In the early morning a Tank started down the portion of the trench held by the enemy from the north-west, firing its machine-guns and followed by bombers. The enemy could not escape, as we held the trench at its southern end. At the same time an aeroplane flew down the length of the trench, also firing a machine-gun at the enemy holding it. These then waved white handkerchiefs in token of surrender, and when this was reported by the aeroplane the infantry accepted the surrender of the garrison. By 8.30 a.m. the whole trench had been cleared, great numbers of the enemy had been killed, and eight officers and 362 other ranks made prisoners. Our total casualties amounted to five."

At noon on September 26 an attack was launched by General Gough's reserve army on Thiepval. Eight Tanks co-operated.

It was the second attack that we had made on Thiepval, of which the Germans had made a most formidable fortress. The ground had been blasted into the familiar alternation of crumbling mounds and water-logged holes, and the shattered houses and splintered trees—particularly a certain row of apple trees—stood up forlornly amid the general desolation.

From the point of view of the Tanks, however, the action was important, because here for the first time Tanks were employed in a surprise attack.

D

No artillery preparation was used, and

> "our men were over the German parapets and into the dug-outs before machine-guns could be got up to repel them."

A large number of prisoners were taken, and in the Somme Despatch the attack was noted as "highly successful," and the Tanks as having given "valuable assistance."

By the middle of October 1916, when Tanks were next in action, the ground was hopelessly sodden, and the story of the month which ensued might, with an alteration of place names, be taken for a narrative of the campaign in Flanders. Than this there is no greater condemnation.

It would be tedious to particularise the five or six minor actions in which Tanks played, or more often endeavoured to play, a part between October 17 and November 18. Excepting in the interesting little action which took place at Beaumont-Hamel, to which we have alluded before, no further light was to be thrown upon the uses and capabilities of the new arm.

The following account of the Beaumont-Hamel fighting was given to the authors by a Tank Officer who was present:

> "At the end of September it became clear that the Somme battle was fizzling out. The ratio of 'cost' to 'results' became more and more unsatisfactory; every advance, too, made the devastated and almost roadless area an ever greater problem.
>
> "It was decided that an attack, if possible a surprise attack, should be launched on the flank of the Somme battle. The position selected was roughly from about Serre to the high ground some half a mile south of the river Ancre. This sector had, of course, been attacked at the beginning of the Somme battle in July, but the attack had been a complete failure, and this front had relapsed into comparative quiet.
>
> "Tanks were collected and again entrained, the new detraining station being Acheux. This was the first of the many flank moves carried out with Tanks in order that a fresh front might be engaged.
>
> "On arrival at Acheux, however, at the beginning of October, very bad weather set in and the preparations for the attack were delayed. Day after day the rain continued, and the ground in the battle zone became steadily worse and worse. It was a trying time for the officers and men of 'C' and 'D' Companies, as they were not in very good accommodation just outside Acheux, expecting daily

to move up to battle. It was not until the beginning of November, however, that a move was made by night via Beausart to Auchonvillers and La Signy Farm. The Tanks having reached these lying-up places, the rain came down even faster than before, and a study of aeroplane photographs of the proposed battle sector showed that all the old shell-holes and many of the old trenches had filled up with water, and that the greater part of the front was in a hopeless condition for that type of Tank (*i.e.*, Mark I.).

"Just before the day of the battle, November 13, it was decided to send back nearly all the Tanks from La Signy Farm, and some of those from Auchonvillers, only a few being held in readiness in case the infantry advance should give scope for their use further ahead on better ground.

"Three Tanks of 'A' Company were due to attack with the main assault on November 13; and one of them succeeded in penetrating into the enemy's position and advancing for some distance along the enemy's support line and nearly reaching the Ancre before it became 'ditched.'

"Further north the attack had met with considerable success, except that the village of Beaumont-Hamel had held out for some hours. Tanks had been called upon to assist, and two of them had advanced along the road to Beaumont-Hamel; just about the time that they reached the village the remainder of the German garrison capitulated. Between Beaumont-Hamel and the river Ancre a considerable body of Germans were holding out in the enemy front and support trenches; although troops of the 63rd Division had reached the outskirts of Beaucourt well in the rear of this body of men, they continued to hold out throughout the day. Tanks were again called upon to deal with this situation. They reached the position the next morning, being led up by a trench mortar officer of the Division concerned. One Tank succeeded in crossing the very large German front trench, but, unfortunately, became stuck soon afterwards; the second Tank came to grief just before it reached the enemy front trench. It appeared that a deadlock had again been reached, and the crews of the Tanks were in a precarious position. On examining the ground about them the Officer Commanding the leading Tank (which incidentally was leading no longer, since it was stuck and all too stationary) noticed that the whole area appeared to be shimmering with white. On opening the front flap of the Tank and obtaining a better view, it was seen that all the German garrison, some 400 in number, appeared to have found something white to wave in token of surrender; those who could not produce anything better were waving lumps of chalk about or bits of board or rifle-stocks which they had rapidly chalked white. The situation was rather an embarrassing one for so small a number as the crew of two Tanks to deal with; fortunately, however, it was possible by signs, and with the assistance of the infantry, to 'mop up' these 400 prisoners before they realised that both the Tanks were stuck and out of action.

" Some of the worst of the ground was now in our line, and an effort was made to get the Tanks through this bad zone in order that they might continue to attack in the neighbourhood of Beaucourt. Efforts were made to prepare a track for the Tanks by means of a considerable digging party, but when the Tanks reached the very broken ground just north of the Ancre, they became one after another firmly stuck; with enormous efforts they were dug out, and succeeded in getting a few yards further, only to stick again. It was heart-breaking work, which would undoubtedly have been rendered far easier if the Tanks had then had the unditching beams which were only introduced some time later.

" Finally, on the evening of the 17th, only one Tank had succeeded in getting through this bad zone and reaching the comparatively good ground beyond. The crew, to whom great credit is due, had already been working continuously for some days and nights, and were not only exhausted, but had had no time to carry out any reconnaissance of the position which was to be attacked at dawn the next day. There being, however, only one Tank, made it of greater importance than ever that it should be made the most of. It was decided that it should be used against the very strong position known as the Triangle, which was a redoubt on the high ground, roughly midway between Beaumont-Hamel and Beaucourt. The ground about this redoubt was, unfortunately, also very heavily shelled, and a frontal approach with the infantry was impossible, and it was necessary for the Tank to go in on the flank while the infantry attacked the position frontally. It was realised that the first necessity was that the Tank should reach this redoubt as rapidly as possible, and during the night a route was taped slightly beyond our front line and directing the Tank straight for the Triangle. The weather was now much colder, and the frost rendered the ground less hopelessly outside the capacity of the Tank.

"Just before dawn, however, a fresh difficulty arose, and tried still further the already severely tried expedition. It began to snow, and the white tape which was to guide the Tank was obliterated."

Captain Hotblack (now Major, D.S.O., M.C.), the Reconnaissance Officer who had done the taping, was the only man who had reconnoitred this piece of ground, and he immediately volunteered to lead the Tank upon which so much depended.

Taking what little cover he could in shell-holes full of ice and water, he walked in front of the Tank past our front line close up to the Triangle. Marvellously enough, not one among the hail of bullets which greeted him and the Tank found its mark. Having succeeded in this arduous enterprise and having guided the machine to its position, he returned to report on the progress of the action. The light was now improving, and the Tank started its " rolling up " movement along the German trenches.

The machine was now so much in the midst of the enemy that the German artillery did not dare to open upon it, and the Tank poured in a devastating fire from its machine-guns not only upon the men in the trenches, but also upon some horse transport behind the enemy lines.

But, meanwhile, the infantry was hung up in another part of the field, and the Tank was urgently needed.

At that time signal communication to the Tanks was very imperfect, and there seemed no way of letting the Tank Commander know of the new development.

Again Major Hotblack came forward and again he crossed the fire-swept zone undeterred. He reached the Tank and piloted it back behind our lines, where a renewed attack was planned.

But before the tired crew could be sent out again, the wind changed and it began to thaw. The ground over which the Tank had passed with difficulty when it was hard became impassable, and the project was abandoned.

It was for this remarkable piece of work that Major Hotblack was awarded his D.S.O.

The incident naturally had far-reaching results. An inspiring deed, especially if it be one demanding skill as well as courage, will influence and " set the tone " of a new unit or a new branch of an old service. It is far more effectual than the most convincing arguments as to the necessity for a high standard of conduct and of competence. Much of the subsequent efficiency of the Reconnaissance Branch of the Tank Corps may be traced to this incident.

Reconnaissance took its proper place, it was recognised as

a fighting service, and its work was seen to be a necessary preliminary to every action.

Of the total of about ten Tanks engaged in other small actions which took place at this period, hardly one machine had satisfactory records to look back upon.

On November 18 ended the Tanks' first short campaign. If it did not close in a blaze of glory, at least it had been sufficiently successful for the authorities to decide not upon doubling but on quadrupling their establishment.

WESTERN FRONT SHOWING BRITISH LINES, XMAS 1916.

CHAPTER V

WINTER TRAINING—EXPANSION AND READJUSTMENTS

I

THOUGH plans for expansion and the complete reorganisation of the unit on a large scale had been begun directly after the results of the action of September 15 were known, little of the actual work of training could be started till the end of November, when the " veteran " Tank personnel were at last available as instructors. They were, as we have said, withdrawn on November 19 and moved to the Bermicourt area, which had been already prepared for them.

They were the leaven—less than one " old " Company to each new Battalion—who must impart their knowledge and experience to the new men.

A subaltern who had seen any fighting with the Tanks would suddenly find himself regarded as the greatest living expert on some obscure technical point, and the newly joined who had never seen a Tank " looked with awe upon these battle-tried warriors."

Men and officers were allowed to volunteer for the Tank Corps from other units either in France or at home. The notion of fighting in a Tank was popular, for on many of the men of the old arms—especially the infantry—the ordinary battle routine had—to put it conservatively—begun to pall.

Therefore, there was no difficulty as to supplies of men whenever the authorities turned the tap.

> * " We came from the infantry, from the cavalry, from the artillery, from the Machine Gun Corps, the Motor Machine Gun Corps, the Flying Corps, the Army Service Corps, and even from the Navy."

At first each individual wore the dress of his original unit, so that there was a strange collection of uniforms at Bermicourt

* Sergeant Littledale of the Tank Corps, writing in the *Atlantic Monthly*,

—Scottish bonnets and kilts, riding breeches, and bandoleers, every conceivable dress, even to naval blue.

> * "The spirit of adventure called us to the Tanks . . . and so the call for volunteers found us ready, and when the word of acceptance came, our hearts beat quickly and our hopes were high . . . some of us were selected because we were machine-gunners, and others because we were motor drivers. But there were many of us to whom the machine-gun and the motor were incomprehensible things. But in the end we did not find this lack of knowledge any handicap; for the Army authorities, who were wiser than we, knew that to men of average intelligence these things were easy to learn; and to our very great amazement we found that a week was all that was necessary thoroughly to master any machine-gun . . . and that it only took us two weeks to grasp the principle of the internal combustion engine and the mechanism of the Tank."

At Bermicourt and at Wool the deficiencies of the old Thetford training were realised. The experience gained on the Somme had been assimilated. Instructors now knew exactly what they must teach, and this time the spirit of the course of training was definite and businesslike.

The whole scheme was most carefully planned to ensure a proper balance, and the right amount of time was allotted to the different courses.

At first the work consisted chiefly in the training of more instructors, for the expansion of the Corps was to be rapid. The "settings" of all the courses showed great advances on the Thetford model, for at last the practice grounds could be made to resemble the actuality. There were old trenches and shell and mine craters, and the men were at once taken over bad ground, until the conditions of this curious progress became things of custom.

> * "There is not one of us who will ever forget his first ride—the crawling in at the sides, the discovery that the height did not permit a man of medium stature to stand erect, the sudden starting of the engine, the roar of it all when the throttle opened, the jolt forward, and the sliding through the mud that followed, until at last we came to the 'jump' which had been prepared. Then came the downward motion, which suddenly threw us off our feet and caused us to stretch trusting hands towards the

---

* Sergeant Littledale of the Tank Corps, writing in the *Atlantic Monthly*.

nearest object—usually, at first, a hot pipe through which the water from the cylinder jackets flowed to the radiator. So, down and down and down, the throttle almost closed, the engine just 'ticking over,' until at last the bottom was reached, and as the power was turned full on, the Tank raised herself to the incline, like a ship rising on a wave, and we were all jolted the other way, only to clutch again frantically for things which were hot and burned, until at last, with a swing over the top, we gained level ground. And in that moment we discovered that the trenches and the mud and the rain and the shells and the daily curse of bully beef had not killed everything within, for there came to us a thrill of happiness in that we were to sail over stranger seas than man had ever crossed, and set out on a great adventure."

The necessity of regularising and systematising the Reconnaissance Branch had not been forgotten, and a separate Reconnaissance Service—really a specially adapted branch of " Intelligence "—was set up, under Major Hotblack.

The first organised work of the Branch was to be done in the preparations for the Battle of Arras, and it is at that period that we shall see the tentative beginnings of the very special system which was later on developed.

For the present " Reconnaissance " spent its time lecturing and being lectured, and in preparing maps or training areas for theoretical or practical exercises in the new art of Tank warfare.

II

By February 1917, when individual courses came to an end and unit training began, the H.B.M.G.C. was about 9000 strong.

Warmed by the sun of official approval, and watered with a kindly dew of Memoranda and official " definitions," Companies had budded into Battalions and later Battalions were to burgeon into Brigades.

Even by this early date the authorities intended that ultimately three Brigades of three Battalions each should be formed.

Each Battalion was to be equipped with seventy-two machines and to consist of four fighting sections, a Headquarters Section and a Battalion Workshop, besides that curious collection of miscellaneous individuals, tailors, barbers, shoemakers and clerks, which is necessary in every unit. General Elles was to command in France, and took over on September 29 with the rank of Colonel. His " charter " was as follows :

"The Headquarters in France is to command the Heavy Branch M.G.C. in the field, to be responsible for the advanced training and for the Tactical employment of the Corps under the command of the C.-in-C."

He was also to have a large Central Depot and Repairing Shop in his charge.

In England there was to be a Headquarters directly under the War Office and which was to administer the Corps as a whole. The home Headquarters was to be responsible for the provision of men, for supplies of "technical material," the preliminary training of units, and the maintenance of units in France as regards men, machines, material and spare parts.

The experienced reader will perceive in this system of dual control a very promising sowing of dragon's teeth.

No one who has had an inside knowledge of the growth of any unit or of any institution whatsoever during the War will be surprised at the fact that the Tank Corps did not escape the common lot. It suffered from growing pains.

Is there a new Ministry, a new Hospital, a new Factory, a new Battalion, nay, a single new Committee, the tiniest Association of Allotment Holders, the smallest Village Ladies' Work Depot, that did not?

Among such organisations there are but two categories—those who have the candour to acknowledge that they went through such a period, and those who still dare not trust themselves to allude to it. Perhaps if we consider the examples that come within our own experience, we shall find that the stronger and more vital the new unit, the more capable and full of character the men who moved it, the more marked was that initial stage of uncomfortable adolescence.

The settling down, before responsibilities and prerogatives had been properly paired and allotted to the right individuals. The time when one department was still irritable from overwork and another exasperated by not being given enough responsibility. We have all of us known such a time, and most of us now look back upon its very real miseries with a kind of mingled wonder and amusement. Not otherwise do the pioneers of the Tanks look back upon their awkward age.

As soon as the programme of expansion had been decided upon * the question of how Tank production could be increased became an exceedingly important one. Owing to the inevitable loss in battle, and still more to the unfortunate defects of the type of the track roller then supplied, there were not enough

* The progress of this decision has been slightly telescoped, the "operative" resolutions only being recorded, and the story of a good deal of proposal and counter-proposal omitted.

Tank Production—"Jorkins"

Tanks even for the training scheme proposed for France, where there were in December 1916 only sixteen machines in working order. The needs of the big training centre which was setting up at Wool could not at present be met at all, and the accumulation of any adequate reserve of fighting Tanks was, for the moment, impossible.

The Mechanical Warfare Supply Department was now responsible for Tank production, and they had the task of arranging for the building of the 1000 Tanks which had been sanctioned on September 29.

In November the M.W.S. Department made an unofficial forecast of the probable rate of production. This forecast they confirmed officially on February 1.

The total output of Tanks was to be roughly as follows:

1917	
January	50
February	50
March	120
April	120
May	140
June	200
July	240
August	260
September	280

Of these, after March at least eighty per month were to be of the Mark IV. type, of which, with the Mark IV.*a*, there was to be a total of over 1000.

In August or September, a proportion of the output was to be of the greatly improved Mark V. type. Actually at the end of March only sixty Tanks could be scraped together for the Battle of Arras, and most of these were machines that had been repaired after the Somme.

Not a single Mark IV. machine arrived in France until April 22, after the Battle of Arras had been fought and won, and no Mark V. machines until March 23, 1918. The entire programme was, in short, many months late.

The M.W.S.D. were, however, not altogether blameable for the occasionally somewhat astonishing discrepancy between their promises and performance.

It is, in fact, related for the defence that even the airy promises had their purpose—that the very discrepancies which the Fighting Side viewed aghast were deliberately created by the wily M.W.S.D. as bogies with which to scare supine manufacturers or reluctant Government Departments.

"What!" the M.W.S.D. would say. "You can't do better

than that! But look what we've actually promised! And just see what sort of names our partners the Fighting Side are calling us already! You *must* do better." A duly enraged Fighting Side must have made an unsurpassable Jorkins.

In any case, however, it was usually only the M.W.S.D.'s promises which could even be called in question. Considering the means at their disposal and the difficulties which surrounded them, their practical efforts were praiseworthy.

Their troubles came chiefly from three sources. Some of the difficulties from each were inevitable, and some were not.

First there were the physical difficulties of manufacture. The shortage both of labour and material was acute, and at the period with which we are now concerned, Tanks came low in the Ministry of Munitions' priority list. Shells, guns, aeroplanes and even transport lorries all took precedence of Tanks.

A second difficulty was the habit which the Authorities had of blowing alternately hot and cold, according as Tanks momentarily did well or ill in the field. This resulted in a tendency towards a see-saw of alternate periods of slackness and overwhelming hurry in the factories.

Tradition relates that Sir Albert Stern (the Director-General of the M.W.S.D.) here played a most useful part. He used his whole influence to maintain a steady output, acting, in fact, as a kind of stabiliser.

The third set of difficulties came from the M.W.S.D.'s own Tank designers, and from the technical experts of the Fighting Side in France. Both constantly asked for small alterations in design. Often these alterations were necessary; frequently they were more or less frivolous, even when they came from what might be considered the best source, that is, from those who fought the Tanks.

If the M.W.S.D. was sometimes accused of adopting an academic attitude towards the results of the "acid test" of battle, it may as truly be said of the Fighting Side that they often underrated the difficulties and problems of manufacture and failed to appreciate how often quality could only be obtained by a disproportionate sacrifice of quantity.

III

About the end of December 1916, when the dual control of Tank affairs had been working for nearly three months, it became obvious that the system was not one that would easily stand the strain of active operations. The Tank Corps had outgrown it, and the shoe would soon begin to pinch. General Elles thus summarised the position in his report of December 31:

Organisation—The Headless Dog

"*In France.* The fighting organisation is under a junior officer who *faute de mieux* has become responsible for initiating all important questions of policy, design, organisation and personnel through G.H.Q., France, and thence through five different branches at the War Office.

"*In England.* Administrative and training organisation are under a senior officer, located 130 miles from the War Office, with a junior Staff Officer (Staff-Captain) in London to deal with the five branches above mentioned.

"The system is working now because Headquarters in France have been free from the questions of operations for most of the last six weeks, and have, therefore, been in a position to deal imperfectly and at a distance with the larger aspects of the whole matter.

"This will not be possible when operations become a more pressing obligation, as they are now doing.

"Then, this duty must devolve either on the five War Office branches, not one of which, I submit with all respect, can have any comprehensive grip of the subject, or on the G.O.C., Administrative Centre, who is out of continued personal touch either with the War Office or the requirements in this country, and is, moreover, debarred by his charter from really having any control or direction except at the instance of his Junior.

"In actual fact, the Director-General of Mechanical Warfare Supply, an official of the Ministry of Munitions, at the head of a very energetic body, becomes the head of the whole organisation. This officer, owing to his lack of military knowledge, requires and desires guidance, which none of the five departments at the War Office can, and which the G.O.C., Administrative Centre, is not in a position to, give him.

"In effect the tail in France is trying to wag a very distant and headless dog in England. We have had one check already in the matter of the increased weight of Mark IV. which it is possible may have serious results as regards transportation.

"In view of the inevitable expansion and great possibilities of this arm of the Service, I wish to urge most strongly that a Directorate (however small to begin with) be formed at the War Office on the lines of the Directorate of Aeronautics. Its functions to be to study possibilities of development, to watch design and supply, to co-ordinate training and administer the Corps as a whole. The officer in charge to be a senior officer, free to travel and empowered to issue definite instructions and decisions as to requirements to the Ministry of Munitions."

As a result of this remonstrance, General Capper was appointed to the War Office, and the first Tank Committee was set up in the following May.

This Committee was commissioned "to systematise and strengthen liaison between the Army and the Ministry of Munitions."

But when we consider the list of its members we do not find a single representative of the still drooping "tail." *

However, the appointment of the Committee proved to be a step in the right direction, and an improvement began to be felt immediately.

Officers of the Tank Corps now took charge of the final running trials of all Tanks. The M.W.S.D. submitted their designs to the Committee, and in several other small particulars the control exercised by the Military side was increased.

But in August the Committee was rent asunder.

A Memorandum was submitted by the two military members, calling attention to the long and serious delays that were still occurring in the preparation of new kinds of Tanks, after the execution of the designs had been approved by the Tank Committee.

The delays, it stated, were largely due to the absence of direct intercourse between the Committee as a body and the actual designer, and they recommended that the designer should be *ex officio* a member of the Committee.

Sir Albert Stern and Sir Eustace Tennyson-d'Eyncourt dissented strongly from this Memorandum—we are not told upon what grounds—and in October a new Tank Committee was formed.

At last—upon this new Committee—the "tail" was fully represented, and the Committee met fortnightly alternately in France and in England, so keeping in touch with both factors in its work. A satisfactory organisation seems, in fact, to have been found, and the interests of all the departments involved in manufacturing and fighting these complex machines seem at last to have been adequately represented. After October difficulties appear to have been halved.

But this happier era did not dawn till after the Battle of Arras had been won, and the long misery of the Flemish campaign had somehow been endured. Meanwhile, as far as Tank control was concerned, things went on much as before.

---

* The list was as follows :
  Chairman.—Major-General Sir J. Capper.
  War Office.—Lieut.-Colonel Sir J. Keane.
     Lieut.-Colonel Mathew-Lannaw.
  Ministry of Munitions.—Lieut.-Colonel Stern.
     Sir Eustace Tennyson-d'Eyncourt.

The reader is to imagine that just such "growing pains" and just such difficulties, correspondences and memoranda filled in the background for the next six months, while the fighting at Arras, at Messines and in Flanders, whose story we are about to relate, was in progress.

CHAPTER VI

THE BATTLES OF ARRAS AND BULLECOURT

I

THE Reconnaissance Officers were the first of the Junior personnel to learn that operations were contemplated for early April, and that the new battle was to be fought before the town of Arras on the banks of the river Scarpe. By the beginning of March, the first small parties of Battalion and Company Reconnaissance Officers had begun to leave Bermicourt.

It was rumoured that this offensive was going to be the blooding of the 1st Brigade; it was to be on a much larger scale than any the Tanks had taken part in on the Somme. It was said that sixty machines would be thrown in in one action. The Tanks were going to have an opportunity of making a name for themselves, and of justifying all the embarrassingly pleasant things that the newspapers had said of them in the previous September. For this lavish praise had spread a gloom over the Tank Corps; they had been unmercifully twitted by unfeeling gunners and infantrymen who knew the real facts.

The newspapers had succeeded in making their intercourse with any but battalions fresh from England one unbearable round of facile jest. Never had any unit, save, perhaps, the London Scottish, been so unmercifully hailed as " Mother's blue-eyed boy."

By March they lusted for blood, and the first whispers of battle were listened to with a satisfied expectancy.

The new 1st Brigade of the Heavy Branch Machine Gun Corps was a very much more assured body than the little band of pioneers who had waited so anxiously for the dawn on September 15, 1916.

Owing to delays in manufacture, they were still only equipped with 60 Mark I. Tanks instead of about 120 Mark I.'s and Mark IV.'s, as had been hoped. Still, the March 1917 Mark I. was very different from the September 1916 Mark I. The most

DIRECT HITS.

BELLIED ON A TREE-STUMP AND SUBSEQUENTLY HIT.

A DERELICT, VALLEY OF THE SCARPE.

A BURNING TANK.

striking improvement was the shedding of the cumbersome and ineffectual " Tail " or hydraulic stabiliser.

Most of the machines had also undergone a most careful overhauling at the Battalion workshops, and those innumerable tiny adjustments, repairs and improvements which constitute " tuning up " had been made.

The machine-gun armament, too, had been modified, the Hotchkiss being replaced by the Lewis gun. A new contrivance for use on soft ground had also been fitted, consisting of stout little cigar-shaped splinter-bars, a yard or so in length, attached to the track by means of chains.

But more particularly crews had had proper time to train and they knew that they knew their work. Their officers, too, were sure that they would this time be properly supplied with maps and detailed orders. Therefore, officers and crews got on with their own battle preparations, or, later, rehearsed the coming action with the infantry, with a good heart.

II

In the front line active preparations had begun. The Reconnaissance Officers, several of whom took up their quarters in the half-deserted town of Arras, had each had his area allotted to him, and they were busy helping " Q " side to find suitable positions for the supply dumps, for at this time there was no system of supply Tanks. Every tin of petrol, every round of ammunition, had, therefore, to be carried by hand from the railhead, and the task was one which took weeks to complete.

It was calculated that had supply Tanks been available each machine would have saved a carrying party of 800 men. The real work of the Reconnaissance Officers, however, was to observe the enemy's lines and the country which lay beyond them.

Much of this country, even within our own lines, was practically unknown to us, as the greater part of the sector selected for attack had only just been " uncovered " by the sudden and unforeseen German retirement. On this portion of the line the retirement had occurred about a month before the battle was due. As in other parts of the line, and as the enemy had intended, the retirement had proved extremely embarrassing. We had carefully selected a site for our battle, and the chosen ground had been thoroughly studied.

The sudden change to a piece of imperfectly known country involved an enormous amount of extra photographing, map-making, sketching and reconnaissance generally. This was merely troublesome; more uncomfortable was the element of uncertainty which the retirement introduced.

Would the enemy stand? And, if so, where? Was there some trap being prepared for us? It was uncanny, for it was contrary to the tradition of more than two years of trench warfare.

The final scheme of the attack was, however, planned on the assumption that the enemy would give battle. For he now held a line of great natural strength which he had improved with extraordinary skill and energy. The scheme, as it affected the Tanks, was shortly this.

The general object of the action was to achieve a rapid success. That is, to inflict a wound in the first twenty-four hours, severe enough to force the enemy to bring up his reserves, thus depleting his line near Soissons and Reims, where the French offensive was to be launched immediately afterwards.

A proportion of Tanks was allotted to each of the Armies taking part.

1. *With the First Army* ("D" Battalion) to the North:

    Eight Tanks were to operate against Vimy Heights and the village and heights of Thélus, considered amongst the most formidable enemy positions in France. Tanks were to play a subsidiary part, as the soil here was a soft heavy loam, highly unfavourable to Tanks.

2. *With the Third Army* ("C" Battalion):

    Forty Tanks were to operate, some north, some south of the river Scarpe. This sector contained several notorious strong points, such as the Harp and Telegraph Hill. The ground here was hard and chalky and afforded good going for Tanks, though it was intersected by old trench lines and had been heavily crumped.

3. *With the Fifth Army* ("D" Battalion):

    Twelve Tanks were to operate in the region of Lagnicourt. Here the ground conditions were bad. The roads especially had been destroyed, and it was found impossible to bring up sufficient artillery for a preliminary bombardment. Therefore, on this sector Tanks were to play a leading part, preceding the infantry and largely replacing the barrage. This action was not to be launched till about forty-eight hours after that on the other two sectors. Zero day was to be April 9, and the attack was to be made at dawn.

III

Till the night before the battle the work of preparation had gone smoothly.

Maps had been issued, stores stood ready, pack animals and limbers were at hand to form advanced dumps.

The Reconnaissance Officers had taken little parties of Tank Commanders to the best observation posts in their sectors, and had there shown them the ground they must cross and expounded their maps to them. All the Tanks had been brought safely to their railheads and successfully detrained, and now they lay waiting in their tankodromes. "C" (afterwards No. 3) Battalion lay in Arras itself. The town had been most carefully prepared for troops to assemble and wait in.

Great chalk quarries underlay it, and these had been linked up and lit with electricity, and here two divisions could lie thirty feet underground secure from the heaviest shelling.

The Tanks had chosen the Citadel as their assembly place. There in the great grassy ditch of the old Vauban Fort they lay, nosing for cover into the re-entrant angles of the tall cliff of mellow brickwork that towered above them.

As soon as it was dark, on the night of April 8-9, the Tanks set off on their journey up the line.

There had been a question as to the route which these Tanks were to follow.

The alternatives were a long detour round the head of a shallow valley or a short cut over ground of questionable soundness.

The short cut had finally been decided upon, and, on the Reconnaissance Officer's report, the Battalion had applied for enough brushwood and sleepers to build a rough causeway.

Owing to transport misunderstandings and difficulties, only a very small proportion of this material arrived in time. It was, however, decided still to chance the short cut. Brushwood had been laid in some of the worst places and the ground had a firm top. It was thought probable that this would, after all, bear the weight of the Tanks.

Alas, the hope was vain! The smooth turf proved to be no more than a crust, covering a veritable bog, and it broke through when the column was about half-way across. In the darkness six Tanks floundered one after another into the morass.

The scene which followed is described by an officer who was present :

"Never shall I forget the scene at Achicourt on the eve of the battle. It was round about midnight when I got there and pitch dark save for the fitful light from the still burning village * near by and the flashes of the guns.

"We had got word of 'trouble near the railway crossing,' and trouble indeed there was.

"There, sunk and wallowing in a bog of black mud, were some half-dozen Tanks—Tanks that should by then have been miles ahead and getting into their battle position for the attack at dawn.

"Instead, here were the machines on which so much depended, lying helpless and silent at all sorts of ominous angles, and turned this way and that in their vain struggles to churn their way out of the morass.

"About them were great weals and hummocks of mud and ragged holes brimming with black slime. The crews, sweating and filthy, were staggering about and trying to help their machines out by digging away the soil from under their bellies and by thrusting planks and brushwood under their tracks. Now and again an engine would be started up and some half-submerged Tank would heave its bulk up and out in unsteady floundering fashion, little by little and in wrenching jerks as the engine was raced and the clutch released.

"Then the tracks of a sudden would cease biting and would rattle round ineffectively, the ground would give way afresh on one side, and the Tank would slowly heave over and settle down again with a perilous list, the black water awash in her lower sponson. No lights could be shown on account of enemy observation, and at any time he might reopen with his heavy artillery, which had already been blasting the immediate neighbourhood earlier in the night.

"Altogether it was a desperate and discouraging business for those of us who knew that there were infantry already assembled for the morning's assault who had practised with us, who looked to us for a lead across the German wire, and who must now do as best they might without us."

In the event, however, it did not turn out as blackly as those at the Achicourt slough had feared.

Had the approach march of the Tanks been run to time, the column would almost certainly have come in for the blowing

* Achicourt.

The Bombardment 53

up of the ammunition dump at Achicourt, which was hit and exploded by a German shell soon after nightfall.

Also, the half-dozen Tanks that were extricated from the bog too late to join in that morning's attack, provided a small local reserve that later proved of the utmost value and had an appreciable effect on the course and ultimate issue of the battle.

The ruins of Achicourt continued to smoulder through the night.

> * "It had just been very badly shelled by the enemy. Two sides of the square were burned and blasted away (it had been all right, nearly, when I passed through it a few days before). The ruins still smoked and glowed, and shadowy working parties shovelled rubbish into shell craters to make them passable for transport and cleared a way through the sorry wreck. Smashed limbers, strings of dead mules, burnt-out and buckled motor lorries, transport wagons, and the like, all rather weird and depressing, the red glow of some other conflagration as a background, and this stabbed with the flicker of white light from our guns, little and great—thousands of them (actually), a throbbing roar in the distance, and fit to deafen you anywhere near. The great thing is to go about with an open mouth. It equalises the pressure on your ear-drums. I am acquiring a permanent droop of the lower jaw. Anyway, a discouraged, shell-shaken sentry told me that one could not go through for the shells, mostly our own, exploding in the fire, and refused to let me take the car in. It did not look anything like as bad as he tried to make out—from the danger point of view—and indeed when I walked through there were the working parties stolidly filling up the craters by the light of the glowing ruins. Having fulfilled my mission, I got back to report at Brigade Headquarters about 4 a.m., and then set out again at 4.30 to follow the battle and note and report the doings of our Willies."

IV

At about 3.30 a.m. heavy rain had begun to fall, and all day the armies fought amid intermittent storms of sleet and drenching rain.

> † "Our bombardment was quite unimaginable—all that

---

* Letter from a Tank officer dated "April 9, evening."
† Letter from an eye-witness written on the evening of April 9.

could possibly be desired, I should think, for accuracy, evenness and intensity. The final barrage was a really wonderful sight; just at dawn the grey sky ablaze with star shells and coloured rockets all along the line, nothing else to be seen.

"Then when it got a little lighter and the barrage had crept on, we could see thousands of our men popping up from their barely visible 'assembly slits' in the ground and pouring up the slope in a slow-moving, loose sort of crowd with no discernible formation, and with and among them, the Tanks.

"They had previously come up across an apparently deserted valley over the heads of our waiting infantry in their shelter trenches. They appeared breasting the hill, and disappeared over the brow together with the attacking waves of troops. The enemy's shrapnel and high explosives that came back were almost laughable in comparison with what we put over them, and our casualties were, on the whole, unusually light. Where I was watching was reported to be the hardest nut on the whole line.*

"What with the barrage and the Tanks the defence appears to have just collapsed, and a few minutes and a few casualties gave us possession of a wonderful redoubt that the enemy had lavished extraordinary ingenuity and industry in preparing for many months past.

"I saw it all from a hedge in a hillside about 1000 yards away. I had determined on the spot, and, as luck would have it, I found when I got there that there was a half-finished observation post with a lovely little pit to jump down into if things got hot. However, there was no need to use it. It was only getting into it that was rather exciting. I got spattered with débris time and again, but by tacking, waiting, and using the country, I got through without any real unpleasantness.

"It's been a real thoroughgoing victory so far as we can see and hear—or rather hear, for I only saw the first phase. Good old Willies, it's partly their victory, too, as all can see. Wonderful messages come in, a dozen or more to the hour, reports, telegrams, telephone messages, kite balloons, aeroplanes, pigeon letters, etc., and nearly all good, *awfully* good.

"'We have reached Z.22.B.64 and are going strong.'

"'Have taken Tilloy Village.'

"'Over 2000 prisoners in our Corps cages already, including thirty officers and a Battalion Commander.'

* The Harp.

" ' Nine hundred prisoners, scared and starved, *moral* rotten.'

" 'Have reached the Blue Line,' *Signed* Daphne, 'Consolidated at Y.13.C.68 to 15.D. Central,' only we don't consolidate, we just hammer on line after line exactly to programme and as never before.

" ' Tanks seen zero plus 5 hours 15 minutes in the " Howitzer Valley " accompanied by infantry. Guns still in position, gunners not.'

" And so on; and our blue cardboard slips representing infantry and my little red flags, denoting Tanks, march on and on and on."

Partly owing to the weather conditions and partly because the sixty Tanks were strung out along so wide a front, Tank Commanders had been told to act more or less independently against the strong points which had been allotted to them. Once zero had struck, therefore, the history of the battle becomes, from the Tank point of view, chiefly that of the exploits of individual machines.

The only exception is the history of the eight Tanks operating with the Canadians at Vimy. Alas! their story is easily summarised.

It had been originally decided that if the weather was wet no Tanks were to operate on this sector at all, as the condition of the ground was already exceptionally bad. The eight were to be sent down to reinforce the 5th Army where the going was good.

As luck would have it, April 7 and 8 were fine, and it was determined that the Tanks should not be sent down, but should go in on the ridge. When a drenching rain set in two hours before zero it was too late to alter the plan of attack. The result was as had been expected.

Every Tank without exception ditched or got stuck in No Man's Land or in the enemy front line.

Therefore, the Tanks claim no share in the Canadians' brilliant and historic taking of the ridge.

So great was the Canadians' *élan*, and so successful was our barrage, that by the time the Tanks were extricated there was happily no rôle for them to play. They were, therefore, withdrawn as quickly as possible, and were, after all, sent down to reinforce the 5th Army.

With the 3rd Army, several Tanks performed interesting exploits.

Second Lieutenant Weber's Tank, " Lusitania," for example, spent an exciting and profitable two days. This machine was some three hours late in starting owing to trouble with the secondary gear. Just as it was getting off, word was brought that the infantry was held up. The arrival of the Tank effected an entire change in the situation, and a machine-gun placed in a wood north of the railway having been silenced by the Tank's 6-pounder fire, it proceeded towards the Blue Line. The infantry advanced at the same time, and both reached the next enemy trench together.

The movement was carried out in such close alignment that the Tank was prevented from making use of its guns and enfilading the trench, but the Germans, unable to face the combined attack, held up their hands and surrendered. The Tank then cruised along the railway towards Fleury Redoubt, firing as it went with its 6-pounder and Lewis guns. The Germans made haste to evacuate the Redoubt, and could be seen to take refuge in a dug-out close to a railway arch.

The Tank drew on towards the arch, firing in its progress at any object suggesting a machine-gun emplacement. Near the arch it found itself under our own barrage and also shelled by an anti-Tank gun. It accordingly wheeled about, re-climbed the slope it had just descended, and signalled to the infantry to come on. Then, returning to the arch, it mounted guard while the infantry unearthed the Germans who had taken refuge in the dug-out. This point disposed of and a steep bank hindering further advance, it was found necessary to take a southerly course to find a more possible place for climbing, the engine having become badly overheated. Indeed, so hot was it that the machine now jibbed at the easiest exit from the valley that could be found, and there was nothing for it but to wait until the engine should cool down.

On the instant that the Tank Commander announced his decision to lie-up, down dropped each man of the crew where he sat or stood, overcome by heat and the cumulative exhaustion of days and nights of almost ceaseless preparation.

Shells whined and droned overhead, and would now and again pitch in the valley on this or that side of the Tank, throwing up a brown cascade of earth with a reverberating crash.

Along the western bank of the valley were the excavated and concreted pits that had sheltered the enemy's guns for two and a half years. From some the pieces had been withdrawn, in others our fire had caught the gunners and their teams in the very act, and the valley bottom was strewn with tragic heaps—guns, limbers, men and horses, huddled together in shapeless tangles of brown and grey, or tossed apart to lie singed and torn amongst the short grass and the shell-holes.

Down near the railway arch through which the valley track led to the river Scarpe, one diminutive Highlander had paraded a drove of some 200 prisoners who had somehow come under his sole charge.

They were neatly lined up in fours, each man with his hands above his head, and as they drooped from weariness or fidgeted from fear of the shells that continued to fall haphazardly about them, their small and solitary escort would flourish, and more than flourish his bayonet. Up would go the 400 hands once more and the parade be restored to order.

Not for nothing had one young Scotsman been taught the value of discipline.

By the time the engine had cooled down, the crew been roused, and the far bank surmounted, the infantry were well on their way to their objective. Dropping into third gear the Tank gradually gained on them, and its commander, observing that they had entered the German trench, swung half right and took a course through the barbed wire parallel to it. On the flank of the 15th Division, the trench was seen to be still in German hands. The Tank opened fire accordingly with 6-pounders and machine-guns, doing what damage it could. It caused a redoubt to be evacuated, it searched out and caused two snipers to surrender, and later in the evening, in answer to an urgent request from a Colonel of infantry, it approached within fifty yards of a trench and silenced two out of four machine-guns. Then, the already defective magneto giving out altogether and the Tank being brought to a standstill, it opened a heavy fire along the trench with Lewis and 6-pounder guns. Having thus killed many Germans, and the engine refusing to restart, the commander at 0.30 p.m. decided to abandon the Tank, after a full twelve hours in action.

It had then been dark for some time, and the Germans had kept up a lively fire on the stranded Tank with rifles and machine-guns, taking aim at the chinks and loopholes through which the lights shone out in tell-tale beams.

For hour after hour, those within had striven laboriously yet vainly to set their engines going, and so to bring their Tank safely back out of its gallant maiden action. But nothing availed, and, the enemy fire becoming more intense and accurate, the lights were switched off and the preparations for evacuation made in total darkness.

It was first necessary to find out where our own line lay and to warn our infantry that the crew would be coming in.

Sergeant Latham at once volunteered for this reconnaissance, and crawled out of the Tank into the lesser blackness of the night. Rifles spat and stray bullets cracked and whined impartially around, and British and German rifles and bullets sound very much alike. However, partly by judgment and partly by luck, Sergeant Latham stumbled into our own lines and warned the garrison of the trench to fire high as the crew from the derelict Tank would soon be coming in.

It was as well that the sergeant succeeded in delivering his message, as a relief had taken place under cover of the night, and the new garrison had been told nothing of the Tank out in front, and would certainly have greeted the returning crew as enemy raiders.

Next day, having procured a new magneto, the Tank Commander and some of his crew set out for their machine with better hope of salving her.

They were approaching the battle front when an agitated battery commander hailed them and sought information as to the Tank out to his front. Hearing that it was a derelict that they were on their way to try to bring in, he exclaimed, "Thank God for that! I've been blasting that part this morning. I didn't know about the Tank, and I've just got a direct hit on it that's crumpled it up. I feared it might have been manned."

So ended the short but valiant career of the avenging "Lusitania." For his very gallant command, Second Lieutenant Weber received an immediate award of the Military Cross, and Sergeant Latham the Military Medal. The specific action for which the latter was decorated is officially described as follows :

> "76441 *Sgt. F. Latham, 'C' Batt., awarded M.M.* for conspicuous gallantry and devotion to duty. During the Battle of Arras on April 9, 1917, whilst passing through a severe enemy barrage, lengths of barbed wire were caught up by the tracks of his Tank which pulled the camouflage cover over the exhaust openings, and caused the whole mass to catch fire. Without waiting for orders Sergeant Latham climbed on top of the Tank and removed the burning material. Later on this N.C.O. displayed the greatest courage whilst attempting to dig out his Tank under heavy fire."

Another Tank, commanded by Second Lieutenant S. S. Ching, in this sector was late in starting, and had barely caught up its infantry when it became ditched. It held out, however, for no less than three days while the fighting eddied about it.

It made most active use of its 6-pounders, thereby effectively protecting the right flank of its infantry.

Another Tank fell bodily into an old gun emplacement near Neuville-Vitasse which had been carefully turfed over.

V

BULLECOURT

By the night of the 9th the force of the first wave was spent, and though, as we have seen, many units were continuously in action for the next three days, for the bulk both of Tanks and infantry April 10 was spent in consolidating positions or digging out and repairing Tanks.

On April 11 the attack on Bullecourt and two other lesser actions were fought. One of the two minor attacks was that on Monchy, in which six Tanks took part.

It was highly successful owing chiefly to the extremely gallant way in which the machines were fought. The Tanks took the village practically unassisted and held it for two hours till the infantry came up.

Unfortunately, there were no further supplies of Tanks to exploit the success or more might have been achieved. The second attack was made from Neuville-Vitasse down the Siegfried Line. Four Tanks took part and did great execution, all the machines returning safely.

The stars in their courses seem to have fought against the success of the attack against Bullecourt, in which eleven Tanks co-operated with the Australians.

It will be remembered that the 5th Army attack was not to be launched till some time after that in the other sectors. Also that the state of the roads was such that it was impossible to bring up enough artillery for a preliminary bombardment. Therefore the Battle of Bullecourt was to have been a first-wave attack in which a small number of Tanks were to play the lead.

The eleven Tanks were to have advanced in line upon the Siegfried defences east of Bullecourt. Some were then to have wheeled west to attack Bullecourt itself, while others were to move east down the German trench system, a third party pushing straight ahead to Riencourt and Hedecourt.

The attack was to have been made at dawn on April 10, and at nightfall on the 9th the Tanks began their move up to their battle positions behind the railway embankment. All day the weather had been cold and stormy, and the Tanks had not gone half a mile before a violent snow blizzard came on, blotting out every landmark. Most of the troops who had moves to make that night were confounded in the swirling darkness, and though the eleven Tanks did not stray far, their pace had to be reduced to a crawl, and at dawn they were still far from their battle stations. The Australian infantry, who had already assembled at the railway embankment, had to be withdrawn under heavy shelling, the whole attack postponed, and the manner of it much modified. All next night the snow fell. When the attack did take place on the 11th, it proved, both for Tanks and infantry, a costly little failure. The day dawned clear, and against the whiteness of the snow every advancing Tank and its broad double track, stood out sharply. Further, the Australian infantry, wading through the snow, found the path made by the Tanks irresistible and followed in long lines strung out along their tracks. Thus Tanks and infantry provided the Germans with the most perfect artillery targets imaginable.

Of the eleven Tanks, nine were knocked out by direct hits before their work was half accomplished. Worst of all, two Tanks which, with about 200 Australians, pressed on nearly five miles to Riencourt and Hedecourt, found their right unprotected owing to our failure to advance the other part of our line. The Germans organised a sweeping counter-attack, and the two villages, the infantry and the Tanks, were surrounded and taken.

* " The First Battle of Bullecourt was a minor disaster—the three brigades of infantry lost very heavily indeed—and the company of Tanks had been apparently nothing but a broken reed.

" For many months after, the Australians distrusted Tanks —' the Tanks had failed them '—' the Tanks had let them down.' " We shall see that it was not till after the Battle of Hamel that their confidence was restored.

Not a single Tank survived to rally after the battle. But our worst loss was that of the two Tanks which were "taken alive," for examination of the captured machines revealed to the enemy how effective a weapon was their armour-piercing bullet against the Mark I.

After this action a German Order was issued that every man should be provided with five rounds of the "K" (armour-piercing) ammunition, and every machine-gun with several hundred. As long as the Mark I. was used, these bullets were to cause heavy casualties among Tanks and their crews.

For the next ten days Tanks were busy refitting. By the 20th thirty of the original sixty Tanks were fit again for action, and on April 23 eleven Tanks were employed in twos and threes to help on the infantry advance on the line of Monchy–Rœux–Gavrelle.

Again the story of the day is one of fine individual work.

The story of a Tank which worked opposite Rœux is told

* Major Watson, the Tank Company Commander, writing in *Blackwood's Magazine*.

in the Honours and Awards List in the note on Sergeant J. Noel's D.C.M. :

> "During the battle of Arras on April 23 this N.C.O. took command of his Tank after his officer had been wounded. He fought his Tank with the greatest gallantry and skill, putting out of action many machine-guns and killing numbers of the enemy, besides taking fifty prisoners. His action enabled the infantry to gain possession of the Chemical Works. He brought his Tank back safely to its starting-point. His skill and gallantry were beyond all praise. He was continuously in action for nine hours."

This was the first time a Tank was commanded in action by an N.C.O.

Another pause followed the actions of the 23rd. Of the sixty Tanks which had gone in on the 9th, not many machines remained that could soon be repaired.

However, twelve Tanks were somehow made "battle-worthy," and on May 3 were sent in for the last time before the Brigade was withdrawn to rest and to be re-equipped at Wailly, their new training ground.

A party of four operated between Croisilles and St. Léger and became heavily engaged in a fight at close quarters against bombs and trench mortars.

The second group of eight Tanks made another assault upon Bullecourt.

Though individuals did extremely well, the attack was once more unsuccessful, as, though Tanks reached their objective, they were obliged to retire again.

No less than ten Military Medals and a D.C.M. were awarded to men and N.C.O.'s of the Tanks who took part in this little action.

The Germans had learnt their lesson, and Tanks and crews suffered heavily from armour-piercing bullets. Several of the decorations were given to drivers who had brought their Tanks safely out of action when themselves severely wounded.

With this second attack on Bullecourt ended, as far as the Tanks were concerned, the Battle of Arras. There were not many 1st Brigade Tanks to withdraw to Wailly nor many unwounded men to man them. It was, however, with feelings very different from those of the "veterans" of the Somme that officers and men left the battle.

The careful training at Bermicourt with its well-planned courses, its boxing, and its games was justified. Men and officers could not have displayed a finer fighting spirit. The value of their work was recognised by all the units with whom they fought.

Major-General Williams, commanding the 37th Division, wrote of " C " Battalion's work in the attack on Monchy:

"It was a great achievement, and in itself more than justifies the existence of the Tanks. Officers and men concerned deserve the highest credit."

Lieut.-General Aylmer Haldane, commanding the 6th Corps, wrote to Colonel Baker-Carr, commanding the 1st Brigade, on April 13:

". . . I am really most grateful for all the Tanks and their commanders have done, and the great success of this Corps is only attributable to the help you have given us. This has been my first experience of the co-operation of Tanks, and I certainly never again want to be without them, when so well commanded and led."

Not only had the personnel done extraordinarily well, their conduct being " a triumph of *moral* over technical difficulties," but on the whole the general work of the Tanks had been a success.

These were briefly the technical lessons of the battle:

Tanks should be used in masses.
They should be concentrated.
A large reserve should always be kept in hand.
Mark I. machines are not suitable for use on very wet or very heavily shelled ground.
Signal and supply Tanks are essential.

In fine, the chief obstacle to a still fuller measure of success had been that there were 60, and not 260, Tanks available.

CHAPTER VII

THE BATTLE OF MESSINES AND THE "HUSH" OPERATION

> "And little would'st thou grudge them
> Their greater depth of soul,
> Thy partners in the torch race,
> Though nearer to the goal."
>
> IONICA.

I

IN many battles in which Tanks later took part, two or more Tank Brigades would be associated. But the Battles of Arras and Messines belong, the former to the 1st and the latter to the 2nd Brigade exclusively.

The 2nd Brigade had been formed exactly like the 1st. That is to say, a nucleus of Somme "Tank Veterans" had been reinforced by picked volunteers from the other branches of the Service. Like the 1st Brigade they trained in France, in the Bermicourt area. The unknown author of the 2nd Battalion history gives an amusing account of this training in which sports of all kinds, rugger, soccer, snow fights, boxing and swimming, helped in the "edification" as well as the more serious courses.

One feature of the period was, as usual, a shortage of instructional machines.

Dummy Tanks were therefore used for several practice attacks. The dummies were made of wood and canvas and were carried from within by their crew of seven.

> "They looked for all the world like some drab-coloured prehistoric monster with as many legs as a centipede. A high wind blew during a certain 'action' in March, and made things most difficult. By the time the final objective was reached many of the Tanks were in a state of collapse, the torn canvas revealing the perspiring machinery to the amused gaze of the onlookers. The

remains of the Tanks were, however, most useful for firewood and the renovation of beds."

The account goes on to relate the delightful keenness of the men, and how their interest in their training was so great that such serious *contretemps* as getting in late for tea " were regarded as nothing."

The 2nd Brigade was to be equipped with Mark IV. Tanks as soon as a supply was available.

The first batch of machines arrived in France towards the end of April.

The Mark IV. Tank was an improved Mark I., and did not differ very materially from its predecessor in design.

These were, briefly, the principal improvements:

First, its armour was of a special steel which was impervious to the German armour-piercing bullet.

Secondly, the sponsons were of a better pattern. In the Mark I. they had to be completely unshipped whenever the Tank was moved by rail; in the Mark IV. they were so constructed that they could be " pushed in " sufficiently for railway transport.

Thirdly, a new and heavier design of track rollers and links was introduced.

Fourthly, danger from fire was reduced by the petrol tank (protected, of course, by special armour-plates) being outside and at the back of the machine.

There were also other minor improvements in armament, and the total weight of the Tank was slightly reduced.

Such was the weapon which was to be first tried at Messines, and such was the unit which was at the same time to make its début.

II

The Battle of Messines did not prove one in which Tanks were able to show to any particular advantage; this not because of adverse conditions, but because of the battle's very success. It was throughout an extremely well-planned little action, and would probably have been perfectly successful even without the co-operation of Tanks.

An expert military critic has said of it:

> " The Battle of Messines, one of the shortest and best mounted limited operations of the War, was in no sense a Tank battle."

It was perhaps a little hard on the 2nd Brigade, who fought

A Model Battle

throughout with particular gallantry, that more of the laurel could not fall to them.

For not only was the 2nd Brigade's maiden battle notable for gallantry in the field, but also for the very high standard of the Staff work—the administrative arrangements indeed long remaining the model for subsequent Tank operations.

So inspiring a little action was it, so well planned and executed in every stage, that the 2nd Brigade themselves felt that they had been privileged in playing even a relatively minor part in such an assault.

Though Tanks proved useful in several phases of the battle, Tank Commanders are the first to attribute the successes of the day to the artillery, the tunnelling companies and the infantry.

They had early established particularly cordial relations with the infantry, and it is said that a Maori Unit of the 2nd Anzac Corps gave expert help to the 2nd Tank Battalion in camouflaging its machines.

Messines was to be a prelude to a more considerable attack in the Ypres Salient. The village of Messines itself and the Wytschaete Ridge were to be taken, thus securing the British Right for the Ypres attack, and depriving the enemy of dominating ground.

The advance was to be a very short one, and the rôle of the Tanks was to be subsidiary to that of gunners, sappers and infantry.

Land Mines were to be a special feature of the action. The explosion of twenty of these containing over a million pounds of ammonal was to be the signal for attack on the morning of June 7.

Some of the mines had been ready for more than a year, and we had constructed nearly five miles of galleries. The Germans too had not been idle.

At the time of our attack we knew that the enemy was driving a gallery leading to our Hill 60 mine. By careful listening we judged that if our offensive were launched on the date arranged the enemy's counter-mine would just fail to reach us. He was, therefore, allowed to proceed.

Altogether seventy-two Mark IV. Tanks were to be employed, and, the lesson of Arras having been learnt, twelve Mark I. and Mark II. Tanks had been converted into supply machines. Each of these was able to bring up sufficient petrol, ammunition and other stores to replenish five fighting Tanks.

Forty Tanks were to cross the parapet at zero hour and the rest of the Tanks were to be held in reserve.

They were to be distributed as follows :—

To the North: twelve Tanks were to work with the 10th Corps, whose objective was the Oosttaverne line.

In the Centre : sixteen Tanks were attached to the 9th Corps, who were to capture Wytschaete.

To the South : twenty Tanks were to fight with the 2nd Corps, who were to take Messines and a strong point named Fanny's Farm, the reserves pushing on to capture the Oosttaverne line in the second phase of the attack.

The weather had been fine and hot for nearly three weeks before the battle, and a heavy thunder shower which fell on June 6 hardly laid the dust which had hung for weeks in a hazy curtain over the approach roads.

The Tanks were as usual moved up during the night before the action. It was very dark, with heavy thunder clouds hiding the moon.

* " The last part of the approach march will never be forgotten by those who took part in it.

" The enemy took it into his head to bombard with lachrymatory and other gas shells, and the night was so black that it was impossible to keep gas-masks on the whole time.

" So with streaming eyes, with no sort of light, with Tank Commanders and drivers coughing and spluttering, the Tanks forged ahead over this area of unseen trenches, barbed wire and shell-holes, the men buoyed up by the knowledge of the shock the Hun would receive in an hour or so."

Zero hour was to be at dawn.

Somewhere north of Wytschaete a German dump had caught fire, and the red flames streamed up against the pale summer sky.

It grew lighter, and our aeroplanes and balloons began to go up, dark against the dawn.

Our unusual activity in the air did not escape the watchful enemy, and his suspicions were soon thoroughly aroused.

He began to send up rockets calling for barrage fire, and soon his guns were responding with growing emphasis.

At seven minutes past three our artillery stopped, and the rattle of machine-guns stood out in the comparative silence.

There was a pause. A low rumbling was heard. The earth rocked and quivered until with a prolonged and rending crash a screen of fire rose where the German front lines had been.

Masses of earth were hurled skywards, and as they rose gleamed for a moment purple and gold in the first rays of the sun. They writhed and shifted, fantastically swaying, and shot through with

* " B " (2) Battalion History.

flames. Balls of fire were hurled in every direction, and the air quivered and vibrated with the shock. Before the tortured earth could fall again, down came the stunning roar and crash of the British barrage; and Tanks and infantry were over the parapet.

By 7 a.m. the Anzacs were in Messines, and both Tanks and infantry had reached Fanny's Farm by noon, their day's objective gained.

One Tank working with the 2nd Corps reached its final objective (at a distance of about two miles) in an hour and forty minutes.

A Tank led the Ulstermen and Southern Irish of the 9th Division into Wytschaete.

By about three o'clock three Tanks had reached Oosttaverne, and they patrolled the ground beyond the village till their accompanying Welsh and West Country troops came up.

By nightfall we held our final objective everywhere, and had besides captured 7800 prisoners and 67 guns, 94 trench mortars and a very large number of machine-guns.

All through the night of the 7th–8th the Germans launched small hastily organised counter-attacks, and in repelling one of these, chance enabled three Tanks to play a curious and useful part.

Three of the Tanks, which had helped in the capture of Oosttaverne, had ultimately got ditched near a place named Joye Farm.

It was impossible to extricate them in the darkness, and the crews stood by, hoping to get them out as soon as it was light again.

Meanwhile towards morning word came that the Germans were going to counter-attack.

In the position in which the Tanks lay, the crews were able to train their 6-pounders against the enemy, who had been seen massing in the Wanbeke Valley. As the Lewis guns could not be brought to bear, they were dismounted, and the rest of the crews operated them from neighbouring shell-holes.

> * "Word was sent to the infantry to warn them of the coming attack, and to ask for co-operation. They replied that they had run short of ammunition for their Lewis gun, and some was supplied to them from the Tanks."

The attack did not develop as early as had been expected, but when it came it was in force.

From about 6.30 onwards the enemy repeatedly attempted

* W.T.N.

to advance, raking the Tanks with a hail of armour-piercing bullets, which, however, failed to penetrate.

They were driven off every time with heavy loss, until at 11.30 a.m. our artillery opened and dispersed them with barrage fire.

III

The failure of their armour-piercing bullets against the Mark IV. must have proved something of a disappointment to the enemy.

It is curious to trace the effort which the Germans made to keep up with our development of the Tank.

For once, we had moved first, and the enemy was always to be a lap behind.

No sooner had he discovered how effective was his " K " bullet against the Mark I. Tank, than we confronted him with the Mark IV., against which it was powerless.

The Germans always had rather hazy ideas as to the capabilities and habits of our current Tank. They had had ample opportunity of examining two Tanks which lay derelict in their lines on the Somme, yet until the Battle of Arras they believed that Tanks were largely dependent on the use of roads, and that therefore pits and other obstacles in roads must form a useful anti-Tank defence.

> * " It was also not till the later stages of the Battle of Arras that the enemy realised from some captured Tanks near Bullecourt that the ' K ' bullet was effective against the type of Tank that had been in use against them since September 1916.
>
> " By the time the enemy had fully realised this, however, the old Tanks were used up, and at Messines the Mark IV. had made its appearance and the chance of the armour-piercing bullet was over. . . .
>
> " After Messines the Germans began to realise the importance of artillery as a defence against Tanks, and ' the chief rôle allotted to the infantry was to keep its head ' and leave the rest to the guns. . . .
>
> " Prominence was given to indirect fire † of guns of both heavy and light calibres on approaching Tanks. In spite of several dawn attacks the enemy laid great stress on

---

* Official paper.

† Indirect fire may be defined as fire directed towards the spot where you believe the enemy to be. Fire is called " direct " when the target can be seen.

what he called 'Distant Defence,' and a few special anti-Tank guns, about two per divisional front, were placed in specially covered positions."

It was not till the Battle of Cambrai in November 1917 that he was to discover by chance the one effective weapon against Tanks. That is to say, Direct Fire by field guns.

The " Hush " Operation

I

Before it was decided to fight the enemy at Messines there had been an idea of an attack near Lens, and most of the reconnaissance for such a battle had been carried out.

Like many another battle of the War, it was never fought, and remained only the shadow of an operation.

Of all these shadows and projected attacks, the one which has attracted more interest than any other was in active preparation while the 2nd Brigade was fighting at Messines.

This was the revised and abridged version of the famous "Hush" operation, that is, of the projected attack on the Belgian coast.

The first time such a notion had been suggested was in the spring of 1916, and elaborate plans were then made for a surprise landing in and near Ostend.

But we were obliged to co-operate with the French, and to fight instead on the Somme. The First Battle of the Somme, however, developed into a " slogging match " and lasted through the rest of that campaigning season.

Next year the idea was again brought up. This time Tanks were to take part. The scheme was a less ambitious one, and the landing was to be effected between Ostend and the Allied line about Nieuport. A special detachment of Tanks was located at Erin, and started training for the difficult manœuvre of climbing the sea wall which here protects the coast. This training was carried out as secretly as possible, and it was given out that its object was the surmounting of some of the Lille fortifications, a figment which for long satisfied the minds of the curious.

The problem to be solved was an exceedingly complex one.

The mere landing of Tanks on an open beach is no light matter. When that beach is heavily defended by an alert and resourceful enemy, when it is commanded and enfiladed by a concentration of artillery of all calibres concealed amongst the dunes, and when in addition the shelving beach is crowned by a steep sea wall of concrete, a landing would seem to have but small chance of success. Still, there was a chance, and the stake at hazard being a big one, big risks might be cheerfully accepted.

The general plans for the enterprise having been approved in the highest quarters, were then very carefully worked out down to the smallest details by a little band of experts, prominent amongst whom were Admiral Bacon, Lieut.-Colonel Philip Johnson, and Major Hotblack.

The whole of the projected landing was elaborately staged, and long and patiently rehearsed—the Tanks playing the lead in what the whole various cast hoped was to be a really notable success.

Immense pontoons 600 ft. in length were specially built to carry the landing parties—armies in little with representatives almost of every arm and branch except the cavalry.

These strange craft were to be lashed between a couple of monitors, and so pushed across the channel and up the beach at certain selected points, points that exhaustive air reconnaissance and photography at all states of the tide had indicated as most suitable.

Actual trials of the pontoons and their monitor escorts were made in the secret waters of the Thames, and officers of the Tank Corps would suddenly disappear on unknown missions, to reappear as suddenly with no memory as to where they had been or what they had seen in the interval.

The sea wall itself might well have been designed as a special defence against sea-borne hostile Tanks, its smooth concave face and projecting coping making it absolutely unscalable by an honest Tank.

The wall was of recent construction, and by a fortunate chance the Belgian architect who had designed it had escaped to France with all his drawings.

From his plans an exact reproduction of a length of the wall was made.

There in the experimental ground it stood, perfectly smooth, and worst of all, ending at the top in a curl-over coping.

At least, however, the engineers now knew the extent of their problem.

In the first place, the Tanks had to get up somehow, and in the second place, when they were up they had to help haul up guns and transport lorries.

After " trying on " various devices, the Tanks at last adopted what was practically a portable ramp for the occasion.

The Tank carried it well in the air on a long spar supported by wire hawsers until it reached the sea wall.

Then the ramp was lowered on to the pair of little wheels

with which it was fitted. On these the Tank pushed it up the incline, wheelbarrow fashion, until further progress was stopped by the coping.

The two wheels were then immediately shed, and steel spikes on the under side of the nose were driven into the concrete by the weight of the Tank, which now, disengaging itself, proceeded to climb up its own scaling ladder which it had thus placed in position. But the lorries and guns had still to be provided for.

The angle formed by the inclined plane and the level ground above the retaining wall was a sharp one.

Besides, it must be understood that the inclined plane used by the Tanks fitted in under the concrete lip. At the point of junction between the ground and the inclined plane there was, therefore, a considerable bump. Both the acuteness of the angle and this " bump " made it necessary to adopt some less back-breaking device for the four-wheeled vehicles. A strong gangway, like a see-saw, was therefore employed, and up this they were hauled, the weight of the gun or lorry gently tipping the board down when it passed the balancing-point.

But the landing was never made, and for this many elaborate explanations have been put forward.

Two circumstances seem, however, sufficient to explain the apparent withdrawal of our hands from the plough.

The first was what seemed a trivial attack which the Germans made on July 10.

It will be remembered that the Belgian inundations stretched inland opposite Nieuport, almost from the mile-wide belt of dry ground next the sea which was formed by the sand dunes. Through these dunes cut the river Yser, and near the coast we held both banks of the river. When the time came, General Rawlinson could have moved his troops forward freely over the numerous bridges which had been made, to join hands with the landing party for whom he had so long been waiting.

In the dune and polder country trenches were impossible, and our defence here consisted of breastworks built in the sand.

Now it had been abundantly and constantly proved throughout 1915 and 1916 that any advanced trench system could be taken at any time by the side which was prepared to mass sufficient troops and guns for the purpose.

The Germans could have stretched out their hands at any moment for this bit of coast.

They chose not to grasp it until they imagined that our plans, whatever they might be, were complete, and when their attack would probably cause us the maximum of inconvenience. Therefore it was on July 10 that, after a tremendous bombardment, they attacked the position in overwhelming force. Our defence was gallant but vain, and by the evening the Germans had captured the northern part of our bridgeheads.

It is true that we succeeded in holding Nieuport itself, but the loss of even the small strip of ground to the north of it rendered the assembly of troops in that area for our own attack, which was to co-operate with the coast landing, almost impossible.

The second and more weighty circumstance was the fatal slowness of our main advance at Ypres.

In the next chapters we shall consider these tragic months, whose slow passage swept away so many schemes and hopes, and made unfruitful so much thought and labour.

Enough that the " Hush " operation was swept silently away with the rest. As late as the beginning of October, however, the men who had planned so cunningly, whose minds had surmounted so many difficulties, still hoped that their work might not prove barren.

But by the middle of the month it had become clear that the landing could not take place, and at the end of October the special Tank detachment was finally disbanded.

CHAPTER VIII

THE FLANDERS CAMPAIGN

PREPARATIONS FOR THE THIRD BATTLE OF YPRES

THE Third Battle of Ypres represented the remaining fragment of what was to have been a great and extensive campaign. It was the stump of a tree shorn down to shoulder height and bare of leaves and branches.

One circumstance after another had postponed the execution of the large design. Troops which had been earmarked for it had had to be diverted to other parts of the front.

We had had to put it off to co-operate more closely with the French, and certain other obstacles had arisen, the full story of which has not even yet been told.

The Battle of Messines was over by June 12, but it was considered that if an attack in the strongly fortified Ypres Salient was to have a real chance of success, it must be an attack in force, a regular full-dress battle, for which the preparations were then held to be necessarily extremely elaborate.

About six weeks were therefore to elapse before the attack was launched. Once launched, however, the attackers must gain their objectives rapidly. That was essential to the plan.

The Russian front was crumbling. Germany was bringing troops and guns westward. We should soon be face to face with an enemy so strongly reinforced that our chance of victory in an attack would be slight.

> * "It was in some degree a race against time. If a true strategic purpose was to be effected before winter, the first stages must be quickly passed. The high ground east of the Salient must be won in a fortnight, to enable the British to move against the German bases in West Flanders and clear the coastline."
>
> * Mr. Buchan's *History of the War*.

Not only must we hasten because we faced an enemy whose strength would be increasing daily, but because we were to attack in Flanders, and the summer would be far spent before we could complete our preparations.

The enemy's lines lay on the slopes of the semicircle of low hills that overlook Ypres. Behind him lay another swampy valley, which rose again to another slightly higher crescent of hills.

In the inner arena lay the ruins of Ypres, and, set in the marshy levels and immediately overlooked by the first semicircle of hillocks and more distantly by the second, lay our lines.

> * " The territory lying within the crescent was practically all reclaimed swamp land including Ypres and as far back as to St. Omer, both of which, a few hundred years ago, were seaports. All agriculture in this area depended on careful drainage, the water being carried away in innumerable dykes. So important was the maintenance of this drainage system considered, that in normal times a Belgian farmer who allowed his dykes to fall into disrepair was heavily fined."

Across this terrain two great armies had faced each other for nearly three years.

The Salient was, after Verdun, the most tortured of the Western battlefields. Constant shelling of the low ground west of the ridges had blocked or diverted the streams and the natural drainage, and turned it into a sodden wilderness.

If August was a wet month, as it had been the year before for the Battle of the Somme, our chance of success was scanty.

> " Much rain would make a morass of the Salient where Tanks could not be used, transport could scarcely move, and troops would be exposed to the last degree of misery." †

However, the previous shelling of the ground was as nothing compared with the bombardment which we now intended to inflict.

Every corner of the enemy's ground was to be drenched with our fire.

> ‡ " The present battle was to be preceded by the longest bombardment ever carried out by the British Army, eight

---

* *W.T.N.*   † Mr. Buchan's *History of the War.*   ‡ *W.T.N.*

days' counter-battery work (begun on July 7) being followed by sixteen days' intense bombardment. The effect of this cannonade was to destroy the drainage system and to produce water in the shell-holes formed, even before the rain fell."

II

The enemy had for long been in no doubt of our intentions. The coming battle was much discussed in Germany.

General von Armin (Commander of the German 4th Army) was to remain strictly on the defensive.

He was to "put in time," to "poke," in fact, until the big movement of troops from the East should have thoroughly reconstituted the Western Front.

We were to be allowed to waste our time and our forces in petty gains of unimportant territory, and to eat our hearts out in the slough.

To this end, and because the waterlogged soil of Flanders did not allow of the making of another Siegfried Line, the enemy had devised a new tactical method.

Directly the theory of this method is understood, many of the once puzzling circumstances of this battle become comprehensible.

It involved the use of but one comparatively new contrivance, the "pill-box." The "pill-box," first seen at Messines, was a small concrete fort. Sometimes it only stood up a yard or two above the ground. More often it stood well up, concealed within the ruins of a derelict farm.

It held a garrison of anything up to thirty or forty men, and bristled with machine-guns.

The tactics themselves in which the pill-boxes figured are admirably described by Mr. Buchan:

> "The enemy's plan was to hold his first line—which was often a mere string of shell-craters linked by a trench—with a few men, who would fall back before an assault. He had his guns well behind, so that they should not be captured in the first rush, and would be available for a barrage when his opponents were entangled in the 'pill-box' zone. Finally, he had his reserves in the second line, ready for the counterstroke before the assault could secure the ground won. . . . Any attack would be allowed to make some advance; but if the German plan worked

well, this advance would be short-lived, and would be dearly paid for. Instead of the cast-iron front of the Siegfried area, the Flanders line would be highly elastic, but would spring back into position after pressure with a deadly rebound."

The thoroughness and success with which this plan was carried out may be read in the story of Glencorse Wood, of St. Julien, and of many another bitterly fought " Minor Action."

In the meantime, the enemy watched us from his vantage ground, and day and night harassed us with his shelling, his aerial bombing, and his gas.

III

On our side the preparations for a formidable attack continued steadily.

> * " The various problems inseparable from the mounting of a great offensive, the improvement and construction of roads and railways, the provision of an adequate water supply and of accommodation for troops, the formation of dumps, the digging of dug-outs, subways and trenches, and the assembling and registering of guns, had all to be met and overcome in the new theatre of battle, under conditions of more than ordinary disadvantage.
>
> " On no previous occasion, not excepting the attack on the Messines–Wytschaete Ridge, had the whole of the ground from which we had to attack been so completely exposed to the enemy's observation. Even after the enemy had been driven from the Messines–Wytschaete Ridge, he still possessed excellent direct observation over the Salient from the east and south-east, as well as from the Pilckem Ridge to the north. Nothing existed at Ypres to correspond with the vast caves and cellars which proved of such value in the days prior to the Arras battle, and the provision of shelter for the troops presented a very serious problem."

It was a problem which in some sectors proved insoluble, and troops and working parties had to come up night by night into the forward area, going back far behind the lines at dawn.

Like their fellows of every other arm, members of the Tank

---

* Sir Douglas Haig's Despatch.

The Oosthoek Wood Betrayal

Corps carried out their battle preparations under conditions of peculiar difficulty.

But the 1st Brigade of Tanks had something more than indiscriminate harassing fire and "area shoots" to trouble them.

The enemy had obtained information of our tankodrome in Oosthoek Wood from a British prisoner, who was either a garrulous fool or a very treacherous knave.

A soldier belonging to a certain infantry regiment had betrayed every detail of the whereabouts of the Tanks of the 1st Brigade, and of the programme of their movements. A German document was captured setting forth the whole of this creature's evidence and explaining its value and significance. The official account of this murderous piece of treachery was periodically read out on parade to all Tank units, and formed the text of many discourses on the vital importance of strict secrecy and high *moral*. The name of this man will for ever have a sinister sound for all who served in the Tank Corps.

Fortunately for us, the Germans seem to have but half believed his story—at any rate, the shelling to which they thereafter periodically subjected the secret tankodrome was, though accurate, never so heavy as such an important target would have seemed to warrant. Perhaps the Germans, having no illusions as to what fighting in Flanders meant, and being reasonably alive to the natural limitations of Tanks, scouted the idea of a Tank attack being possible or being even seriously contemplated. Be that as it may, they certainly failed to act on the very valuable information given them in anything like an adequate way.

Still, after some days of well-directed shelling and bombing, it was decided to withdraw the whole of the personnel from Oosthoek Wood, and to lodge them in camps in the plantations just north of Château Lovie, where the Headquarters of the 1st Brigade was already established.

Hither, too, had come the Advanced Headquarters of the Tank Corps, the original intention of occupying a most eligible house in the town of Poperinghe being given up, in view of the inconvenience caused by the periodic shelling of the place and the consequent interruption of communications.

The advance Reconnaissance party had spent some weeks in the town, and had been considerably annoyed by frequent and accurate high-velocity shelling.

The concentration of personnel which thus came about seemed inconvenient enough at first, but turned out most usefully, and liaison between the Brigade and its battalions had never been so good.

There were forward dumps to be established with the aid of the supply Tanks.*

Very special preparations had to be made in order to bring the Tanks within striking distance of the enemy. The roads were reserved for lighter traffic. The enemy shelling was too heavy for railway making to be possible beyond the detraining camps at Oosthoek Wood.

Tentative attempts to push the line further on were constantly made, and as constantly detected and discouraged by the enemy.

The Tanks must have some sort of independent routes of their own over the innumerable small waterways that must be crossed.

The Kemmelbeke, the Lambardtbeke, and in some places the Yser Canal, all lay in the way. Miles of rough causeways over the marshes had to be built; splinter-proof shelters for the various advanced Headquarters, and, further back, camps, Tank " stables," storage sheds, kitchens and so forth, had all to be constructed.

Such a programme of work was beyond the unaided power of the Tank Corps, and therefore the 184th Tunnelling Company was allotted to the Corps, one section to each Brigade.

Much of the canal bridging and of the track making was done under fire, shrapnel, gas and H.E.

Often a series of shells bursting on the newly laid causeway would undo a day's work in a few minutes. Half the time the men had to wear gas-masks, and almost always they worked knee-deep in liquid mud or in the oozy bed of some little " beke."

Yet in no instance did the 184th Tunnelling Company fail to carry out the work allotted to it.

One very ingenious piece of mechanism for use on the Tank itself had been evolved at Central Workshops in view of the Flanders mud. This was the " Unditching Beam." It was a massive baulk of teak, iron shod at the ends, and having heavy chains whereby it might be secured to the tracks when it was needed.

---

* The size of these dumps was now always computed in " Tank Fills."
    1 fill consisting of :
        60 galls. of Petrol.
        10 galls. of Oil.
        20 galls. of Water.
        10 lb. of Grease.
        10,000 rounds of S.A. Ammunition for a Female Tank,
  or
        200 rounds of 6-pdr. Ammunition
  and
        6000 rounds of S.A. Ammunition for a Male.

Its length was somewhat greater than the width of the Tank over its tracks, and therefore ordinarily it was carried lengthwise along the back of the machine.

Its battle position was across the Tank, where it rested on the raised guide-rails which served to lift it clear of the conning-tower, the silencer and the other excrescences above the armoured back.

To these guide-rails it was secured by special holdfasts to prevent it from breaking adrift when the Tank pitched or rolled amongst the shell-holes.

When the Tank got "bellied," these holdfasts had to be released and the drag-chains attached to the tracks by one of the crew climbing out on to the roof—the feat being one of some danger when in the near presence of the enemy.

The beam having been duly attached, the differential gear would be locked and the clutch released, when the revolving tracks would carry the beam over the nose of the Tank, from which it would dangle by its two track-chains until dragged beneath the Tank itself.

If the ground proved loose and boggy beyond a certain point, the beam would merely be dragged under the Tank to come up again behind, clogged and dripping with mud and leaving the " ditched " Tank still wallowing on its belly.

Sometimes Tanks would thrash away with their unditching beams until their vain efforts to struggle out of some quaking quagmire on to better ground overheated the engines or caused the machine to settle down so hopelessly in the oozing mud as to be flooded out.

Save on the very worst ground, however, the unditching beam proved a most effective contrivance, and but little could have been done in the Ypres fighting without it.

IV

The Reconnaissance side had also been busy during the weeks of preparation.

To facilitate the movement of Tanks over the battlefield a new system was made use of, by which a list of compass bearings from well-defined points to a number of features in the enemy's territory was prepared, thus enabling direction to be picked up.

This system was to prove invaluable when, later, the tides of battle had obliterated all the nearer landmarks, and men wandered hopelessly lost in the increasing desolation.

The Reconnaissance Officer's methods of observation did not differ from those they had employed at Arras.

They used artillery O.P.'s, they flew over the enemy lines, a " supply of prisoners " for special examination was allotted to them, they talked to refugees, they observed, made and annotated maps, and drew many panoramas, and made detailed raised maps in plasticine.

By early July they had collected a great mass of information that was not only vitally important to the Tank Corps, but also of great use to the other arms.

Very carefully constructed from information collected from all sources, a huge sand model was laid out by the 19th Corps in Oosthoek Wood. Every hillock or depression, every road, railway, trench, stream, ruin, spinney, or other landmark, was faithfully reproduced to scale. The miniature trenches were formed in lengths of cast concrete, the trees were represented by little evergreen bushes, and real water lay in the pools and shallows of the Lilliputian Steenbeck.

The model covered nearly an acre—a man to the same scale would have been about the size of a normal mouse.

At one side of the model was a high wooden platform raised on a scaffolding and reached by a ladder, and from this point of vantage this Ypres Salient in little could be overlooked and memorised as from a kite balloon.

For several weeks before the day appointed for the battle, the platform was almost constantly occupied by groups of officers. Indeed, it was seldom unoccupied during daylight from the time it was erected to the eve of the great attack, and round and across the model perpetually wandered little groups of officers and N.C.O.'s with maps and notebooks and orders—discussing, pointing, explaining. Generals personally conducted their immediate subordinates over the mimic battlefield, whilst N.C.O.'s were coached by their Company Commanders.

From a liaison point of view the model was invaluable. Individual Tank Commanders there met the infantry officers with whom they were actually to fight, and would walk and talk over " the ground " together, until they were perfectly clear about their own and each other's rôles, routes, objectives and time-tables, after which mutual esteem and confidence would be cemented and reinforced at the dinner table.

In this and similar ways a close and cordial *entente* was established between the Tanks and their partners the infantry, and there were many battlefield incidents that showed vividly how much success depended on this personal liaison and good fellowship.

V

There was to be nothing novel in our general plan of assault.

> * "The 5th Army attack was to be carried out on well-recognised lines; namely, a lengthy artillery preparation followed by an infantry attack on a large scale and infantry exploitation until resistance became severe, when the advance would be halted and a further organised attack prepared on the same scale. This methodical progression was to be continued until the exhaustion of the German reserves and *moral* created a situation which would enable a complete break through to be effected."

Tanks were everywhere to be auxiliary, and were to be employed to deal with strong points and for "mopping up" behind the infantry.

There was, however, one great improvement in the method of using them.

They were to be used in definite "waves." That is to say, supposing thirty-six Tanks were to be employed on a sector where the Germans had established the usual three lines of defence, twelve Tanks would start at zero and be used to take the first objective. Meanwhile the second wave would have been advancing, and as soon as the first objective had been taken by the first wave, the second wave would pass through them and on to the second objective. The third party of twelve would advance in the same way—a wave to each objective.

The method did not, as a matter of fact, have a good trial on this occasion, for, in the first place, the Tanks' first objective was only the infantry second objective; and as we have seen, the enemy did not this time employ his usual method of three set lines at all.

Altogether three Brigades of Tanks were to be employed with the 5th Army.

Tank Brigade Commanders were to keep in touch with Corps Commanders, Tank Battalions were to act with Divisions, Tank Companies (twelve fighting Tanks) with Brigades, and individual Tanks with Battalions.

The three Brigades were to be distributed as follows :—

A. 2*nd Corps* (consisting of the 24th, 30th, 18th, 8th and 25th Divisions).
    2*nd Tank Brigade* ("A" and "B" Battalions).

* *W.T.N.*

72 Tanks to be allotted as follows—

1st Objective	16
2nd „	24
3rd „	24

The remainder to be held in reserve.

The main objective was to be the Broodseinde Ridge.

The ground in this area was broken by swamps and woods; only three approaches were possible for Tanks, and these formed dangerous defiles.

B. 19*th Corps* (consisting of the 15th, 55th, 16th and 36th Divisions).

3*rd Tank Brigade* ("C" and "F" Battalions).

72 Tanks to be arranged as follows—

1st Objective	24
2nd „	24
Reserve	24

The main objective was to be a section of the Gheluvelt-Langemarck line.

On the 19th Corps front the valley of the Steenbeek was in a terrible condition, innumerable shell-holes and pools of water existed, the drainage of the Steenbeek having been seriously affected by the shelling.

C. 18*th Corps* (consisting of the 39th, 51st, 11th and 48th Divisions).

1*st Tank Brigade* ("D" and "G" Battalions).

36 Tanks to be allotted thus—

1st Objective	12
2nd „	12
Corps Reserve	12

They were to seize the crossings of the Steenbeek and establish posts beyond it.

On the 18th Corps front the ground between our front line and the Steenbeek was cut up and sodden. The Steenbeek itself was a difficult obstacle, and the only good crossing was at St. Julien, thus forming a dangerous defile.

Thirty-six Tanks belonging to the 1st Brigade were held in Army Reserve.

Such was the battle order of the Tanks.

Zero was fixed for 3.30 a.m. on July 31. By the last week

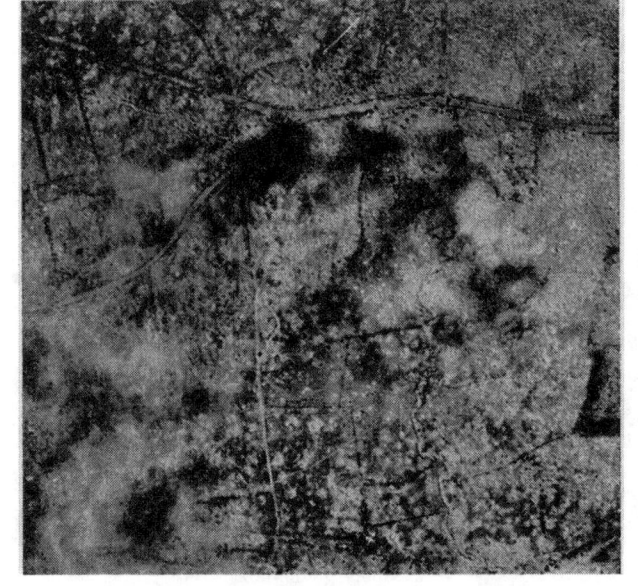

THE SAME AFTER BOMBARDMENT.

THE STEENBEEK VALLEY BEFORE THE BATTLE.

A FLANDERS "PILL-BOX."

THE "UNDITCHING BEAM" IN ACTION.

in July misty weather with often a drizzle of rain at night had set in.

Our preparations were complete, but it was perhaps not without a certain anxiety that our commanders awaited the issues of the engagement.

By none might such an uneasiness have been felt with better reason than by General Elles.

The Army had staked much upon a gamble, but at least it had not been forced to stake its prestige. General Elles must have been conscious that the very existence of the Tank Corps might hang upon the fortunes of the coming attack.

CHAPTER IX

THE THIRD BATTLE OF YPRES

" Quenched in a boggy Syrtis, neither sea
Nor good dry land—nigh foundered, on he fares,
Treading the crude consistence; half on foot."
Paradise Lost.

1

THE night of July 30 was dark and wet, and towards morning a fine mizzling rain blurred the outlines of the star shells that lit up the lines. Along fifteen miles of front the English and German guns had roared against each other all night.

The waiting men shivered in their wet assembly trenches.

About three o'clock on the morning of the 31st there was a lull in the firing. A low soaking blanket of Scotch mist had crept up and lay heavily enfolding the opposing armies. Zero hour was drawing near. All along the front, men were feeling for the little footholds above the fire-step.

At 3.50 the streaming darkness was rent along the seven miles of attack. Thermite and blazing oil flared out, and such a barrage as had not yet been, crashed upon the enemy's line, and infantry and Tanks scrambled and lurched in the darkness in and out of shell-holes over the torn and slimy ground.

The German front line fell at once along the whole seven miles. Until nearly eight o'clock men and Tanks could hardly get through the mud fast enough to come to grips with the enemy. On each Corps front there were many machines that got ditched on the enemy front line as they nosed about here and there, seeking to mop up lurking machine-gun nests and snipers.

There some of them remained stuck fast, not having seen the main body of the enemy at all, so immediate had been his retreat.

His artillery was, however, active enough, and as the Tanks floundered or stuck utterly in the mud, his guns and his low-flying aeroplanes took steady toll.

"Cyprus," "Culloden," and "Cumbrae"

All morning we pressed on, the enemy Command patiently conserving the power of its armies.

The doings of a group of Tanks belonging to the 3rd Brigade give an extraordinarily good idea of this part of the action. They were fighting on the 19th Corps front.

> * At 11.30 a.m. message was received that a Battalion of Argyll and Sutherland Highlanders were held up on the right. Tank 'Canada' moved in this direction and silenced enemy machine-guns in the Railway Embankment, assisted by the Tank 'Cuidich'n Rich.' When patrolling in front of the infantry whilst they were consolidating, Tank bellied.
>
> "At the same time enemy barrage came down, and both Tank 'Canada' and Tank 'Cuidich'n Rich' received direct hits. Five of the crew remained with the infantry, and assisted in repelling a counter-attack, two of the men being wounded.
>
> "... Tank 'Cape Colony' arrived at Low Farm and proceeded in front of the infantry. Came under heavy shell-fire and bellied. Whilst unditching, Tanks 'Cyprus' and 'Culloden' were observed under heavy fire from anti-Tank guns, which were in position on the high ground beyond. Both 'Cyprus' and 'Culloden' were seen to be hit.
>
> "'Cape Colony' then came under heavy M.G. fire from both flanks. On request of infantry 'Cape Colony' proceeded to a wood on right flank, where they were held up.
>
> "Although not fired upon from the Tank, several enemy machine gunners surrendered to the infantry, on seeing the Tank approach. 'Cape Colony' now turned N.E. towards Beck House, where a good view of anti-Tank guns, which had been shelling 'Cyprus' and 'Culloden,' was obtained. Whilst manœuvring to take these guns in flank or rear, the Tank sank in a swamp, water rising to the engine cover. Boche aeroplanes circled low overhead whilst unsuccessful attempts were made to unditch. Enemy shelling then became very heavy, so Lewis guns were taken out and Tank locked up.
>
> "... Flag Tank 'Cumbrae' was delayed half an hour by bellying in a trench near Bill Cottage, went in front of the infantry towards second objective. Opened fire on enemy who were disappearing in direction of Delva Farm. Ground was quite water-logged, and Tank bellied in a borrow pit. Whilst digging out was fired at by a sniper,

* "C" (3rd) Battalion History.

and by an aeroplane flying low overhead. Time was then zero plus 9 hours (*i.e.*, 12.50 p.m.).

". . . Tank 'Caithness' came under sniper and machine-gun fire near Beck House. No bullets penetrated armour-plating. Proceeded in company with Tank 'Carstairs,' which silenced enemy M.G. fire. Cameron Highlanders then advanced, and Tank followed, bellied near Zonnebeke Stream. Mud was up to floor level and door of sponson was pushed off its hinges. Enemy aeroplane circled overhead, and fired on them whilst attempting to unditch. Eventually Tank 'Carstairs' came to the rescue, and Tank was got clear.

". . . Tank 'Culloden' had her unditching gear carried away by barbed wire near Hill Cottage. Unditching beam was recovered, but again broke loose, until secured with rope. Just west of Frost House shell burst under front of Tank. Whilst crossing light railway half-way between Frost House and Square Farm, a second shell hit roof door and killed one gunner. Tank stopped, and it was found petrol pressure pipe was cut. Time 9.15 a.m. A third shell struck behind right sponson. Crew were withdrawn from Tank, and took up a position in shell-holes near Square Farm. Tank was still being shelled, undoubtedly by an anti-Tank gun, about ten shells being fired at it in five minutes, six of which hit the Tank.

"Tank 'Cyprus' was then seen to be hit by the same anti-Tank gun. At 10.15 a.m. survivors of Tanks 'Culloden' and 'Cyprus,' together with undamaged Lewis guns, withdrew to Battalion Rallying Point, after pigeon messages had been despatched reporting the situation.

". . . Tank 'Carstairs' arrived at Black Line near Beck House, but infantry had not then arrived.

"Tank soon bellied in boggy ground, but was unditched successfully. Just west of Borry Farm Tank 'Caithness' was found badly bellied, and with unditching gear lost.

"Having been informed by 6th Cameron Highlanders that the second objective had been captured, Tank 'Carstairs' hitched on to Tank 'Caithness' and towed it out. Enemy shell-fire was extremely heavy, and an aeroplane flew over, firing at crew with machine-guns during the operation.

"Instructions were then received to return to Battalion Rallying Point."

Another very gallant action was fought by a Tank crew also belonging to this Battalion.

They started the battle in a Tank named "Ca' Canny" under

command of Lieutenant H. P. M. Jones, who was killed near Wilde Wood. The crew carried on under command of Corporal Jenkins until about 11 p.m., when the Tank " bellied " hopelessly. Corporal Jenkins withdrew his Lewis guns and crew, and, placing some of them on the top of the Tank and some on the ground, kept up an effective fire on the enemy, who were then attempting a small counter-attack.

He then transferred his men to another Tank, " Clyde," whose crew had all been wounded. They fought this Tank for a further two hours, but at about three o'clock " Clyde," too, stuck in the mud and proved inextricable. He and his crew then returned on foot to their Battalion Rallying Point.

With the 18th Corps, the 1st Brigade Tanks were on several occasions signalled for by fairly distant parties of infantry, who proceeded to " set " them at strong points that were giving trouble. This system worked extremely well, and had a particularly impressive moral effect on the enemy. Several occasions are recorded on which enemy garrisons did not wait for the Tank which had been thus " whistled up " to get near enough to fire, but surrendered as soon as they saw it coming.

Our advance had continued for about ten hours, that is, till nearly three in the afternoon, when our enterprise seemed to have succeeded.

As early as nine in the morning we held the whole of our second objective north of Westhoek.

By the afternoon we had entered St. Julien, Frezenberg and the Pommern Redoubt, and had taken the crossings of the Steenbeek and Stirling Castle.

Glencorse Wood and Inverness Copse had proved more difficult, but even here we held a footing on the ridge.

We had " riven the oak," we were now to feel the force of the rebound.

That afternoon in a downpour of rain the enemy counter-attacked along the fronts of all three Corps. There was a fierce struggle, in which in many instances Tanks were able to do a good deal of execution.

We were shelled out of St. Julien. North of it we withdrew to the line of the Steenbeek, and we were obliged to fall back from all but the western outskirts of Westhoek.

All afternoon we slowly lost ground, yet when night fell we could still boast a battle well begun. It was, after all, never meant to be a one-day attack, and to-morrow we should start well. We had everywhere taken and held our first objective, that is, the low muddy ridge from which the enemy had so closely threatened the original Ypres arena.

The second flat valley and the higher ridge from Passchendaele to Staden now lay before us.

At least we were in a good position for to-morrow's attack.
Mr. Buchan thus in effect analyses our gains:

Along two-thirds of our line of attack we held our first objectives. On half of the remaining third we had only fallen just short of our final objective. On the remaining sixth we had even slightly exceeded our final objective. We had besides taken 6000 prisoners and a quantity of machine-guns.

II

All that night the enemy counter-attacked us doggedly, resolved upon driving us down again. All night we fought to keep what we had won, and prepared the redoubled blow that we meant to deliver next day.

That blow was destined never to be struck. The wind that brought the rain blew out our hopes of victory.

> * "The weather had been threatening throughout the [first] day, and had rendered the work of our aeroplanes very difficult from the commencement of the battle. During the afternoon, while fighting was still in progress, rain began, and fell steadily all night.
>
> "Thereafter, for four days, the rain continued without cessation. . . . The low-lying, clayey soil, torn by shells and sodden with rain, turned to a succession of vast muddy pools. The valleys of the choked and overflowing streams were speedily transformed into long stretches of bog, impassable except by a few well-defined tracks, which became marks for the enemy's artillery. To leave these tracks was to risk death by drowning, and in the course of the subsequent fighting on several occasions both men and pack animals were lost in this way. In these conditions operations of any magnitude became impossible, and the resumption of our offensive was necessarily postponed until a period of fine weather should allow the ground to recover. As had been the case in the Arras battle, this unavoidable delay in the development of our offensive was of the greatest service to the enemy. Valuable time was lost, the troops opposed to us were able to recover from the disorganisation produced by our first attack, and the enemy was given the opportunity to bring up reinforcements."

It was nearly a fortnight before the 5th Army could again attack.

* Sir Douglas Haig's Despatch.

The disappointment of the Higher Command was acute; acute, too, were the physical and mental miseries suffered during that fortnight by the Tank Corps and all the other arms engaged.

Their magnificent efforts, their sacrifices, were of no avail. There they lay day after day, drenched by the inexorable rain, those in the forward area half choked in the rising streams of liquid mud.

It was in no sunny frame of mind that the 5th Army Headquarters Staff read the verdict of the three Corps upon the day's work done by the Tanks.

The three Summaries were agreed that the courage and perseverance shown by Tank personnel had been admirable.

One Corps, however, had given way thoroughly to the spirit of the time. They practically reported that Tanks had been of no use to any one, and moreover that they were never likely to be. With the 30th Division they had been unable to deal with certain machine-gun emplacements; with the 24th they had been late, they always drew enemy shell-fire; and with the 8th Division one Tank had even lost direction and been reported as firing on our own men.

Another Corps had found Tanks helpful, and said all they could for them.

Tanks had greatly assisted the Gordons and Black Watch at Frezenberg, they had dealt effectively with concrete dug-outs; with the 55th Division they had broken the wave of an enemy counter-attack at Winnipeg, and everywhere their moral effect on the enemy had been of great assistance. Twenty-four Tanks had been put out of action by bad going or shell-fire.

A third Corps with fewer machines had in many cases reached their objective without being held up. The Tanks had in these cases merely followed the infantry, but they reported that without Tanks the capture of the strongly wired position of Alberta would have cost the 39th Division dear, and that on the Steenbeek near Ferdinand Farm the enemy, who had bolted at the mere sight of a Tank, had been "dealt with" at ease with a machine-gun by infantry of the 51st Division.

Upon these Summaries and upon later failures the Commander of the 5th Army was subsequently to base a generally unfavourable report upon Tanks.

The report may be condensed into a simple syllogism :—

    1. Tanks were unable to negotiate bad ground.
    2. The ground on a battlefield will always be bad.
    3. Therefore Tanks are no good on a battlefield.

He added to this, that being no longer a surprise to the enemy, he considered that Tanks had lost their moral effect, and had no value used in masses.

This report was not officially presented for some weeks, but the Higher Tank Command must early have perceived the drift of affairs. The events of the first day and the manner in which those events were interpreted gave only too much data to the prophetic spirit. The junior Tank personnel knew little of what was going on. Like Burns's mouse, they were only touched by the present, the throwing away of what had cost them so many weeks of toil. To the Higher Tank Command was reserved Burns's own fate :

> " But, och ! I backward cast my ee
> On prospects drear !
> And forward, tho' I canna see,
> I guess and fear."

What would be the results of the initial ill-success of the battle, and of the further Tank failures which seemed only too probable when an advance which had begun so ill was continued, after perhaps two or three inches more rain?

How were the final arbiters, G.H.Q. and the War Cabinet, going to regard such failures? Tanks had been employed under grotesque conditions, and after all, they had failed in common with every other arm. Were the events of the next few weeks to be disastrous enough to consign them irrevocably to Bottomless Perdition?

At best their hopes of expansion would most probably be nipped. Their establishment would be reduced, and Tanks would be used in *petits pâquets* again, by ones and twos as they had been in the past, because, once more, there would never be enough machines for an effective action.

As the days wore on, and the rain continued (at the rate often of an inch a day), one of these alternative fates seemed inevitable.

The gloomy surmises of the Tank Headquarters Staff were only too well founded. The authorities were in fact suffering from one of the worst cold fits which the pilots of the Tank Corps at home and abroad ever endured.

Tank Corps Headquarters heard it all. They knew well enough that in well-informed but irresponsible London circles the remark, " I hear the Tanks are going to be abolished," was a common one ; that often in such gossip circumstances of person and date would be added.

For all this they had no certain refutation. If only Tanks could even now do something that would catch the eye of authority. Some little " show " exploit. Something that would at least make a summary condemnation unlikely. The battle would have to be continued some day. Tanks would have to play their part, but in that intolerable swamp was it likely that they would do anything except engulf themselves—literally and metaphorically—yet deeper than before?

There, however, lay the Tanks' best hope. Chance and their own exertions might bring them a success even in Flanders.

III

Thirty-six Tanks belonging to the 1st Brigade had remained in Army Reserve. On August 16, the weather having been less wet for a day or two, the first and most considerable of a series of renewed attacks was to be made.

Twelve Tanks were to co-operate with the infantry on the Langemarck–St. Julien front.

On the night of the 13th the Tanks began to move up. The roads were already congested with other traffic, and the Tanks were not to be allowed to make use of them.

> * " The country they had to traverse was all very deep in mud, and the Tanks wallowed on their bellies in ground too soft for the tracks to hold. The approach was continued during the following night, but in spite of the repeated use of unditching beams, the mutual help of Tanks in towing each other, and the valuable assistance of a Tunnelling Company, it was recognised on the 15th that none but the four leading Tanks could hope to reach the line in time to take part in the battle. These four made strenuous efforts to complete the journey the next night, but without success. None of them could overcome the difficulties of the ground, and the infantry had to go into attack without them."

The infantry attacked, and after the action a nest of pill-box strongholds north-east of St. Julien still remained untaken.

Like most of these little fortresses, they had been extremely skilfully placed. An unwary advance would be trapped in their wire just within convenient range of their machine-guns.

They were so small, scattered, and well concealed as to be almost impossible targets for heavy guns, and as they were built of reinforced concrete at least three feet thick, the ordinary high-explosive shell thrown by a field gun had no effect upon them.

* " G " (7th) Battalion History.

This particular nest consisted of four pill-boxes of more than average size.

Three of them were hidden in the ruins of farmsteads. That in the Mont du Hibou was manned by a garrison of about eighty men, and the Cockcroft was still more strongly held. Triangle Farm and Hillock Farm were slightly smaller. It was essential that they should be taken, and General Sir Ivor Maxse, commanding the 18th Corps, was informed by the Brigadiers concerned that their capture would probably cost us 600 to 1000 casualties. He and Colonel Baker-Carr (commanding 1st Brigade of Tanks) then considered the possibility of a Tank attack.

Colonel Baker-Carr, admirably undismayed by the dismal events of the 16th, optimistically guaranteed the fortresses at half the estimated cost to the infantry, and the attack was arranged. One innovation he specially asked for. There was to be no shelling, but he was to be granted the concealment of a smoke barrage. Having once decided to entrust the affair to the Tanks, General Maxse was zealous to give them every possible chance of success and did not hesitate to modify his orders to suit their considered demands. Only twelve Tanks were to be employed, and they and their infantry were to use the roads for as far as these served them. Colonel Baker-Carr decided to form a composite Company from " G " (7th) Battalion under the command of Major Broome.

The resulting action, small as were the numbers engaged, will ever find a place in the annals of the Tank Corps.

> * "In spite of the appalling condition of the ground, for it had now been raining steadily for three weeks, a very memorable feat of arms was achieved."

The four strong points were triumphantly captured.

> * " Phenomenal results were obtained at very little cost, for instead of 600 to 1000 casualties, the infantry following the Tanks only sustained fifteen ! "

At 4.45 a.m. on the morning of August 19, the artillery isolated the doomed strongholds in clouds of dense smoke.

The action had been carefully rehearsed. Two Tanks were to be used against each pill-box, and they were to take them in rear, so striking where the forts were most vulnerable, and at the same time cutting off the garrison's retreat.

Just before six o'clock the enveloping manœuvre was com-

* W.T.N.

plete, and the first pill-box—Hillock Farm—fell, nearly all its garrison having fled.

At 6.15 two Tanks reached the Mont du Hibou, and fired forty rounds from their 6-pounder guns into the back door of the stronghold. Sixty of the garrison fled, of whom about half escaped or were shot down, and the rest surrendered to the infantry as soon as it came up.

Triangle Farm fell ten minutes afterwards. The garrison had put up a fight against the Tanks, and our infantry killed them all, mostly with the bayonet.

At the Cockcroft the attacking Tank * got ditched within fifty yards of its victim. But at sight of it the garrison of over 100 " withdrew." The Tank and its infantry immediately opened fire with their Lewis guns, and more than half the fugitives fell.

> † " Our infantry then consolidated the Cockcroft. This completed the capture of all objectives.
> " The Tanks waited till consolidation was well forward before returning.
> " *Casualties*—Infantry : no killed, 15 wounded.
> "Tank Personnel—Killed : Officers, none ; other Ranks, 2. Wounded : Officers, 2 ; other Ranks, 10."

In one of the strong points we found a German officer who had been hanged by his men.

The St. Julien attack, as it was afterwards called, proved a sufficient counterblast to the 5th Army report.

The friends of the Tank Corps made the most of it. It was a brilliant little exploit, and once brought to notice, the casualty figures pleaded too loudly to be ignored.

It is probably no exaggeration to say that it was in some measure to the Tanks which won the little Battle of St. Julien that the Tank Corps owed the opportunity of winning the Battle of Cambrai.

IV

From August 22 till October 9, by which time hope of a British success at Ypres had been more or less abandoned, the Tanks fought in about a dozen minor actions. They made almost as many more unavailing attempts to fight. Like the rest of the Army, they spent much vain labour and knew the

---

* The second Tank detailed for this strong point had—in common with the two reserve Tanks—bellied or become ditched on the way up.
† Official Summary.

weariness of much frustrated effort. They made elaborate and toilsome movements in preparation for attacks which were never launched. They struggled night after night to get up to some battle which eventually had to take place without them. Tanks had now invariably to move upon the roads, as the ground between had finally and definitely been reduced to impassable swamp. The roads naturally formed standing targets for the German gunners. We lost heavily in men and machines. General Elles had originally estimated that one machine in two would get into effective action. Now, in view of the appalling ground conditions, he revised this, only reckoning on one machine in ten getting into effective contact with the enemy. This modest estimate was as a matter of fact seldom exceeded.

Whenever Tanks did get into action, however, they usually did well, though rarely decisively, in spite of the standard of extraordinary courage which was steadfastly maintained by the crews.

The briefest review of most of these depressing little engagements is all that need be given. They were remarkable for nothing except the heroic patience shown day after day by every arm of our attacking forces.

On August 22 a minor attack was launched by all three Corps. Small parties of Tanks fought with each.

With the *2nd Corps* in Glencorse Wood four Tanks of the 2nd Brigade were of some service, and did considerable execution.

With the *19th Corps* eighteen Tanks of the 3rd Brigade were used on the off-chance of their being able to reach the objectives. The going was more than ordinarily atrocious, the whole of the Frezenberg–Zonnebeke road having been shot away. One Tank fought a very remarkable action, engaging the enemy near " Gallipoli " for sixty-eight hours.

With the *18th Corps* twelve Tanks of the 1st Brigade headed an attack on Bülow Farm, Vancouver, Winnipeg, and other strong points. They proved useful, and several Tanks were in action for longish periods.

Two things are remarkable about this operation : first, that every Tank which ventured to leave the road instantly bellied. One was " drowned " in six or seven feet of water.

Secondly, the remarkable way in which they affected enemy *moral*. In several instances parties of the enemy surrendered at the sight of them. Prisoners in their examination said that they could have held up infantry, but " felt helpless against Tanks."

Next day, on August 23, four 2nd Brigade Tanks went into action near Inverness Copse. The operation had had to be

A DEADLY SWAMP. (THE WRECKS OF SIX TANKS MAY BE COUNTED.)

THE SALIENT.

"CLAPHAM JUNCTION" NEAR SANCTUARY WOOD.

undertaken in a hurry, liaison was bad, and the attack a failure.

On August 26 four Tanks fought with the 33rd Division in the neighbourhood of Jerk House (near Glencorse Wood). The morning was misty, and an enemy shell unfortunately exploded a dump of smoke bombs just behind our lines. The attack was a failure. That night an inch of rain fell, and four Tanks which were to have operated with the 14th Division next day, August 27, never reached their starting-point. Thirteen men were wounded and an officer killed on the way up.

Nearly three weeks elapsed before Tanks were again in action, and several battalions from the 2nd and 3rd Brigades were moved back to a new training area near Arras. A certain number of "Replacement Tanks" were issued to remaining battalions. The 1st Brigade stood ready in case they should be wanted at short notice, but no attacks of any sort were launched, probably partly on account of weather, and partly because a section of the 5th Army front was in process of transfer to the 2nd Army.

By the middle of September the relief had been completed, and again we endeavoured to press on.

On September 20 a fairly successful assault was made along the whole line. 2nd Brigade Tanks took part near Inverness Copse, and 1st Brigade Tanks near Triangle and Wurst Farms. But the ground being known to be unusually appalling in both areas, they had been given minor parts. These parts they played with fair success, and they undoubtedly scared the enemy a good deal. On the 18th Corps front 3rd Battalion Tanks had rather better luck.

The efforts made by the crews to get to the battle at all were superhuman.

Trees had been felled across the road by the enemy, resting breast high on their branches and the tall stumps from which they were not completely severed. At Wurst Farm also this kind of obstacle had been opposed to the Tanks—the butts of the trees lying obliquely and at a slope, forming a barrier very difficult to surmount.

If one leading machine got into difficulties struggling in the dark through or over these obstacles, the whole string of Tanks behind would be hung up, the deep swamps on either hand making it impossible to leave the road.

The Tanks, however, arrived, and are reported to have "inflicted many casualties."

On September 26 fifteen Tanks operated near Zonnebeke Village. The attack was not a success, though the Tanks did a great deal of good work.

On October 4 took place the last two actions of this battle in which Tanks succeeded in playing a part. The first was fought by twelve Tanks of the 1st Brigade, who had the honour of taking part in the capture of Poelcapelle. It was a most successful little attack, and after reducing three strong points which guarded the outskirts, the Tanks hunted through the main street and out beyond the village.

In the other action four Tanks of the 1st Battalion were to take part in an attack upon Juniper Cottage on the line of the Reutelbeek.

Not only was this, like the other, a successful little action, it was ennobled by affording the background to one of the most patiently courageous actions of the War.

It was on October 4 that Captain Robertson fell upon completing a service for which he was posthumously awarded the V.C.

Tanks and infantry were to endeavour to cross the Reutelbeek and drive the enemy from the positions which they held on the further bank.

There was only one bridge over the marshy stream. If, in the half-light of the early morning and in the confusion of battle, they missed this crossing-place, their one chance of success was gone.

Captain Robertson, the officer commanding the section of Tanks, early realised that here lay the crux of the little operation for whose success he was responsible. For three days and nights he and his servant, Private Allen (subsequently awarded the D.C.M.), went carefully backwards and forwards over the ground under heavy fire, taping the routes for the Tanks.

Working without a break, this task took them until half-past nine on the night before the action.

It was time to get the machines up.

Captain Robertson started out at once again with his Tanks. The weather was dark and misty, and from inside a Tank it was impossible to see the way over the heavily shelled ground. Captain Robertson therefore walked ahead; they reached the assembly point in good time, and at 6 a.m. on October 4 he led them into action.

In imagining the rest of the story we are to remember that Captain Robertson had already been continuously under fire and without sleep for three days and nights.

The roads and every other landmark had all been wiped out by the shelling, but the bridge still stood. Captain Robertson still led his Tanks on foot, facing besides the shells an intense close-range machine-gun and rifle fire. He must have known that to go forward on foot meant certain death.

He and his convoy were by now well ahead of the infantry.

Captain Robertson's V.C.

Still he led his Tanks on, carefully and patiently guiding them at a foot's pace towards their objective.

They reached the bridge, and one by one the Tanks crossed over. He led them on towards a road that would take them straight up to the enemy positions, the machine-gun fire growing more and more intense as they advanced.

They reached the road, and as they reached it Captain Robertson at last fell, shot through the head.

But the Tanks went on, and succeeded in their mission. The object for which Captain Robertson had so deliberately sacrificed his life was achieved.

The 2nd and 3rd Brigades had by now gone back to Arras to refit their machines, and to replenish their ranks. The 1st Brigade, however, made two more efforts to take part in the fighting. The battle was by now recognised as a serious British check. The Germans' " elastic tactics " and the weather had together delayed us for so long that they had defeated us.

We had inflicted heavy losses on the enemy, and had in the act suffered still more severely ourselves.

Our hopes of clearing the coast were gone.

At the end of ten weeks we had achieved gains which had been on the programme for the first fortnight.

The whole plan of campaign had to be reconsidered, and to take Passchendaele must now be our ultimate ambition.

On October 7 two Tanks were to operate ahead of their infantry and endeavour to capture two fortified farms. Half-way to their objective a derelict Tank blocked the way, and the two advancing machines became ditched on trying to make a détour. By the time they had been unditched it was too late to go on.

On the 9th eight Tanks were to have attacked strong points on the Poelcapelle Road. At midnight on the night of the 8th–9th they started for their objectives.

The road was everywhere encumbered with blown-up limbers and the bodies of dead teams.

Large shell-holes had been blown in it.

The Tanks managed to get on as far as the Poelcapelle cross-roads, but the enemy then began to shell the road heavily. The leading Tank ditched in a new shell-hole, the second Tank as it waited to pass was set on fire by a direct hit.

These two wrecks formed a complete barrier to the advance of the rest of the column.

No way being found by which the surviving Tanks could circumvent the obstacle, and the shelling having grown hotter, it was decided to return.

But they had not gone far on the return journey when they discovered that on the way up the last machine of the column had somehow fouled an old derelict Tank. The remaining machines were trapped, and could neither go forward nor back.

The efforts of their crews proved vain, and they were all five lost, some being hit by enemy shells and the crews killed or wounded, and some ditched in vain efforts to make their escape across country.

The enemy continued to shell the road, which was one we were obliged to use, and it was a work of extreme hazard and difficulty to clear it of the wrecks by which it was completely blocked.

The work was, however, performed. Every night for a week Major G. L. Wilkes,* the 1st Brigade Engineer, used to go up the road as far as he could in a Tank. Then he would get out and work till morning. Most of the wrecks he blew up, some he and his small party of men were able to tip over into the swamp.

The scene on the first of these expeditions is thus described by an engineer officer who accompanied him:

> "I left St. Julien in the dark, having been informed that our guns were not going to fire. I waded up the road, which was swimming in a foot or two of slush; frequently I would stumble into a shell-hole hidden by the mud. The road was a complete shambles and strewn with débris, broken vehicles, dead and dying horses and men; I must have passed hundreds of them as well as bits of men and animals littered everywhere. As I neared Poelcapelle our guns started to fire; at once the Germans replied, pouring shells on and around the road; the flashes of the bursting shells were all round me. I cannot describe what it felt like; the nearest approach to a picture I can give is that it was like standing in the centre of the flame of a gigantic Primus stove. As I neared the derelict Tanks, the scene became truly appalling: wounded men lay drowned in the mud, others were stumbling and falling through exhaustion, others crawled and rested themselves up against the dead to raise themselves a little above the mud. On reaching the Tanks I found them surrounded by the dead and dying; men had crawled to them for what shelter they would afford. The nearest Tank was a Female. Her left sponson doors were open. Out of these protruded four pairs of legs; exhausted and wounded men had sought refuge in this machine, and dead and dying lay in a jumbled heap inside."

* Major Wilkes was awarded the D.S.O. for this piece of work.

So ended the tragedy of October 9, the last of a series of hopeless adventures.

A few Tanks were later moved up to a new railhead, with the hope that better weather might enable them to take part in the final attack on Passchendaele, the attack which was to end the Flanders offensive. But the weather did not mend, and it was without the help of Tanks that by a final effort the heights of Passchendaele were stormed and taken in the first week of November. We held our gains. The high ground was ours, the weary armies might rest, and the tragic nightmare of the Third Battle of Ypres was over at last.

When time brought the verdict of the Official Despatch upon the work of the Tanks, it was neither an unjust nor an unkindly one :—

> *" Although throughout the major part of the Ypres battle, and especially in its later stages, the condition of the ground made the use of Tanks difficult or impossible, yet whenever circumstances were in any way favourable, and even when they were not, very gallant and valuable work has been accomplished by Tank Commanders and crews on a great number of occasions. Long before the conclusion of the Flanders offensive these new instruments had proved their worth, and amply justified the labour, material and personnel diverted to their construction and development."

It was not to be long before the Corps had an opportunity of proving their worth indeed.

* Sir Douglas Haig's Despatch.

CHAPTER X

THE FIRST BATTLE OF CAMBRAI

> "On they move
> Indissolubly firm; nor obvious hill
> Nor straightening vale, nor wood nor stream divides
> Their perfect ranks."
>
> *Paradise Lost.*

PART I

I

ALL through the later part of the Ypres struggle the Tank Corps had turned their eyes towards certain other parts of the line with a longing as for The Delectable Mountains.

They imagined places in dry rolling chalk country where a Tank could travel on the surface of the ground. They dreamed of battles in which the artillery had neither given the enemy weeks of warning nor helped him to reduce the ground to a swamp or the likeness of an ash heap.

A starving man does not picture every circumstance of a meal, a drowning man the sensations of warmth and solidity, more vividly than did the Tank Corps call up their dream battle.

General Elles and his Staff had several places in mind in which such a battle might be fought. Perhaps they dwelt most affectionately on the thoughts of some sector of the Hindenburg Line, some high rolling chalk plateau anywhere south of Arras.

Several such delightful spots lay in the domain of General Sir Julian Byng's 3rd Army. Perhaps he had some sort of operation in view already! In September General Elles hopefully paid him a visit as he lay at Albert. They conferred.

The Army Commander had, indeed, an idea of attacking.

More, he had already independently worked out the place, and many of the details, of just such an attack as the Tank Corps had been sighing for.

Together the two Generals worked at the scheme and a draft plan was forwarded to G.H.Q.

G.H.Q., however, could not allow the attack for the present. The Ypres affair must first be thrashed out, but when that was ended, say by early November, then such an attack would have their blessing.

Meanwhile the two conspirators waited eagerly, all the while working out and perfecting their plans.

At last, on October 20, the scheme was finally sanctioned, and Z day was fixed for November 20. Still only four members of the Tank Corps Staff knew of the project, and these four immediately stole off to our lines near Havrincourt to make a preliminary survey of the new site.

II

The First Battle of Cambrai was to be a single-minded battle. It was to fulfil in the simplest way the prime function of war, that is, to destroy the forces of the enemy.

To attain this end it was to rely upon surprise, audacity, and rapidity of movement.

Its main action was to be completed in about twenty-four hours, during which time it was proposed to penetrate the Hindenburg Line, which here consisted of four systems of trenches. Territorial gains were not to be so much considered as were the destruction and capture of enemy personnel and material. In other words, we were out to kill and chivvy Germans. The system of attack was to be one completely new for a full-dress battle. There was to be no artillery preparation whatever. To all appearance the front line was to be perfectly normal up to the very moment of attack, when two Army Corps and three Brigades of Tanks were suddenly to hurl their whole weight against the enemy.

Such tactics demanded that the most complete secrecy should be maintained up to zero hour itself, and for the second time in the history of the Tanks a vital secret was successfully kept.

The area to be raided lay just south of Cambrai. It was an open rolling chalk plateau, which had lain uncultivated for two years, and was now covered with a thin growth of wan grey grass.

From north-west to south-east the low ridges ran, save where the dominating hump of Bourlon's wood-crowned Hill ran across the grain of the country.

On either flank of this area, sometimes at right angles to the curve of our lines, sometimes running parallel to the German lines, ran the Canal du Nord and the Canal de l'Escaut.

The slopes were nowhere very steep, but the levels were everywhere varied by spurs and—so-called—" ravines." One of these, which lay just within the German lines, and parallel to our front, for some time gave grave concern both to the Tanks and to other arms, who apparently coupled it in their minds with the Grand Cañon of Colorado. Its name sounded so formidable, and it was marked so large on the map! It might well prove a serious obstacle to the progress of Tanks. A series of exhaustive reconnaissances carried out by the Tank Corps, however, dispelled this alarming legend, and the " Grand Ravine " stood revealed as being no more than a shallow dry field ditch which could be jumped by any rabbit of reasonable activity.

The German defences, the famous Hindenburg Line, lay wide and strong across the spurs. The main line of resistance had been everywhere well placed on the reverse slopes of the main ridges, and was invisible from our lines. Only from the air and from rare posts of vantage could we see a length of it. There were three lines of trenches, each trench anything up to 15 ft. wide, with an outpost line thrown forward to screen these main defences. In front of the main line lay band upon band and acre upon acre of dense wire; nowhere was it less than 50 yards deep, and here and there it jutted out in great salients flanked by batteries of machine-guns. Never had we before been faced with such a wilderness of wire.

It was calculated that to cut it with artillery would have taken five weeks and cost twenty millions of money.

Not only was the actual " ditch " of the trench believed to be in most places some 12 ft. wide and 18 ft. deep, but at either side, the parados and parapet (each about 2 ft. 6 in. high) were, we had reason to believe, so sloped as to increase the effective width to about 16 to 18 ft.

These were the dimensions of some trenches captured by us at Arras, and for such trenches we had to be prepared.

The space to be cleared was too wide for a Tank. A special means of crossing was, however, devised by the Staff of the Central Workshops at Erin.

This was a special huge fascine made of about seventy-five ordinary bundles of brushwood, strongly compressed and bound by heavy chains.

It was carried on the nose of the machine, and could be released by a touch from inside the Tank by a specially ingenious releasing gear, and dropped neatly into the trench.

The manufacture of the 350 fascines and the fitting of the Tanks with the releasing gear was a piece of work of which the Central Workshops have reason to be proud. They received the order for 350 fascines and 110 Tank sledges on October 24, when they had already for some months been working at high pressure, chiefly upon Tanks salved from the Salient.

Making the Fascines

To fulfil the new order the shops worked day and night for three weeks.

To make the fascines, 21,000 ordinary stout bundles of brushwood, such as are used for road repairing, were unloaded at the Central Workshops.

Here eighteen Tanks had been specially fitted up, for binding and fastening these into bundles of sixty or seventy.

The Tanks acted in pairs, pulling in opposite directions at steel chains which had been previously wound round and round the bundles.

So great was the pressure thus exerted that, months afterwards, an infantryman in search of firewood, who found one of these fascines and gaily filed through its binding chain, was killed by the sudden springing open of the bundle.

When they were ready, each bundle weighed a ton and a half, and it took twenty of the Chinese coolies employed at the Central Workshops to roll one of them through the mud. On one occasion 144 fascines had to be loaded on to trucks within twenty-four hours. Concurrently with the fascines the Central Workshops achieved the making of the 110 Tank sledges. The whole of the timber needed for this work had to be sawn out of logs. Besides this they repaired and issued 127 Tanks.

III

Each Tank could only carry one fascine, and once it had dropped it into a trench had no means of picking it up again. There were, however, three broad trenches to be crossed.

This circumstance had to be taken into account in the general scheme of attack. Every detail of this plan had been most ably worked out either by Lieut.-Colonel Fuller himself (G.S.O.I. to the Tank Corps), or by the Staff whom he inspired. Every movement and formation which we are going to describe had been reduced to an exact drill, several special exercises being evolved for the occasion. One of them, a simple platoon drill for the infantry, was, we are told by an official historian, based upon a drill described by Xenophon in the *Cyropædia*, and attributed by him to Cyrus of Persia (*circa* 500 B.C.).

Very briefly the main plan was as follows :—

The whole line of attack was divided into areas for three Tanks who formed a section and worked together.

Of these one was an " Advance Guard Tank," and the other two were " Infantry Tanks."

The advance guard Tank was to go straight forward through

the enemy's wire, and, turning to the left without crossing it, to shoot along the fire trench which lay in front of it.

Its object was to keep down the enemy and protect the two infantry Tanks. These the while both made for one selected spot in the trench; the left-hand one cast in its fascine, crossed the trench on it, turned to the left and worked down the fire trench; the right-hand Tank crossed the fire trench on the first Tank's fascine, and made for the second trench, dropped in its fascine, and crossing, worked down this second trench. Meanwhile the advance guard Tank had swung round and crossed over the first and second trenches on the fascines of the two infantry Tanks, and it therefore moved forward with its own fascine still in position for the third line.

The infantry were also divided into three forces and worked in single file. The first force were "Trench Clearers." They worked with the Tanks, and helped to clear up trenches and dug-outs. They carried small red flags with which they marked the paths which the Tanks had made through the wire. The second were the "Trench Stops," who, as it were, played the net over the rabbit hole to the Tank's ferret. The third force were the "Trench Garrisons," who took over the trenches as they were captured.

One feature of the combined Tank and infantry training for this battle was particularly interesting.

They had not very long to work together, yet it was essential that the infantry should have confidence in the trench-spanning and wire-cutting power of the Tanks.

Infantry units were therefore invited by the Tank Corps to build their own defences and entanglements, the Tanks guaranteeing to cross the trenches and chew up the wire of their best efforts.

Some very formidable and ingenious defences were made.

The Tanks, however, everywhere carried out their guarantee, to the great edification of the infantry.

The following table gives briefly the allocation of Tanks and infantry to the various objectives:

ALLOCATION OF FIGHTING TANKS

1st Brigade Battalions.	Tanks (No.)	3rd Corps Divisions.
D (4)	42	On Right : 51st,
E (5)	42	51st and 62nd.
G (7)	42	On Left : 62nd.

Objectives : Havrincourt, Flesquières.

Of each battalion: thirty-six Tanks for 1st, 12 (plus survivors) for 2nd Objective.

The Detailed Plans

Exploitation towards Fontaine, Bourlon Wood, the Bapaume–Cambrai Road, Bourlon Village and Graincourt. Bridges over Canal du Nord.

2nd Brigade Battalions.	Tanks (No.)	4th Corps Divisions.
B (2)	42 on Right.	6th.
H (8)	42 on Left.	6th.

Objectives: Beaucamp, Villers, Plouich Road.
Exploitation towards Marcoing, Preny Chapel, and Nine Wood.

3rd Brigade Battalions.	Tanks (No.)	4th Corps Divisions.
C (3)	42	12th.
F (6)	42	,,
I (9)	42	20th.
A * (1)	42	,,

Objective: La Vacquerie.
Exploitation towards Crèvecœur, Masnières, and Marcoing.

The part to be played by the artillery was carefully worked out. There was to be no preliminary bombardment, but as soon as the attack was launched the heavy guns were to begin counter-battery work and were to shrapnel the bridges along the Canal.

At the same time a jumping barrage of smoke shells and H.E. was to cover the advance of the Tanks and infantry.

The secrecy of the attack made it impossible for any registering shots to be fired, and the ranges could be worked out in theory only.

Several squadrons of the R.A.F. were to co-operate, flying low; their especial work being to bomb enemy Headquarters.

The cavalry were also billed to co-operate. Special wire-pulling Tanks fitted with grapnels were employed to clear convenient broad lanes through the wire for them, and their needs were throughout carefully considered.

For one reason and another, however, the cavalry did not, after all, find it possible to take much part in the fighting.

The preparations for the battle were of the thorough and laborious kind always requisite for a " full-dress " attack.

An immense amount of railway movement was necessary in order to bring up the three Tank Brigades, whose component parts were a good deal scattered. Thirty-six trainloads of twelve Tanks each had to be dealt with, and their stores besides.

For the sake of secrecy all this movement was done after

* " A " Battalion was borrowed from 2nd Brigade.

dark. There were only two minor accidents, otherwise the whole scheme was worked out exactly to programme.

The usual huge dumps of petrol and grease and special stores had to be formed. Most of them were made in neighbouring woods, where the Tanks also lay up. Havrincourt Wood and Desert Wood were, for instance, used for main dumps, and as lying-up places for the 1st and 2nd Brigades, for in these woods the hornbeam undergrowth had not yet shed its leaves, and the Tanks and their stores could lie in perfect secrecy.

For the 3rd Brigade, however, there was no wood conveniently near, and the Tanks lay out in a village with camouflage clothes thrown over them, painted to represent bricks and tiles.

For the forward dumps splendid work was done by the 3rd Army's light railways, who handled astonishing masses of stores; for example, 165,000 gallons of petrol, 541,000 rounds of 6-pounder ammunition, and 5,000,000 rounds of S.A.A.

Beyond the light railways the Tank fills were transported by supply Tanks.

All these preparations had to be carried out as secretly as possible. Moves were made after dark.

No new wheel tracks must be made. There must be no reference to the battle over the telephone. There must be no extra horse or mechanical transport seen about in daylight.

The concentration of Tanks in the background was explained by the establishment of an alleged new training area. Tank Corps Headquarters established with the army at Albert was disguised under the plausible alias of " The Tank Corps Training Office."

There must be no increase in aeroplane activity for reconnaissance purposes.

The same troops were to continue to hold the line, the attacking forces passing through them, and those in the line were as far as possible to be kept in the dark as to the new operations. There was always a danger of men in the trenches being taken prisoner in some raid, and the less they knew the better. Oosthoek Wood had not been forgotten.

All the Reconnaissance Officers and the Tank Staff who had to frequent the line wore non-committal burberries and discreet tin hats; one well-known Staff Officer even went to the length of affecting blue glasses; in fact, in the matter of disguise the line was only drawn at ginger whiskers. The cars they came in had their distinguishing badges taken off, and their drivers were carefully primed with cock-and-bull stories with which to explain their presence. Staff and Reconnaissance Officers slunk about, above all avoiding Headquarters and those other social centres which etiquette enjoins must be first called upon by all who visit other people's trenches. Friends

Stealthy Preparations

were stealthily avoided, and a curious jumble of assorted and obvious lies was gradually put into circulation.

At the Lyceum the villain conducts his affairs in this sort of way without arousing the least suspicion in any one, but in real life, and particularly in the line where a look-out must constantly be kept for spies, such conduct is apt to cause remark.

Before Cambrai embarrassing situations frequently arose which could be elucidated only by the drawing aside of some justly indignant Commanding Officer for a few minutes' whispered conversation.

At the 1st Brigade Headquarters in Arras there was a locked room with " No admittance " written large upon the door. Here were ostentatiously hung spoof maps of other topical districts and a profusion of plans lay spread about.

The Reconnaissance Officer always hoped that this room was duly ransacked by the " unauthorised person," for whose visit he had taken such pains to prepare.

One more precaution was most carefully observed in the line itself. Exactly the amount of artillery fire to which the enemy was accustomed must be continued, and from guns of the calibre which he expected. It was considered that more or less shooting, or the use of guns to which he was not accustomed, would be sure to alarm him.

For more than a week before the battle there was no rain. Low, creeping mists screened our movements and made it almost impossible that the enemy should have seen us from the air.

But the time was, nevertheless, an anxious one.

On the night of the 18th–19th the enemy raided our line and captured some of our men.

We were uncertain how much these men knew, and how much information they would give under examination.

If under prompt examination they gave away the gist of our plans the enemy would have twenty-four hours in which to bring up reserves. There was, however, nothing to be done except to await the event.

There was yet one other particular in which the Battle of Cambrai was to differ from other battles.

In modern warfare the place of the General commanding any considerable body of troops is almost invariably in the rear at some point where communications are good and whence he can effectively control his reserves.

His leadership is more a matter of the spirit and *moral* which he can infuse into his troops, than of his actual presence in the forefront of the battle. But General Elles had determined to lead his Tanks in person. All the available machines were to be used, there would be no reserves for him to handle. He would be best placed, he argued, in his Flag Tank where he could keep his hand on the pulse of the battle. It must have been with great satisfaction that he perceived that he would here once more be able to indulge his remarkable penchant for battles, a penchant from whose gratification his responsibilities as a commander had now long (officially) debarred him.

On the evening before the attack he issued his Special Order to the Tank Corps. It was not the incitement to "do their damnedest" which the contemporary Press fathered upon him. That spurious fosterling he hated the worse, the more he perceived its popularity.

His authentic Order was as follows :—

"*Special Order, No. 6*

"1. To-morrow the Tank Corps will have the chance for which it has been waiting for many months, to operate on good going in the van of the battle.

"2. All that hard work and ingenuity can achieve has been done in the way of preparation.

"3. It remains for unit commanders and for Tank crews to complete the work by judgment and pluck in the battle itself.

"4. In the light of past experience I leave the good name the Corps with great confidence in your hands.

"5. I propose leading the attack of the Centre Division.

"November 19, 1917.

"(*Signed*)   HUGH ELLES,
"B.-G.: Commanding Tank Corps."

The statement that the G.O.C. was to lead the attack came as a great surprise to every one; it was probably a greater surprise to some of the authorities than it was even to the Tank Corps themselves. This decision was generally accepted with pleasure by the fighting troops, but many of the more thoughtful were filled with very great anxiety. It was clear that the General's Tank, the "Hilda," was going to be thrust close behind the barrage in a conspicuous position flying the flag; the dangers that it ran were, therefore, greater than those run by any of the other Tanks. On the other hand, it was generally realised that the Tank Corps had, in this action, a very great deal at stake; it risked not merely machines and the lives of its officers and men, but its very existence. If the Tanks failed to make good this time there is little doubt that this type of mechanical warfare would have been abandoned for some time at least. On November 20, therefore, the Tank Corps was "all in" in every sense of the word.

IV

At 4.30 on the morning of the 20th a heavy burst of firing from the enemy made us fear for the integrity of our secret, but to our great relief it died away, and for an hour before zero (6 a.m.) quiet reigned along almost the whole front of attack.

From documents captured during the battle we found that up to the 18th the Germans had issued such reports as " The enemy's work is confined to the improvement of his trenches and wire." But the prisoners whom the Germans had taken on the night of the 18th had yielded more interesting information. On the strength only of their preliminary examination the Germans moved reserve machine-guns up to Flesquières.

At the last moment a higher enemy authority seems to have again examined the prisoners, and, too late, an urgent warning was sent down to all units in the line to maintain a sharp lookout and to issue armour-piercing bullets immediately.

This message we found half transcribed in a front-line signal dug-out.

Six o'clock had struck.

Under cover of the mist the whole line of 350 Tanks moved forward, led by General Elles' Flag Tank, the " Hilda." As they moved a thousand concealed guns hailed down their fire upon the German line. Even through the din of the barrage and the clamour of their own engines the Tank crews could hear, as they advanced, the tearing and snapping of the German wire as they trampled it under them. The bewildered enemy was overwhelmed. He had only one last hope. Perhaps the wide trenches themselves would hold back this inexorable company!

But when each of the second line of Tanks stopped, ducked its head, laid its " stepping stone " in the trench and crawled easily over it, the enemy completely lost his balance.

All along the line men fled in panic. Only at a few tactical points did our onrush meet with any real opposition. The surprise, the novel tactics, the crushing onrush of the Tanks proved too much in those first confounding minutes for one of the best fighting armies the world had ever seen.

The " Hilda " reached the outposts line in the van of the battle; the resistance here was only slight, but General Elles succeeded in picking up a few targets which he pointed out to the gunners. It is reported that he did most of his observing with his head thrust up through the hatch in the roof of the Tank, using his feet in the gunner's ribs to indicate targets.

Once the Tanks were astride the enormous Hindenburg ditch, the enemy only offered resistance in a few places. The

"Hilda," still carrying the flag which had been several times hit but not brought down, went on to her first objective line, which included the main Hindenburg front and support lines.

But the General's holiday was over. The great problem had been triumphantly solved.

The next most pressing need would be for reorganisation.

If any of the Tanks were required to operate again the next day, that reorganisation must be begun at once. So reluctantly leaving the "Hilda" to carry on to further objectives, the General came back on foot, somewhat impeded by various parties of "unmopped up" Germans who insisted on surrendering to him. By the afternoon, General Elles was back at his Headquarters, functioning by telephone and shorthand-typist in the manner usual to Generals.

Here and there, after the first rush, a desperate handful of the enemy would be rallied by their officers to defend some point of vantage.

At Lateau Wood on the right of the attack heavy fighting took place, including a duel between a Tank and a 5.9 in. howitzer. Turning on the Tank the howitzer fired, shattering and tearing off most of the right-hand sponson of the approaching machine, but fortunately not injuring its vitals; before the German gunners could reload, the Tank was upon them, and in a few seconds the great gun was crushed in a jumbled mass amongst the brushwood surrounding it.

A little to the west of this wood the Tanks of "F" (the 6th) Battalion, which had topped the ridge, were speeding down on Masnières. One approached the bridge, the key to the Rumilly–Seranvillers ridge, upon the capture of which so much depended. The bridge had, as the Tank Commander knew, been damaged either by shell-fire or by the German sappers. It was, however, most important that he should cross, and he very pluckily, therefore, went for it. As the Tank neared the centre of the bridge, there was a rending of steel girders—the bridge had broken, and as it collapsed the Tank disappeared into the waters of the canal. Other Tanks arriving, and not being able to cross, assisted the infantry to do so by opening a heavy covering fire.

The Tank that had fallen into the canal had been let down quite gradually into the water as the bridge slowly subsided.

There was but one loss. The wig of one of the crew got knocked off as his head emerged from the manhole, and it floated away down the canal and was never seen again. Lost to view, its memory was kept green for many months by its injured owner's claims for compensation.

The dilemma which most cruelly racked the official mind was the question whether a wig came under the heading of

The Comic Relief at Masnières

"Field Equipment," "Loss of a Limb," "Medical Comfort," "Clothing," "Personal Effects," or "Special Tank Stores." Finally, however, its owner did receive monetary compensation for his loss.

But the genius of Comedy had not done with the Tanks.

> *" The town had been evacuated so suddenly by the enemy that some civilian population still remained.
>
> "Two cows belonging to the German Town Major were solemnly presented by their French civilian keeper to Major Hammond as a token of the joy that the inhabitants felt at their liberation."

These absurd camp followers remained for long the most cherished possessions of the Battalion, and accompanied them wherever they went.

At Flesquières the 51st Highland Division, which was using an attack formation of its own, was held up; it appears that the Tanks outdistanced the infantry, or that the tactics adopted did not permit of the infantry keeping close enough up to the Tanks. As the Tanks topped the crest, they came under direct artillery fire at short range and suffered heavy casualties.

No less than sixteen Tanks were knocked out by a single field gun.

This gun was at the west end of the village, and from its position the Tanks were each outlined against the sky as they topped the ridge. Its story is told in Sir Douglas Haig's Despatch, with a generosity which might well have encouraged what the Tank crews considered a most undesirable spirit in enemy gunners :

> "Many of the hits upon our tanks at Flesquières were obtained by a German artillery officer who, remaining alone at his battery, served a field gun single-handed until killed at his gun. The great bravery of this officer aroused the admiration of all ranks."

There was stiff fighting at Havrincourt, and before nightfall the 62nd Division and its Tanks had captured Graincourt. Several Tanks even pushed on beyond towards Bourlon Wood and the Cambrai road, but by this time the infantry were too exhausted to follow.

By 4 p.m. on November 20 one of the most astonishing battles in all history had been won, and as far as the Tank Corps was concerned, tactically finished.

* " F " (6th) Battalion History.

There were no reserves of Tanks, and the crews that had fought all day were now very spent and weary.

The infantry were still more exhausted and a further advance was impossible. The night was spent by Tank crews and infantry in resting, and by the Staff in planning a renewed attack for the next day.

A letter home from a Tank officer describes a typical scene:

"We had captured the village of Havrincourt that morning, or rather its ruins, and it was in the one remaining room of the once magnificent Château that General John Ponsonby, commanding the 40th Division, established his Headquarters and convened a conference for ten o'clock in the evening.

"The road thither had already been sufficiently restored to permit of cars getting through, granted skilful driving and good luck.

"Felled trees, wire, breastworks, and other barriers had been cleared aside, trenches and craters on both sides of No Man's Land had been roughly filled in, whilst the notorious 'Grand Ravine' had been made passable for carriage folk by the judicious placing of a few fascines.

"There were a round dozen of us at the conference, a muddy, rather blear-eyed party, some in tin hats and trench coats, revolver girt—some in honorific red and gold—all with slung gas-masks.

"General Ponsonby and his G.S.O.I. sat on an old packing-case with a map spread out before them on another, lit by the dancing flicker of two guttering candles stuck into German beer bottles. General Elles and Colonel Baker-Carr were there with a chorus of Commanding Officers, Company Commanders and Reconnaissance Officers from the 1st Tank Brigade.

"An armed sentry stood at the breach in the wall that served for doorway—signallers and orderlies entered and left the little circle of yellow light, stirring up the dust from the fallen débris on the broken floor.

"One felt uneasily conscious of forming part of a *Graphic* picture entitled 'Advanced Headquarters,' or 'Planning the Battle.'

"Anyway, the battle *was* eventually planned and to the satisfaction of all parties present. The G.S.O.I. finished writing his operation orders for the morning's attack, the conference dissolved, and we stumbled out once more into the night, each of us with some job to get done before the dawn.

"To me it fell to push on to the advanced Headquarters

of the Infantry Brigades concerned to explain the plans for the morrow's battles and to deliver certain necessary maps to the Tank Commanders who would be co-operating.

"I slung the maps for easier porterage along a pole that I and my orderly shouldered and from which they dangled in swaying white packages to the great interest and mystification of passing troops, to whom the bearers and the pole were invisible in the inky dark.

"It was a weary way up to Graincourt with nothing but gun flashes and infrequent star-shells to light the way, but at last we reached it.

"Two of the Infantry Brigades had, we found, established their Headquarters in a sort of catacomb underneath the ruined church—a wonderful place, part mediæval and part the work of the industrious Hun.

"Down and down you went—the old vaulted brickwork giving place to stout German timbering—until at the very bottom, some hundred feet below the floor of the church, the steep stairway ended in a gallery off which opened a whole street of little chambers.

"The place was insufferably hot and stuffy to one fresh in from the cold of the outer night; there was haze and reek of tobacco smoke and cooking, half drowning the stale dank smell, inseparable from a deep dug-out that has been long occupied—especially by Germans.

"Graincourt had been taken by surprise and had changed hands so quickly that we had taken over these very eligible Headquarters as a going concern 'ready furnished for immediate occupation.'

"So sudden, indeed, had been the change of tenancy that the two Boche engineers whose job it was to run the electric lighting plant had been captured in their own subterranean engine-room and were even now stolidly carrying on their old duties, seemingly but little concerned by the fact that they were now 'under entirely new management.'

"As it turned out, it was very well for us that we did capture and retain this precious pair, for when they found that they were going to be kept on to run the lighting as before, they quite shamelessly said:

"'Well, if that's the case, there's just one little point we ought to warn you about, and that is, if any one moves what looks like the main switch—as any one would who didn't know, when starting up the plant—the demolition charges would be blown. If you would like these removed in case of accidents, we can show you where to dig for them—we know exactly where to find them, as it was our job to lay them.'

"Even whilst I was there, I saw these ruffians superintending the removal of case after case of high-explosive from cunningly concealed chambers behind the timber linings and under floors.

"The cramped stairways, galleries and cubby-holes were crowded with odd specimens of all ranks and arms, some eating or talking, others huddled uneasily asleep, with the constant tide of traffic pouring over their sprawling limbs.

"Electric lights burned brilliantly, and the engine sent a steady shiver through the timbered walls like the vibrations of a steamer.

"Like a ship breasting the waves, too, were the intermittent thud and tremor of bursting shells in the village high overhead, or the replies of our own artillery.

"Telephones buzzed, a typewriter rattled away, and the clatter of plates being washed in a bucket made one wonder wistfully whether it would occur to any one to suggest that you might be hungry.

"One Brigadier, presumably the first come, sat in the utmost pomp and luxury in a sumptuous arm-chair of crimson plush, a ci-devant drawing-room table before him, on which was spread a large-scale detailed map of Bourlon Wood—a very valuable legacy left behind by the overhasty Boches.

"On the walls were framed oleographs of Hindenburg and the Kaiser, whilst a gilt clock still kept German time as it ticked above the door.

"Two tiers of wire rabbit-net bunks lined one side of the little chamber, and a smart little stove surmounted by a fine old mirror adorned the other.

"They are pretty sound on Home Comforts are the Boches, and they don't think twice about pinching anything they fancy from the unfortunate natives.

"Like another much-advertised system of furnishing, 'It's so simple'! 'Deferred Payment,' if they will have it so—deferred, but payment at the last—payment good and plenty or I'll eat my tin hat—including visor and lining."

V

The next day (November 21) saw composite companies of Tanks fighting in co-operation with new infantry.

But though the infantry was new, it was unfortunately not

fresh. Sir Julian Byng had no rested troops at all at his disposal. It may be said that the whole of the subsequent history of the battle and its sequel hinges upon these two points. All our infantry was weary in the extreme, and most of it had never co-operated with Tanks before.

Consequently many strong points, though they were finally captured, gave us more trouble than they should.

On the 21st, Tanks attacked several villages and strong points with success.

Thirteen Tanks of " B " (2nd) Battalion surrounded the village of Cantaing. They met with a stubborn resistance as they closed in upon it. To this they replied vigorously with machine-gun and 6-pounder fire, and by noon the enemy had been driven out.

Two Tanks also, of " B " Battalion, were sent for by the infantry, who were held up by heavy machine-gun fire outside Noyelles. In half an hour they succeeded in crushing all resistance, setting fire to an ammunition dump and patrolling the village till the infantry took over.

Neither Tank was in the least hurt, and there were no casualties among the crews.

Twelve Tanks of " H " (8th) Battalion received orders soon after 8 a.m. to attack Fontaine-Notre-Dame.

The village was six miles distant, and the Tanks came in for severe fighting on the way there.

They reached their objective at about 4.30. By 5.30 they had captured it and were withdrawn after handing it over to the infantry.

But next day a furious German counter-attack dislodged our garrison.

We were determined to possess it, and on the 23rd attacked again in force.

The enemy was prepared, and a desperate battle ensued among the houses. Twenty-four Tanks from " B " and " H " Battalions had entered the village first, whereupon the enemy retired to the tops of the houses and rained down bombs and bullets upon the roofs of the machines.

The Germans were in force, and in the narrow streets it was difficult for the Tanks to bring an effective fire to bear upon them.

The infantry was too weary to clear the place, and after patrolling the streets the Tanks withdrew, as soon as darkness covered their retreat.

On the same day thirty-four Tanks of the 1st Brigade supported a brilliant attack made by the 40th Division upon Bourlon Wood. The wood was captured after a sharp struggle. The Tanks then pressed on towards the village, but as at

Fontaine, the infantry, who had suffered severe casualties in the taking of the wood, was too exhausted to follow up.

On November 25 and 26 we renewed our attack upon Fontaine-Notre-Dame and again tried to capture Bourlon Village.

In the end, however, both these important points remained in enemy hands.

A week had now elapsed since the launching of the battle.

According to the original scheme, the action should not have been continued for more than three days, but in spite of our original " Self-Denying Ordinance " as to ground, when desirable posts of vantage were actually in our hands, we had fallen a prey to "land hunger," and had still fought on and continued to advance in order to consolidate these new and delightful possessions.

But now we held the extremely important tactical point formed by the heights of Bourlon Wood, and it was plain that to take Fontaine and Bourlon Village would cost us more than they were worth to us.

We had done all and more than all we set out to do. The troops urgently needed resting. They had had no proper rest before the battle, and now, despite their sense of victory, they were extraordinarily spent.

The Tanks' crews, too, were almost fought to a standstill, and owing to the constant daily necessity there had been for hurrying composite companies into action, their units had become inconveniently disorganised.

So on November 27 we rested from our labours and counted the spoil.

> * "Whatever may be the future historian's dictum as to its value, the First Battle of Cambrai must always rank as one of the most remarkable battles ever fought. On November 20, from a base of some 13,000 yards in width, a penetration of no less than 10,000 yards was effected in twelve hours (at the Third Battle of Ypres a similar penetration took three months), 8000 prisoners and 100 guns were captured, and these prisoners alone were nearly double the casualties suffered by the 3rd and 4th Armies during the first day of the battle. It is an interesting point to remember that in this battle the attacking infantry were assisted by 690 officers and 3500 other ranks of the Tank Corps, a little over 4000 men, or the strength of a strong brigade, and that these men replaced artillery for wire-cutting, and rendered unnecessary the old preliminary bombardment. More than this, by

* *W.T.N.*

A TANK CRUSHING DOWN THE ENEMY'S WIRE.

PREPARING FOR CAMBRAI.
(A Train of Tanks with fascines in position.)

THE BAPAUME-CAMBRAI ROAD.

keeping close to the infantry, they effected a much higher co-operation than had ever before been attainable with artillery. When on November 21 the bells of London pealed forth in celebration of the victory of Cambrai, consciously or unconsciously to their listeners they tolled out an old tactics and rang in a new—Cambrai had become the Valmy of a new epoch in war, the epoch of the mechanical engineer."

It was a weary but satisfied body of men that General Elles inspected at Havrincourt on November 29 when the party broke up.

The 1st and 3rd Brigades were entraining immediately for Mult and Bray respectively, and the 2nd was to follow them in a few days' time.

Good-byes were exchanged, and, as every one thought, the curtain rung down upon the First Battle of Cambrai.

Part II

(November 30)

In order to understand the events that followed, we have to imagine a victorious but very weary British Army holding a newly consolidated salient against an enemy whom they have just roused to a revengeful fury by a sudden stinging slap in the face.

The enemy had been horribly frightened, and now that he had recovered he realised how urgently his prestige demanded signal vindication. We were, it would seem, half expecting in a tired unimaginative sort of way that he might hit at us on the new Bourlon Wood flank of our salient. On the Gouzeaucourt side were old-established defences. These we held thinly—it never entering our heads apparently that he would attack an old piece of the line.

But the German Army Commander, General von der Marwitz, had an ambitious scheme in his mind. He meant to pinch off our salient and, if possible, to capture the entire 3rd and 4th Corps, who held it. His right wing was to operate from Bourlon southward, and his left from Masnières westwards, the two attacks converging on Havrincourt and Metz.

The attack was launched shortly after daylight on November 30, and failed completely on the right against Bourlon Wood; here the enemy was caught by our artillery and machine-guns and mown down by hundreds. On the left, however, the attack succeeded; first, it came as a surprise; secondly, the

Germans heralded their assault by lines of low-flying aeroplanes, which made our men keep down and so lose observation. Under the protection of this aeroplane barrage and a very heavy trench mortar bombardment the German infantry advanced and speedily captured Villers Guislain and Gouzeaucourt.

It was not till nearly ten o'clock on November 30 that Brigadier-General Courage of the 2nd Tank Brigade received a telephone message warning him of the attack.

The Tanks had been definitely "dismissed," and were busy refitting, and at that moment every machine was in complete *déshabillé*. Many of the engines were in process of being tinkered with, and not a single Tank was filled up or contained its battle equipment. Those whom some emergency has obliged to get out an ordinary car on a cold winter's morning when it has neither petrol, oil, nor water in it, and has half its engine strewn about the garage, will understand the difficulties that faced the Tank Corps. They will realise that when no less than twenty-two Tanks of "B" (2nd) Battalion had started for the battle by 12.40, a very smart piece of work had been done. Very soon fourteen Tanks of "A" (1st) Battalion followed them, and by two o'clock twenty Tanks of "H" (8th) Battalion were able to move up in support.

In the words of Sir Douglas Haig's Despatch, "Great credit is due to the officers and men of the (2nd) Tank Brigade for the speed with which they brought their Tanks into action."

By the time the first twenty Tanks reached Gouzeaucourt, however, the Guards, who had been hurried up with all speed, had managed to retake it, and the Tanks were therefore pushed out as a screen to cover their consolidation.

Here they remained all day, beating off enemy counter-attacks.

All day along both sides of the salient the enemy hammered fiercely at our lines. Here and there he penetrated them. Cooks, servants, and signallers, every available man, was given a rifle and put into the line, and the Despatch tells of wonderful individual deeds that were done as the battle surged and eddied confusedly. We did not propose to allow the Germans to hold their new possessions, the points of vantage out of which they had hustled us.

On December 1, Tanks, Guards, and dismounted Indian cavalry hit back against Villers Guislain and Gauche Wood.

> "Tanks were," the Despatch notes, "in great measure responsible for the capture of the wood. Heavy fighting took place for this position, which it is clear that the enemy had decided to hold at all costs. When the infantry and cavalry finally took possession of the wood, great

numbers of German dead and smashed machine-guns were found. In one spot four German machine-guns, with dead crews lying round, were discovered within a radius of twenty yards. Three German field guns, complete with teams, were also captured in this wood.

"Other Tanks proceeded to Villers Guislain, and in spite of heavy direct artillery fire three reached the outskirts of the village, but the fire of the enemy's machine-guns prevented our troops advancing from the south from supporting them, and the Tanks ultimately withdrew."

For two more days the enemy pressed on against us, and the battle raged round Bourlon, Fontaine, Marcoing, and La Vacquerie.

Everywhere he dented in our line, and by December 4 the outline of our front showed an impossible series of irregularities. We must either renew the attack on a big scale, or make up our minds

* "to withdraw to a more compact line on the Flesquières Ridge.

"Although this decision involved giving up important positions most gallantly won, I had no doubt as to the correct course under the conditions. Accordingly, on the night of December 4–5 the evacuation of the positions held by us north of the Flesquières Ridge was commenced. On the morning of December 7 this withdrawal was completed successfully without interference from the enemy."

It is as well that the enemy did not "interfere," for through some oversight the Tanks did not receive due notice of the intended withdrawal, and certain salvage parties, busily at work on disabled Tanks, in forward positions, knew nothing of the evacuation until, to their astonishment, they found our infantry streaming back past them in the darkness. There was then nothing for it but to abandon the wrecks and to get back themselves with such gear as they could carry.

So ended the second phase of the battle.

It had been an exceedingly vexatious business.

Putting the best construction we could upon it, we had to admit to having been caught napping. The German attack had thrown us into complete, if momentary, confusion. But afterwards, when the situation could be calmly reviewed, contemporary criticism was unanimously agreed that we had, after all, suffered little but moral damage. And from that sort of damage the British have the art of deriving wholesome

* Sir Douglas Haig's Despatch.

instruction in a unique degree. We braced ourselves up, and determined that this sharp rap over the knuckles should do us good.

But to the Tank Corps the exploits of the 2nd Brigade were more directly advantageous.

Amid the hubbub and confusion the Tank crews, like the Guards and the 2nd Cavalry Division, had known but one impulse—they had gone straight east against the enemy. That was the pole to which their compass pointed.

While everything had been doubt and hesitation they had had but one thought, to fill and adjust their machines and hurry them forward. At 9 a.m. the Tank crews had been peacefully preparing to break camp and leave for their training area. By four in the afternoon seventy-three Tanks had been launched with decisive effect against the enemy.

To many High Commanders who had believed that Tanks could only be used in a "full-dress" attack after weeks of preparation, the events of November 30 came as a joyful revelation.

So for the Tanks ended the 1917 campaign.

CHAPTER XI

THREE NEW TYPES OF TANK—THE DEPOT—CENTRAL
WORKSHOPS

I

THE "Fighting Side" had now been for many months almost exclusively engaged with "operations," and having fought themselves nearly to a standstill at the Battle of Cambrai, were now in as urgent need of reorganisation as were their machines of overhaul and repair.

The present chronicle has also for long followed their fortunes, with not a glance to spare for the activities of the manufacturing and other organisations which played the supporting parts "Aaron and Hur" to the Fighting Side's "Moses."

At the period we have reached it is high time to pick up the dropped histories of the other persons of the drama. For while the Tank Corps had been fighting, manufacturers had been busy, and a huge network of auxiliary services and organisations had grown up, by means of which the whole Corps was to rise rejuvenated from its ashes.

Before the Tanks fought their next pitched battle the Mark V. had come into being, Whippet Tanks had been issued, a heavy type of infantry-carrying Tank had been designed, and for fast work on good roads a Battalion of Armoured Cars had grown up.

Besides this, a complete system of Supply Tanks and Field Maintenance Companies for salvage and supplies had been gradually evolved during the course of the last campaign.

The Tank Corps Depot had been enormously enlarged, and had moved to its final " location " on the coast near Le Tréport.

The Home Depot at Wool had also increased, and there had been changes and developments at the Ministry of Munitions and in the Tank production side generally.

It is in fact impossible in a single chapter to give more than a brief indication of this universal and increasing "back area" activity.

To begin with the changes in the home organisation and in the production of Tanks.

The "New" Tank Committee was, as we have already related, a success.

In December 1917 and January 1918 it saw a rather interesting new phase, when Majors Drain and Alden, of the U.S. Tank Corps, attended certain of its meetings, and when the manufacture for the British and American Armies of the Mark VIII. or "Allied Tank" was decided upon. This Tank was never fought, but its projection is perhaps interesting as an example of inter-Allied solidarity.

By January 1918 proposals for an expansion from nine to eighteen Battalions and for a reorganisation of Tank control had been put forward.

These proposals were eventually (in April 1918) discussed by the Inter-Allied Tank Committee, a sort of sub-committee of the Versailles Conference, on which the British, French and American Tank Corps were represented.

But neither men nor really constructive thought could then be spared from the immediate needs of meeting the German onrush, and nothing was done to realise their proposals until that onrush was finally stemmed.

But in July 1918 the business was taken up again. It was decided to expand the Tank Corps to thirty-four Battalions armed with about six thousand machines.

II

In December 1917 the manufacturing situation was not particularly satisfactory. As late as August 20 the Commander-in-Chief had, it will be remembered, laid down, in an official letter, an order of priority in which there were four categories preferred to Tanks.

> "The manufacture of Tanks should not be allowed to interfere in any way with:
>
> "(1) The output of aeroplanes.
> "(2) The output of guns and ammunition.
> "(3) The provision of mechanical transport, spare parts therefor, and petrol tractors up to the scale demanded.
> "(4) The provision of locomotives up to the scale demanded."

And though by December the views of the authorities had

changed considerably, the sudden expansion of the Tank building programme was not easy.

In October 1917, 700 Mark IV. Tanks had already been delivered in France, and a balance of about 500 was still due. But the Fighting Side was anxious that these should not all be of the unimproved Mark IV. pattern. For up to now no change in the design had been made since the first Mark IV. had been delivered. It was decided, therefore, that some of the 500 should be given Ricardo engines and Epicyclic gears, and that others should be fitted as Supply Tanks.

The M.W.S.D. hoped to build about 1600 new Heavy Tanks, 800 of which were to be of the Mark V. type and ready by May 1, and the others to be of other heavy types, probably Mark V. star and Mark VI., while 385 Whippet ("Medium A") Tanks were also to be ready by May 1918.

Further, there was to be a small cadre of Salvage Tanks and of special infantry Supply Tanks, two of the latter being able to carry complete supplies for an infantry Brigade for one day.

A large number of these Tanks were as before to be built by the Metropolitan Carriage and Wagon Company.

A very brief account of most of these new types of Tank has already been given in Chapter I., and it is not necessary to repeat here the details of their speeds, armament, and so forth.

Salvage Tanks were usually Mark IV. Tanks on which special gear, such as winches and small cranes, had been fitted for hoisting wrecks out of the mud, or for towing.

The Supply Tank was a Mark IV. fitted with very capacious sponsons. In order to save weight these carriers were not made as fully armoured as the fighting Tanks.

The Gun Carrier Tank was a machine with an elongated tail which formed a platform whence it was intended that a 60-pounder gun or a 6-in. howitzer could be fired.

The Tank Corps Armoured Cars were of the usual turreted pattern, and were armed with machine-guns.

But more important than any other new development was the improvement in the main issue of heavy Tanks, an improvement which is very well described by the historian of the 13th Battalion :

> "The old Mark IV. type had serious disadvantages. Its engine power on bad ground was insufficient, and the clumsy secondary gears made turning slow and difficult, as well as requiring the services of at least two members of the crew in addition to the driver. This, in battle, **became a heavy handicap upon the fighting powers of**

the Tank. The officer was hampered by the need to attend to brakes, and a gunner called upon suddenly to help alter gears would lose the fleeting chance of firing at favourable targets. In the new Mark V. Tank these troubles largely disappeared. An engine of new design gave both greater speed and greater turning power, while a system of epicyclic gears made turning easy and under the sole control of the driver. The officer was free to supervise his crew, the gunner was free to use his weapons to the best advantage. Add that a greatly increased field of view was obtained by the addition of an observer's turret, and it will be understood that an immense advance in type had been secured."

The Mark V. had, however, one serious drawback. Its ventilation was extremely faulty. We shall see later how serious a disadvantage this was to prove.

III

There were also to be changes in the technical and mechanical engineering side of the Tank Corps itself, by which an economy of man-power was to be effected.

When the Tank Corps was first formed each Company had its own workshops, and this system lasted to the end of 1916. Then in the course of the winter reorganisation, Company Workshops were abolished and Battalion Workshops were substituted.

By the autumn of 1917 the experiment was tried of centralising still further and merging Battalion into Brigade Workshops, and early in 1918 it was decided to take the last step and to concentrate all repairs in the Central Workshops.

This system, which achieved a great economy of skilled men, was made possible by a very clear line of demarcation being drawn between Repairs and Maintenance, a principle which had been laid down by Colonel F. Searle, D.S.O., the chief engineer of the Corps and the head of the whole mechanical side of the Tanks.

No damaged part was ever to be repaired on the field; mechanical efficiency was to be maintained by the broken bit of mechanism being immediately replaced by a complete new part.

This replacement was carried out by the crew, whose efficiency as mechanics was enormously increased by being thus made responsible for their own machines.

GUN-CARRYING TANK TAKING UP A HOWITZER.

A WHIPPET GOING IN.

BERMICOURT CHÂTEAU, NEAR ST. POL.
(Tank Corps Main Headquarters.)

SLEDGE-TOWING TANK TAKING UP SUPPLIES.

One point had, of course, to be carefully attended to in carrying out this system. There had to be a very efficient supply organisation by which the necessary spares were quickly available in the field.

When the crew had removed the damaged part from the Tank, it was sent back to the Central Workshops to be repaired.

Here a specially skilled man would be always employed upon damages to one particular part.

> * " For example, broken unions of petrol pipes commonly occur in all petrol engines, and if a small unit workshop exists, the brazing out and repair of such broken unions can be carried out there. But in order to do this a coppersmith must be kept at the unit workshop, and only part of his time will be employed in this work of brazing petrol unions. If now, however, all broken unions, from every unit, are sent back to a Central Workshop for repair, there is a sufficient amount of work of this description to keep one man, or possibly two or three men fully employed all their time.
>
> " These men become absolute experts in brazing broken unions, and before very long can do in a few minutes a job which would take a coppersmith with the unit workshop an hour or two to carry out."

It is interesting to trace what might have been the itinerary of a Tank from the time it left the manufacturers in about Midsummer 1917, till after going into action in, say, the Third Battle of Ypres.

On completion every Tank was first sent to testing grounds at Newbury, where it was manned by No. 20 Squadron R.N.A.S. From here it was forwarded to Richborough, whence it was shipped by the Channel ferry and received at Le Havre by another detachment of Squadron 20. Thence it went to Bermicourt, was again tested, this time by Tank Corps personnel, and then handed on to the Central Stores at Erin. These stores were first established in 1917, and eventually consisted of over seven acres of railway siding and six acres of buildings. The Central Workshops were at one time also installed here, but as more accommodation became necessary they were moved to Teneur, about a mile and a half away.

From the Central Stores the Tanks would be issued to Battalions as needed.

For example, during the Third Battle of Ypres a large number of Tanks were supplied to Companies actually in the

* W.T.N.

line. We will suppose that a particular Tank was so supplied, and received a bullet through its carburettor during one of the small actions of the end of October.

The crew would immediately draw a new carburettor from the neighbouring mobile advanced store, which was run by one of the two Tank Salvage or Field Companies.

Thus re-equipped the Tank would again go into action, perhaps within a day of being damaged.

This time we will suppose that the Tank got knocked out between the first and second objective by a direct hit, the unwounded members of the crew going forward with their Lewis guns and leaving the Tank stranded and immovable.

The position of the derelict having been reported, men from a Tank Salvage Company would go up that night, probably under shell-fire, and possibly in full view of the enemy whenever a Véry light went up.

The experts would arrive at the wreck with their favourite set of repairing tools, possibly consisting of the specially designed Tank-repairing outfit, but more probably of a few pet spanners, some odd lengths of tubing and a coil of copper wire. They would toil at the Tank till dawn.

Sometimes after one or more nights spent like this they would induce the Tank to go. In the Ypres area Tanks were sometimes salved that had completely disappeared into the mud. Sometimes it was possible to tow a machine away, particularly after the special salvage Tanks with their hoisting gear came into use. Sometimes only *disjecta membra*, such as engine parts, 6-pounders, or parts of the gears or transmissions, could be saved.

During the two years of their existence the Field Companies, at the lowest computation, saved two or three million pounds' worth of stores, a work which they did not accomplish without heavy cost to themselves.

We will suppose that the Tank whose history we have followed was salved whole.

The next step would be that it would be entrained by the Field Company and sent back to the Central Workshops at Teneur.

This was really a vast engineering works covering about twenty acres of ground, where, besides a very large number of trained and expert mechanics, more than a thousand Chinese coolies worked.

These coolies often became very dexterous artisans.

Here, in endless ranks down the long shops, they would toil indefatigably, in the summer stripped to the waist, their brown bodies gleaming in the white light of the arc lamps or in the glow of the forges, or in the winter dressed in their loose blue quilted jackets and close caps with curious rabbits' fur ear-lappets.

Possibly the shattered or burnt-out Tank would have to be almost entirely rebuilt, two wrecked Tanks providing, perhaps, parts enough to make one good one. Here, finally, the reconstructed Tank would be tested and sent back to the Central Stores.

Possibly it would have been reduced to a sort of "C. III." category, and made into a Supply Tank. Possibly it would have been fitted with all the latest gadgets, and come out from its reforging a better weapon than it was originally.

For the activities of the Central Workshops were not confined to mere repair. It will be remembered how they distinguished themselves in the matter of the lightning delivery of fascines, releasing gear, and supply sledges for the Battle of Cambrai.

A large proportion, too, of the experiments which led to improvements in the design of Tanks were carried out here; for example, the long Tank and the unditching beam were of Central Workshops origin, and here the officers who fought the Tanks could have their ideas for gadgets sympathetically reviewed and put to practical proof by the band of expert engineers that Lieut.-Colonel Brocklebank had brought together. But they were more than mere experts; they were enthusiasts whose unflagging zeal had created the marvel of Central Workshops where there had been bare ploughland so short a time before.

IV

We have traced a Tank from its setting forth from home with unscratched paint through the vicissitudes of battle to its remoulding as a greatly improved machine or to its relegation to "Permanent Base."

How would the military history run of a member of a Tank crew which had fought, say, at the Battle of Cambrai?

We have already related how the Tank Corps was chiefly recruited in early days, that is, either from among mechanical experts or from volunteers from other branches of the Service. Later men with no special qualifications were taken by direct enlistment. We will suppose, however, that 1234 Pte. John Smith got his transfer from the West Surreys when in the line in about June 1917, and that at that moment the training schools in France had no vacancies. To their great joy, therefore, Pte. Smith and his batch would be sent home for training to the Tank Depot at Wool.

Here was a huge camp where men like themselves, who had

seen fighting, and also men fresh from the Recruiting Depots, were being formed into the new Tank Battalions. By July about nine of these new Battalions were in training. The men went through the usual recruits' curriculum. First of all, drill, discipline and physical training; then individual courses in Tank Gunnery, Driving and Maintenance. Then they would go through the Signalling, Revolver and Compass Schools, the Gas and Reconnaissance Schools.

There was also here an Officer Cadet Preliminary Training Company where the same sort of instruction was given. Gunners at this time did all their firing practice with 6-pounders at the Naval School of Gunnery, Chatham, or rather, to be exact, on " H.M.S. Excellent," Whale Island. All the other courses were gone through in and around the camp.

Practically, only individual instruction was given at Wool, and their collective and tactical training was done by the men at Bermicourt, after their arrival in France. At Wool it was reckoned that, with this important omission, nearly four months would usually be occupied in raising and training a Tank Battalion. It would, therefore, be towards the end of September that Pte. Smith found himself in France.

He was, he found, to be detailed to one of the old Battalions, and was, therefore, despatched to the Training and Reinforcement Depot, then established at Erin, and later to be moved to Le Tréport.

Here he was attached to a Reception Company, put through a kind of examination in the subjects he had studied at Wool, but passing satisfactorily and his records being duly completed, he was issued with his kit and equipment and posted to his Company. He was soon sent to join it at an improvised training area where it was at this moment " resting " from the Battle of Ypres. It was not actually having a particularly restful time, as tactical training with the infantry was in progress, and there was more than enough night work in the programme.

This phase did not last long, however, for the Company was soon sent back to join its Battalion in the Salient, where they executed an astonishing number of moves and were considerably shelled, but never succeeded in getting into action.

After that they were hurried off to do intensive training for Cambrai. Then came the battle, in the last three days of which a very much exhausted 2nd Driver Smith was wounded in the face by a bullet splash. The trouble was not serious enough to get him to England, and on his return from an all too brief stay in a Hospital in France, he again found himself at the Depot. This time, after only a day in the

Reception Company and after a medical examination, he was posted for fourteen days to the Seaside Rest Camp at Merlimont.

This Rest Camp consisted of rows and rows of rather pretty bungalows built among the sand dunes. Here both men and officers were given a very pleasant time, though they were still under military discipline and had a certain number of parades to keep. For the officers there was a comfortable club, and for the men an exceedingly well-run Y.M.C.A. hut, where there were concerts or pierrot shows almost nightly—either home-grown or imported.

Games and, in summer, swimming and bathing were great features. There is no doubt, first, that the Camp was immensely popular, and, secondly, that the Tank Corps owed a good deal of its cheerful spirit and high *moral* to the refreshment which the Camp afforded to many a weary body and mind.

After this fortnight by the sea Smith rejoined his Battalion, and was, with the rest of the Tank world, plunged into winter training.

V

The general organisation of the 1917–18 training, though, of course, on a much larger scale, was very much like that of the previous winter. New training centres had been established and old centres extended.

But perhaps a chronicle of the numbers who passed through these courses of instruction at Wailly, Le Tréport, Bermicourt and Merlimont, and of the sequence in which the different Brigades took their turns at the different areas, might prove less interesting than a brief account of what was actually taught and of the sort of way a syllabus would be carried out.

In the official "Instructions for the Training of the Tank Corps in France" these are the sort of general principles we find laid down :

> "All work must be carried out at high pressure. Every exercise and movement should, if possible, be reduced to a precise drill.
>
> "Games will be organised as a definite part of training (see S.S. 137, 'Recreational Training').
>
> "Order is best cultivated by carrying out all work on a fixed plan. Order is the foundation of discipline. Small things like marching men always at attention to and from work, making them stand to attention before dismissing them, assist in cultivating steadiness and discipline. Each day should commence with a careful inspection of the billets and the men, or some similar formal parade. Strict

march discipline to and from the training grounds must be insisted upon.

"It is an essential part of training for war that the men are taught to care for themselves, so as to maintain their physical fitness. To this end the necessity for taking the most scrupulous care of their clothing, equipment and accoutrements will be explained to them."

The following is the syllabus (slightly condensed) of a Maintenance Course for Tank Commanders :

How to drive a Tank.
How to set a magneto.
When an engine is misfiring or overheating.
When an engine is knocking too badly to continue working or is not pulling.
When carburation is bad.
When a Tank is at such an angle that it is dangerous to run the engine.
The causes of engine failures and how to correct them.
How the autovac works.
The correct tension for fan belts.
When an engine bed is loose.
How much petrol, oil, grease, and water should be used during average hour's run.
When road chain sprocket wheels or pinions should be changed.
How long it takes to change a set of sprocket wheels and pinions.
When a track or the Coventry driving chains are too slack.
When a clutch is too fierce, and how to correct it.
When a clutch is slipping, and how to adjust it.
When secondary gears are too much worn for further service, and what is the effect of their not being fully in mesh.
How long it takes to change such gears.
When tracks or secondary gears are over or under lubricated.
When brakes are operative or not.
How long it takes to prepare a Tank for a day's run.
How long it takes thoroughly to clean and adjust a Tank after a day's work.
How long it takes to detrain Tanks and adjust sponsons.
How the equipment of a Tank should be stowed.
The appliances which are necessary to dismantle various sections of a Tank, and how it should be done.

Technical Courses

That it is just as necessary for a Company Commander to inspect Tanks daily as it is for a Cavalry Squadron Commander to inspect his horses.

For an interesting " Immediate Action Course," *i.e.*, first aid to the engine, the following directions are given to instructors :

" In order to inspire confidence at the outset, particular stress should be laid upon the fact that in a Tank there are practically only three causes of engine failure—Valves—Ignition—Petrol.

" If this is borne in mind, a very little experience in the simple operations connected with these three functions, coupled with a little training in diagnosis, will enable students to deal very easily with troubles as they occur.

" Drivers should know by the ' feel ' of their engine whether it is firing correctly or not, and any member of a crew ought to be able to detect and report at once any irregularity in the sound of an exhaust from outside the machine.

" When the students have been through a course (using the book) of what to do when :

" 1. The Engine won't start,
" 2. Engine starts and stops after a few Revs,
" 3. Irregular sound of exhaust—machine will not climb,
" 4. Popping back of Carburettor,
" 5. Overheating and knocking,

the Instructor is to set up faults for the students to remedy."

He is given ideas for nearly fifteen ways of producing the symptom " Engine won't start."

" It is suggested that the Instructor should insert a piece of paper between the platinum points in the little magneto, or fit a faulty contact breaker with a stiff rocker in the big magneto, or smear segments and outside of the distributor with a little dirty oil; if he desires to queer the plugs, he may insert one with its gap closed up or bridged with dirt or with a cracked insulation. To produce symptom No. 2, he may insert a punctured float in the Carburettor or insert a piece of rag in the passage between the float chamber and the jets, or block a cock under the Autovac. Or in order to produce an irregular sound in the exhaust and to make the machine refuse to climb, he may remove the roller and pin from one or more inlet valves; or place two faulty plugs in the engine. To make the engine overheat, he is to insert an extra link in the Radiator Fan Bolt, open the Air Slide, or start a leak in one or more of the water outlet elbows. He may make the engine tap and rattle by adjusting the valves with abnormal clearances, and so on with the number of other defects, which each student in turn is to be called upon to diagnose and remedy."

For the conduct of a " Refresher " Battle Practice Course the following points are suggested for the guidance of instructors :

" The ammunition required for each man firing will be 20 rounds of shell, 5 rounds of case shot, and 250 rounds of S.A.A.

" Before beginning a Battle Practice, the following points must be seen to :

" That each practice or scheme is of a practical nature, *i.e.*, that it should bring out certain lessons under as near battle conditions as possible.

" All ports, etc., in the Tanks will be closed during the practice. Targets should represent as nearly as possible those met with in action. The practice must not be hurried and the Tank must never contain more than the normal crew. Students should be allowed to ride on the top of the Tanks, in order to observe the fire effect. In this way, by observing the faults of others, they should be able to avoid committing the same errors themselves, when their turn comes to fire.

" Battle Practice exercises must be regarded by the Tank Crews as what the Field firing practices are to the Infantry.

" Vizors and Gas-Masks must frequently be worn during a Battle Practice Course.

" Before the Battle Practice begins, Crews and Gunners will form up outside the Tanks and the scheme of attack will be explained to them; also how it is intended to carry out the attack and what are their objectives. All drivers and gunners must fully understand the scheme of attack and what is expected of them; they must be told to ask their Tank Commander to explain any point that does not appear clear to them. Positions where Anti-Tank guns are expected must be pointed out to them on a map, and other information of this type may be given. This will add to the keenness and interest of the men.

Battle Practice

"Drivers must be reminded that the goodness or badness of the shooting will probably depend upon their driving.

"The Gunnery Officer must see that the targets are sited properly; he should always go over the Course in a Tank previous to the practice to satisfy himself on these points.

"If flashes are to be used, or moving targets employed, he must see that the fatigue men know their work, and the Gunnery Officer should always give these fatigue men one rehearsal before a Battle Practice Course, as it is most important for everything to go smoothly on the day.

"N.C.O. Instructors must be told off, one to each gun in the Tank which is firing, and their duty will be to see that points taught in the elementary training are brought into play and that the necessary safety precautions are adhered to.

"There will always be a conference at the end of each Battle Practice exercise. All members of the crews, students, instructors, etc., will attend. Constructive criticism and encouragement should be the tone of the conference. Faults brought to light should be carefully explained so that all can hear, learn and correct, in the future. The Gunner is as anxious to learn and to improve his shooting as is the Instructor to have a pupil who will do him credit."

Very excellent courses were also arranged in the Reconnaissance Schools. But almost the most interesting of the Reconnaissance Side's activities was the series of improvised courses—outdoor schemes, indoor practices and lectures which they arranged during the weary time while the Tank Corps "stood to quarters" through January, February and early March 1918.

The events of this time we propose to chronicle in the next chapter but one.

There had by this time been many other Tank activities which we have not at present chronicled at all. The French had trained and equipped a Tank Corps. The Americans were busy with Tanks, and a Detachment of our own Corps had fought in two engagements in Palestine.

Note to Chapter XI

Stories of the early days of Wool are related in the 6th Battalion History.

When the first few consignments of Tanks were sent to the

Camp at Bovington from Wool Station the most elaborate precautions were taken to secure the machines from the eyes of the profane.

The route was guarded by military policemen marshalled by A.P.M.'s. All civilian traffic was stopped, and—as if the Tanks had been so many Lady Godivas—all the blinds in the front rooms of the farms and cottages which bordered the roads had to be drawn, and all the inhabitants were relegated to the back rooms.

This ritual was observed every time a batch of Tanks arrived.

One farmer remarked that he was delighted to help keep the secret in any manner that seemed good to the authorities, but he thought they might like to know that a day or two before a Tank had broken down and that he and his horses had helped to tow it into his yard, where it had remained for forty-eight hours.

CHAPTER XII

THE FRENCH TANK CORPS—AMERICAN TANKS AND BRITISH TANKS IN EGYPT

The French Tank Corps

It is said that there is something in the Anglo-Saxon mind which has a special affinity for committees.

"Enough," said the logical Asiatic when the doctrine of the Trinity was being explained to him by the English missionary, "I understand you perfectly. It is a Committee of three."

At least, there is no doubt that the British Tank sprang from committees, and was matured and licked into shape entirely by a large assortment of these excellent bodies.

So with the American Tank Corps. Three or four names are equally illustrious in its early annals.

But with the French, one man, and one man only, stands out as the Father and Mother of Tanks. He was the General Swinton, the Sir Albert Stern, and the General Elles of the French Tanks. That is to say, he was first the principal independent inventor, deriving his inspiration (in early 1915) from Holt Tractors which he saw at work with the British. Then he was for long the principal "propellant" of the Tank idea in official quarters, and was the Commander-in-Chief's delegate to the Ministry of Munitions in the matter of Tanks. Finally, on September 30, 1916, he was gazetted " Commandant de l'Artillerie d'Assaut * aux Armées."

So much did the personality of this remarkable man permeate and vitalise the French Tank Corps that we offer no apology to the reader in setting forth the following delightful miniature biography of General Estienne by the hand of Major Robert Spencer, the British Liaison Officer to the French Tank Corps :

"Jean Baptiste Eugène Estienne was born at Condé en Barrois (Lorraine) on November 7, 1860. Owing to the trend of events during the Franco-Prussian War of

* " Artillery of Assault," *i.e.*, Tanks.

1870–71 his school, the Lycée of Bar le Duc, was forced to shut, and it was whilst enjoying an enforced holiday at the age of ten years at Condé with his parents that his idea of embracing a military career was born. He was one day an interested spectator of the passage of a column of Prussian artillery through the paved streets of his native town, and was lost in youthful admiration of this display of military power. He hastened back to tell his parents of his decision one day to enter as a conqueror into a town with his guns clattering behind him.

" From this hour he became wedded to an artilleryman's life, and in due course passed in and out of the famous École Polytechnique, where his mathematical ability enjoyed full scope.

" In due course, too, he passed through the artillery school of Fontainebleau, and in 1884 entered the garrison town of Vannes as a Second Lieutenant.

" Promoted Captain in 1891, he completed his studies in the use of the *collimateur* * and became the apostle of the use of direct fire for field artillery, which he eventually succeeded in introducing in the French Army. In 1909 he was summoned to Vincennes with a view to determining if any use could be made of aeroplanes in conjunction with field artillery, and succeeded in establishing a part for F.A. aircraft service. This, however, was transferred to the R.E., and Lieut.-Colonel Estienne consequently asked to be returned to regimental duty.

" In 1913 he was again summoned to Vincennes to continue his research, and was here at the outbreak of war, when he obtained command of the 22nd Regiment of Artillery. This he commanded in Belgium and throughout the retreat from Charleroi to the Seine. He had with him his two experimental aeroplanes, which rendered invaluable service during the Battle of the Marne, where he served under General Pétain.

" It was during the retreat that Colonel Estienne first spoke to members of his Staff of the future which would attend a machine capable of crossing ploughed fields and trenches, transporting arms and men. With this thought in his mind he was wont to invite his casual visitors and members of his Staff to assume all manner of peculiar attitudes under tables, etc., with a view to determining how many human beings could conveniently be crammed in a certain cubic area.

" His last command before being selected to father the future *Chars d'Assaut* was at Verdun, when he did not

* An aiming instrument.

Colonel Estienne 137

hesitate to employ a barrage of his heavy guns to break up a threatening German attack.

"As a man he appears to enjoy perpetual youth. He is short of stature, with no neck and a large round head. His hair is white, plentiful and worn *en brosse*, and he appears to be clean-shaven, so short is his clipped white moustache.

"Two things strike one immediately, the charm of his perennial smile and the quick brilliance of his brown eyes.

"As a raconteur he is inimitable, whilst as a lecturer his marvellous power of expression, his command of vocabulary and his convincing use of simile make it possible for him to communicate to his less erudite audiences a certain measure of his vast knowledge. This is by no means confined to military subjects, and his power of quotation from the classics is marked, whilst he has at least once published a lengthy poem in a volume dealing with the mathematics of gunnery.

"As an ardent philologist he bristles all over at the sound of the word 'Tancque' from French lips, and opens a violent crusade against the use of foreign words as a substitute for good French equivalents.

"His voice is loud and resonant and his speech accompanied by frequent gestures, his favourite being the placing of his left hand flat upon his chest as if he implies that his utterances emanate from his heart.

"He possesses many characteristic attitudes, and when in conversation is often to be seen tossing his *képi* from one side of his head to the other. In fact, it is scarcely ever to be seen except jauntily tilted over one ear.

"His admiration for the cavalryman at the head of a triumphal entry into a town is reduced to nothingness by his conviction that he is useless in modern war. He would prefer to see a victorious General enter a town on foot, escorted by a section of *Chars d'Assaut*, as being more typical of the present-day battlefield.

"He is himself a great walker, and may frequently be seen alone, wearing, as is his wont, a pair of pale blue spats or gaiters, a relic of the Empire uniform, and in summer no socks.

"This latter habit was recommended to him by a friend, and its adoption by him is typical of the man in that he is always prepared to give careful thought and personal trial to any scheme laid before him.

"To this quality, added to his immense personal charm and vast experience, is due his undoubted right to rank amongst the big men of this war, a successful issue to which has ever been the dream of his life."

On December 1, 1915, Colonel Estienne wrote an official letter to the Commander-in-Chief of the French Armies in which he outlined the idea of a new engine of war exactly as Colonel Swinton had done earlier in the year to our own War Office. A few days later he was given an interview at French General Headquarters, when he was able to enlarge upon his theories as to the new arm. Here he must, one conjectures, have received some encouragement, for about a week afterwards he visited the Schneider Engineering Works in Paris and discussed mechanical details with the management.

But the good seed which Colonel Estienne had sown at Headquarters would, he knew, take some time to germinate. He returned to his command, now the artillery of the 3rd Corps, at that time before Verdun. All the while he kept unofficially in touch with the Schneider Works.

At last, about February 25, 1916, he learned that the Under-Secretary's Department for Artillery had decided to place an order for 400 armoured vehicles with Schneider's.

But about two months later, at the end of April, he heard a more surprising piece of news.

The Under-Secretary's Department had, without the approval of the Commander-in-Chief or any notice to him, Estienne, placed an order for a further 400 vehicles of a different and heavier type, driven by a petrol-electric motor.

Curious as was their parentage, these 400 machines were actually made and were known as the St. Chamond Tanks. It is said to have been upon stolen drawings of this type that the Germans afterwards based their still heavier " Hagens " and " Schultzes."

In the course of the summer, the new French Ministry of Munitions formed an experimental and instructional area at Marly-le-Roi, and in the early autumn, Colonel Estienne was gazetted to the command of the French Tanks, and, as we have said, to be delegate, as far as this arm was concerned, from the Commander-in-Chief to the Ministry of Munitions.

Like the British, the French were beginning to need a name for their new engine of war.

But more logical than we, instead of an absurd, if pleasant, nickname, they chose "Artillerie d'Assaut," which they contracted into the letters " A.S.," as being more agreeable to the ear than " A.A."

Apparently Colonel Estienne had no preliminary inkling of what our activities had been in the " Land Cruiser " direction.

It is interesting to conjecture how eagerly he must have

A New Light Tank

read of what was happening on the Somme during the fortnight before he was finally gazetted to his new post. His "heart" must, indeed, have been "at our festival" when the British Tanks were everywhere acclaimed by the public, and when even the most conservative soldiers had to admit that the new weapon had at least earned a right to further trial.

In October 1916 a training centre for personnel was established at Champlieu, on the southern edge of the Forest of Compiègne, and here in December the first lot of sixteen Schneider Tanks were delivered, other batches both of Schneiders and St. Chamonds following them during the succeeding months, until, in April 1917, nine Schneider Companies and one St. Chamond Company and their crews were ready for action.

On April 16, 1917, French Tanks took part in their first battle, fighting with the 5th French Army in the attempted penetration of the Chemin des Dames.

Of the eight Schneider Companies employed, five succeeded in reaching their third and final objectives, but owing to lack of previous training with the infantry, the attack as a whole was not very successful, and the Tanks, though they played an exceedingly gallant part, suffered severely.

A week or two later, one St. Chamond and two Schneider Companies took part in a hurriedly prepared operation with the 6th Army.

The Schneiders did extremely well, but of sixteen St. Chamond machines, only one managed to cross the German trenches. All through the summer months, the 6th French Army was preparing another attack on the west of the Chemin des Dames, and for this battle, warned by their previous experiences, infantry and Tanks trained diligently together, special detachments known as *troupes d'accompagnement* being taught how to help the Tanks over trenches.

But the agile mind of Colonel Estienne was not content. He had had another idea. This time his mind had worked at the idea of the armoured attacking force from a slightly different standpoint.

He envisaged waves of armoured skirmishers attacking in open order, each man possessing besides his armour a quick-firing weapon with which he could shoot as he advanced.

Now, armour which will protect from machine-gun and rifle fire is too heavy for human legs. The armour must be independently propelled. More, if its occupant is to fire as he advances, it must carry him as well as itself. This postulates an engine, and if there is an engine, there must be a second man to look after it. This set of propositions he laid before the Rénault firm in July 1916, and the design of the famous Rénault Tank was evolved.

But the Ministry would have none of it.

However, the designs were worked out in greater detail, and at the end of November 1916 Colonel Estienne proposed to the Commander-in-Chief that a number of such machines should be constructed. A few, he explained, had already been ordered to act as " Command " Tanks for the heavy Battalions. The Commander-in-Chief consented to a trial.

This, however, was not held until March 1917, and when it had been held the Ministry were still not convinced.

Therefore, still further demonstrations were arranged in May, when at last they ceased to doubt, and finally, in June 1917, ordered 3500 of the new machines.

In October the five Companies of heavy Tanks, which had been in training all summer, were launched when the 6th Army delivered its blow at Malmaison.

As before, the Schneider Companies were successful, and again the St. Chamond Tanks were nearly all unable so much as to get into action.

Still, at the end of October the general verdict was that the French heavies had justified themselves, though many soldiers of the old school still doubted their utility.

But in November the British Tanks fought the Battle of Cambrai, and all doubts were finally dispelled from the French mind.

It is to be imagined that Colonel Estienne did not fail to rub in the facts proved by that engagement.

They were facts which it was impossible to deny or to overlook. The Ministry removed its hold from the brakes, and from that moment life behind the scenes of the French Tank Corps became happy. It was decided to form thirty light Tank Battalions, each Battalion to consist of seventy-five machines, and the firms of Schneider, Rénault and Berliet were all set to work upon their manufacture, while over a thousand machines were ordered in America.

All the winter of 1917-18, the French Tank Corps, like the British, continued to train and to organise.

For the future of the French Tanks was to be a brilliant one.

Those matchless givers of " unsolicited testimonials," the German General Staff, attributed the great victories which the late summer of 1918 brought to the French arms, chiefly to the employment of " masses of Tanks."

Naturally the annals of the French Tank Corps are full of stories of individual deeds of gallantry.

Chevrel, R. C., Brigadier, 505th Regt., Chars Légers.

" In the course of an attack he refused to abandon his Tank, which remained isolated in the German lines. Protected by his turret, he ceaselessly opened machine-gun fire on the surrounding enemy, and shot down with his revolver those who succeeded in approaching the Tank and who called upon him to surrender. For thirty-six hours he never slackened. Finally rescued by our advancing troops, he immediately undertook the unditching of his Tank and volunteered to support the further advance of the infantry, and then brought his Tank to the rallying point.

Médaille militaire and Croix de Guerre with Palm."— Official Gazette, dated October 26, 1918.

Cellier, Pierre, Brigadier in 35th Co., 11th Heavy Battery.

"This soldier, on July 18, when his Tank had been hit by a shell, placed himself at the head of fifteen American soldiers and stalked a position whence the Germans were using many machine-guns to resist the attack. These he engaged with an automatic rifle and forced the Germans to surrender after an hour's struggle. This act resulted in the capture of fifteen officers, including one Colonel, guns and numerous machine-guns.

Chevalier de la Légion d'Honneur and Croix de Guerre with Palm."—Official Gazette.

Dr. Gilles, Raoul Jules Gustave, Cte. in the 506th Regt., Chars Légers.

"Although blinded by wounds, brought his Tank back into French lines guided (by signals tapped on his shoulders) by the Tank Commander Maréchal de logis Joseph, who was himself wounded in the stomach.

Médaille militaire and Croix de Guerre with Palm."— Official Gazette, No. 2127 " D," July 26, 1918.

Colonel Estienne was promoted to the rank of General of Division and received the Cravat de la Légion d'Honneur, and the Commander-in-Chief of the French Armies issued the following special Order of the Day to the French Tank Corps:

" Vous avez bien mérité (de) la Patrie."

American Tanks

By the time the United States of America declared War (April 1917) the value of Tanks had already been demonstrated in battle by the British in the Somme Offensive, and by the end of October 1916 the French were already training with their first machines. It is not, therefore, surprising that the

Americans, with their great experience of Tractors (it was, the reader will remember, an American Tractor that was the chief ingredient in the make-up of the Mark I.) had a strong desire to include this new arm in their Expeditionary Force. Colonel Rockenbach, who was later to command the American Tank Corps in the field, was detailed to initiate preliminaries. He arrived in France in June 1917, and followed General Pershing to Chaumont, the United States General Headquarters, where he immediately occupied himself with the future organisation of the Corps. By September 23, 1917, the provisional American Tank Corps establishment had been approved. It was to be of a size to match the original Expeditionary Force, which was to be limited to twenty Divisions and ten replacement Divisions —that is to say, to one Army. The American Tank Corps in France was to consist of five Heavy and twenty Light Battalions, with the usual complement of Headquarters Units, Depot Companies, instructors and Workshops; and in the United States a Training Centre accommodating two Heavy and two Light Battalions was to be maintained. When the American Expeditionary Force was increased to three Armies, a new Tank Establishment was authorised to match it. There were to be five Brigades per Army. These Brigades were to consist of one Heavy and two Light Battalions. The Light Tanks were to be of the French Rénault type, and the Heavy were to be of the British pattern. The first Tanks with which the Americans were equipped were, in fact, actually of French or British manufacture, but as soon as an establishment was sanctioned, Tank manufacture was pushed forward in America, and by the time the Armistice was signed there were several thousand American-made machines ready for shipment.

So keen on the Tanks were Americans, that private enterprise was not idle, and early in October 1918 a three-and-a-half-ton Ford Tank arrived in France. This Tank, indeed, had the honour to be the first American-made Tank to appear in France. But though it was extremely agile and handy, its designers had not quite succeeded in producing a genuine fighting machine. It could, however, be turned out quickly and in great quantities, and in spite of its defects, it was thought in America that it would be worth while to continue its construction, and tradition has it that no less than 10,000 of these little Ford Tanks were ordered.

In the autumn of 1917 a number of American officers who were later on to have charge of the organising and training of the new Tank Corps were sent on visits to the British and French Brigades, to learn as much as they could, both from the mistakes and successes of the two older Corps. By February 1918 there were a large number of volunteers for the American

Tank Corps, some in England at Wool, who were to form the American Heavy Section, and others (about 500) at Burg in France, where a Training Centre was being formed for instruction in the Light French Rénault machines. At Burg were ten French Tanks which were used for training purposes, and in the course of the summer, as the personnel to be trained increased, this number was added to, and at the end of August 124 Rénault Tanks were delivered to the Training Centre for impending operations.

Two Light Battalions were formed into a Brigade under Colonel G. S. Patton, Junr., and they proceeded to the St. Mihiel Salient. Here they went into action with the First American Army on September 12, the first occasion on which United States Forces fought independently.

But, alas, it was our First Battle of the Somme over again! Nobody quite understood the habits of the new beasts, and unfortunately both Battalions were called upon to trek over twenty kilometres to their lying-up places from the railhead, and, the ground in the back area being very difficult, they did not succeed in catching up the infantry at all on the first day. The enemy resistance was, however, very feeble, as they had already decided to give up the Salient, but misfortune still dogged the unhappy Tanks. They had run out of petrol, and no supplies being immediately available, they were not able to get into action on the second day.

On the third day, however, they did get into the fight, but by this time the enemy had been thoroughly demoralised by the American infantry, and there was little more for them to do than to receive the surrender of a number of prisoners. The two Battalions suffered hardly at all in casualties and were withdrawn practically intact.

The American Light Tanks next appeared at the beginning of October in the Argonne, in operations where they fought side by side with French Tank Units. This time the two Battalions had much better luck, and though they must have been a good deal handicapped by the fact that they and the infantry with whom they were to co-operate had had no opportunity of training together, the Tanks rendered good service.

All the machines were launched on the first day, although in the original plan of the battle it had been proposed to hold back a reserve for the second day; but the infantry had been held up, and the reserve Tanks had, instead, to go to the rescue in the afternoon of the first day. From this time to October 13 these two Battalions were continuously at the disposal of the infantry. But, as with us in the early days, the infantry do not seem to have had a very clear idea of the uses and limitations of the Tanks, and the Battalions were frequently called upon to traverse many weary miles—much to the detriment of their machines—without finally being ordered into action. On one or two occasions they were used for independent reconnaissance and for unsupported assaults upon positions which the infantry had failed to capture. By the middle of October the long distance covered and losses in battle had caused the numbers of the two Battalions to dwindle exceedingly, and they were formed into a provisional Company which accompanied the advance of the American Forces right up to the Armistice.

A Third Light Battalion had also been mobilised and supplied by the French with seventy-two Tanks. Recruiting, too, had been continued, and there were no less than 7000 officers and men awaiting admission to the Corps at Burg alone.

Meanwhile, on August 24, 1918, the 301st U.S. Heavy Battalion had left Wool for France, and was almost immediately sent to the forward area, where it was attached, to begin with, to the 1st and later to the 4th and 2nd British Tank Brigades. With the 4th Brigade and still later with the 2nd Tank Brigade the 301st was, as we shall see in Chapters XX and XXI, destined to take part in several successful actions.

The 301st had based its methods of training almost entirely upon British lines, and though the American Tank Corps would undoubtedly have struck out improvements and methods of its own had the war gone on, the 301st, being throughout its active service brigaded with British Tanks, very wisely adopted a battle organisation practically uniform with the British. Only in minor details did their habits vary. Their reconnaissance procedure, for instance, was almost exactly like ours, except for one improvement. Special Reconnaissance N.C.O.'s relieved Reconnaissance Officers, Tank Commanders and Section Commanders from the work of guiding the machines on approach marches. From the tankodromes to the lining-up points the Tanks were in charge of these N.C.O.'s, who were directly under the orders of the Battalion Reconnaissance Officer. This system worked out extremely well.

In later chapters we shall see how worthy a representative both of the arms of the United States and of the best traditions of the British Tank Corps the 301st Battalion proved themselves in the supreme test of battle.

In February 1919, to the regret of their British colleagues, the men of the 301st sailed for America, when General Elles expressed the sentiments of all ranks of his Corps in a special Order.

"*February* 15, 1919.

" 1. On the departure of the 301st American Tank Battalion, I wish to place on record my appreciation of the services it has rendered.

"2. The Battalion has practically formed part of the British Tank Corps since April 1918, and while fully maintaining its national identity, has co-operated with British troops and adapted itself to British methods with a spirit that deserves fullest recognition.

"3. In the field the 301st Battalion, after experiencing heavy casualties in its first engagement at Bony, which might have deterred less determined troops, volunteered for the next action, in which, as in subsequent ones, it inflicted heavy casualties upon the enemy at Brancourt, the Selle and Catillon.

"4. I feel I am voicing the opinion of all commanders and troops who have been associated with them, in expressing sincere regret at the departure of our American comrades and in wishing them all good fortune in the future.

"(*Signed*) H. J. ELLES,
"Major-General,
"Commanding Tank Corps in the Field."

TANKS IN PALESTINE

The Second and Third Battles of Gaza, April and November 1917

> "Gaza yet stands, but all her sons are fallen,
> All in a moment overwhelmed and fallen."
> *Samson Agonistes.*

The Tanks that had fought in the Battle of the Somme, in the autumn of 1916, had proved successful enough for the authorities to consider that a test ought to be made of their capabilities in some other theatre of war.

Accordingly a small—a very small—detachment of Tanks was sent to "assist our troops in the Sinai Peninsula."

Unfortunately only eight Tanks were ultimately sent, and further, *"through an unfortunate error, old experimental machines were sent out instead of new ones as intended."

The experiment was thus upon so extremely miniature a scale that it cannot be said to have proved anything save what was already clear, that is, the general proposition that with a few mechanical modifications Tanks are perfectly suitable to desert warfare.

The Tanks were, of course, too few to exert any influence upon the fortunes of war in Palestine, and the two actions in which they fought amid palms and cactuses and lay up in groves of fig trees, form a curious, rather than an important, little incident in their history.

* *W.T.N.*

The field on which they fought was like the plain of Flanders, one of those ominous lands which seem predestined for ever to witness the strife of men.

> * "The land from the Wadi el Arish—the ancient 'River of Egypt'—to the Philistian plain had for twenty-six hundred years been a cockpit of war. Sometimes a conqueror from the north like Nebuchadnezzar, Napoleon and Mehemet Ali, or from the south like Ali Bey, met the enemy in Egypt or Syria, but more often the decisive fight was fought in the gates. Ascalon, Gaza, Rafa, El Arish, are all names famous in history. Up and down the strip of seaward levels marched the great armies of Egypt and Assyria, while the Jews looked fearfully on from their barren hills. . . . In this gate of ancient feuds it had now fallen to Turkey's lot to speak with her enemy."

In December 1916 a little company of 22 officers and 226 other ranks, under Major Nutt, embarked with their eight Tanks at Devonport and Avonmouth and landed in Egypt in January.

The first business was to show the Staffs of the various fighting units, with whom they were to co-operate, exactly what Tanks could and could not do.

Demonstrations were therefore given among the sand dunes near Kilban, a village which lies between Port Said and El Kantara on the Suez Canal.

One day in February—the exact date seems uncertain †— the detachment received orders to entrain immediately for the fighting zone, and within three hours of receiving the message, the whole little force with its Tanks and accessories was travelling towards the forward area. A delay occurred half-way, at El Arish, which had only recently been captured, but next morning the Tank Train arrived at its destination, Khan Yunus, an old Crusaders' stronghold, surrounded by fig groves and lying inland about fifteen miles south-west of Gaza.

Here the detachment remained for about ten days.

During these ten days the First Battle of Gaza had come to an end.

Gaza had not been captured, as, though we had fought in its streets, we had just not been able to keep up the attack long enough to keep what we had gained owing to lack of water.

* Mr. Buchan's *History of the War*.
† Major Forsyth-Major (the Second in Command of the E.T.D.), on whose report through Colonel Fuller this summary is largely based, was torpedoed on his return to England in 1918 and all his maps and documents were lost.

In his despatch, General Murray, the Commander-in-Chief of the Egyptian Expeditionary Force, characterised it as a most successful operation which only the waterless nature of the country had prevented from being " a complete disaster to the enemy."

We had been obliged to withdraw again to our water supplies, but we immediately began to prepare a second attack in greater force.

This time great cisterns were set up forward, and filled with rail-borne water. Three weeks of careful preparation were allowed for what was to prove one of the most hotly contested actions fought in the Eastern theatre.

We were to attack a Turkish force of about 30,000 men which lay upon a front of some sixteen miles, between Gaza on the north and Hereira and Sheria to the south-east.

Two ridges, Sheikh Abbas and Mansura, run almost at right angles to the coast and command the town of Gaza from the south, and the capture of these heights was allotted to the 52nd, 53rd, and 54th Divisions.

On their left flank was the sea, and their right, on the Hereira front, was protected by the Desert Column, consisting of cavalry units and of the Imperial Camel Corps which was manned by Australian, New Zealand, and British personnel.

The eight Tanks were to be widely spaced along the crucial five miles of attack. The 53rd Division nearest to the sea was to have two Tanks, which were to be held in reserve until the infantry had taken their first objective. Next to them the 52nd Division was to have four Tanks, which were to support the infantry in the attack on the Mansura Ridge. With the 54th Division, two Tanks were to support the attack on the Sheikh Abbas Ridge. The battle was to be in two phases; the Turkish outer defences were to be taken in the first phase, and in the second his inner ring was to be broken through and Gaza itself taken.

It was a country of sand dunes, deep nullahs, and criss-cross ridges, a labyrinth admirably adapted to defence and containing endless natural machine-gun positions. Between Gaza and the sea the enemy had built a double line of trenches and redoubts * "strongly held by infantry and machine-guns well placed and concealed in impenetrable cactus hedges built on high mud banks and enclosing orchards and gardens on the outskirts of the town."

The Tank Detachment had been able to do little or no reconnaissance; routes had been arranged to the starting-places, and petrol and ammunition dumps had been formed

* General Murray's Despatch.

in convenient places, but no forward preparations had been possible.

All eight Tanks reached their assembly places before daybreak on April 17, and at zero hour, the dawn of what promised to be a day of scorching heat, the first phase of the attack was successfully launched.

The advance of the 53rd and 52nd Divisions came as a complete surprise to the Turks, and the six Tanks did not come into action at all on the first day, as the enemy fled from his trenches and strongholds in complete confusion, and the slow Mark I.'s and Mark II.'s had no chance of getting in at him. The outer defence line had fallen by seven that morning. The two Tanks, however, on the 54th Division's front saw a good deal of fighting. One received a direct hit and was destroyed, but the other did admirable work in clearing the enemy out of his trenches, north-west of the Abbas Ridge. The Tank inflicted heavy casualties, and our infantry had only to come up and occupy the defences which the Turks had abandoned.

By the evening the three attacking Divisions found themselves in satisfactory positions on high ground, and proceeded to entrench themselves and to prepare for the second phase.

On the morning of April 19 we again attacked, this time upon a wider front, a French man-of-war and two British monitors supporting on the left, and the Australians on the right. The three original Divisions were, however, once more to deliver the main blow.

A very stiff programme was outlined for the seven surviving Tanks.

The four with the 52nd in the centre had finally four lines of defence to attack, and their orders were changed during the night before the action.

With the 53rd Division two Tanks were to work separately, each having a succession of objectives, while with the 54th the single Tank had only one redoubt allotted to it.

This time the Turks were ready for us.

One of the Tanks with the 53rd Division, the "Tiger," led the infantry advance on its sector. The enemy was quickly driven from our first objective, Samson Ridge. The Tank went on to the second objective, the El Arish redoubt, but the infantry being unable to follow, after being in action for six hours and having fired 27,000 rounds from its machine-guns, the Tank withdrew, all its crew being wounded.

On the front of the 52nd Division, our advance was hotly contested.

The Turks had massed hundreds of machine-guns along their entire front, but on this sector their fire was particularly

An Unsuccessful Action

intense. One Tank was able to do good service at Outpost Hill, which it helped to clear before receiving a direct hit.

Of the other three Tanks, one fell into a gully, the sides of which unexpectedly crumbled under its weight; another was put out of action by a direct hit, while the third eventually rallied.

The objective of the Tank fighting with the 54th Division was a particularly strong redoubt. The work was held in force, but the garrison soon surrendered on the advance of the Tank. Our infantry immediately took over the position, which the Turks forthwith proceeded to shell.

It was not long before the Tank was hit and one of its tracks broken, and the Turks, counter-attacking, eventually captured Tank, infantry and redoubt.

By nightfall our position all along the line was unfavourable. The left of the 54th Division was more or less in the air. We had, in several parts of the line, been forced off the lately won main ridges. We had lost 7000 men, and our troops were worn out by the dust and heat, and were once more short of water. The battle had to be admitted as a failure. The Tanks had been too few and of too old a type for the work they had been given.

Their co-operation was, however, much appreciated, and they were considered to have given a good deal of protection to the infantry.

It is interesting to note that by the time the battle was over these antiquated machines are said on an average, each to have covered forty miles of country.

The Third Battle of Gaza

The Second Battle of Gaza had been so completely unsuccessful that the troops who had been engaged in it had to be withdrawn from their advanced positions.

The Tanks were concentrated in a fig grove to the rear. Here, no work being found for them, they stayed till October, being reinforced by three Mark IV. machines.

General Allenby had now succeeded to the command, and there was to be another attack upon Gaza, for the town and its defences effectually barred our further advance along the coast or towards Jerusalem.

We were this time to operate upon a still wider front. The usual shock troops, the same three Divisions and their eight Tanks, were to attack nearest the coast.

Next to them, a mixed force of French, Italian and West Indian troops were to make feint raids near Outpost Hill.

Opposite Gaza itself several cavalry Divisions, mounted and dismounted, were to attack, and from Hereira to Beersheba a synchronised assault was to be made by the Australians. The position was, in fact, to be turned by an extensive flanking movement.

On October 23, 1917, the Tanks moved up to a new station on the beach.

From here, on horseback and by boat, the new area was thoroughly reconnoitred. This was the special country of cactus hedge and strong mud bank, and in it had been dug a veritable labyrinth of trenches. It had been a country of small fig groves and of little irrigated gardens, and its close boundaries afforded unending cover to the enemy. However, it was divided into Tank sectors, and by dint of patient toil, the Tank Commanders at last formed a more or less coherent picture of the intricacies. Tank Officers and N.C.O.'s were attached to each Brigade with which they were to work, for ten days before the battle.

Most of the Tanks were detailed to bring up R.E. stores, such as wire, pickets, shovels and sandbags for their infantry. These things they were to carry on their roofs.

The first phase of the attack, timed in consideration of a full moon for an hour before midnight, was to be independent of Tanks, and was to consist of an infantry attack protected by a creeping barrage. While this attack was going on, six of the Tanks were to move to their starting-points, in order to be ready to advance at 3 a.m. Two Tanks were held in reserve. It will be observed that the plans, preparations and liaison were in general much more complete than for the Second Battle of Gaza, but unfortunately one mistake of that battle was repeated.

The six first-line Tanks were given among them no less than twenty-nine objectives to attack.

At eleven o'clock on the night of November 1-2, the first phase of the battle began.

The 156th Infantry Brigade attacked Umbrella Hill, the first objective. The Turks were taken completely by surprise, there was little resistance, and even their artillery seemed too startled to fire.

Unfortunately, however, the smoke of the battle and a dense haze made so thick an atmosphere that not a ray of the expected moonlight reached the combatants, and the infantry had to fight and the Tanks to manage their approach march in profound darkness.

Also, when the enemy's artillery at last woke up, it was to open a heavy fire on our back areas, where the second wave was gathering. All the Tanks, however, came safely through and were at their stations half an hour before the second zero at 3 a.m.

The Turkish resistance had by now stiffened, and when the Tanks and the fresh infantry advanced behind a heavy barrage it was to meet with dogged opposition.

The two Tanks detailed to the El Arish redoubt were, after a stiff fight, successful in driving the enemy out of the enclosed stronghold, and were making their way through the maze of trenches, cactus hedges and gardens beyond, when one received a direct hit and the other got ditched in the darkness. Both crews at once joined the infantry. Slowly, scrambling up the mud banks, often fighting hand to hand in the darkness, we advanced. The Turks were fighting stubbornly, but inch by inch we pushed them back. The remaining Tanks lumbered slowly on.

At last all along the coast all the objectives were taken. No. 6 Tank captured Sea Post, and, followed by the infantry, moved along the enemy's trenches, crushing down the wire as far as Beach Post. It successively attacked three other strong points and deposited its R.E. stores at the appointed place. It was again moving forward to attack a certain isolated Turkish trench when one track broke, so ending a brilliant innings. The crew went on, but the Tank had to be temporarily abandoned.

The two reserve Tanks both caught fire through the empty sandbags with which their roofs were loaded being set ablaze by the heat of their exhaust pipes.

The coastal attack had done its work, and the Turks' hold upon Gaza had been loosened.

The other attackers, the troops who had advanced from Beersheba, broke through the enemy's resistance completely, and drove them back for nine miles on an eight-mile front.

The battle was decisive, and after about three days' fighting our troops at last entered Gaza. Our persistency in attack was well rewarded. The *Spectator*, commenting on the battle, said, "Samson took away the gates of Gaza, but General Allenby has secured the gates of Palestine."

On the whole the Tanks had been a success.

All machines except one reached their first objectives; four reached their second, third, and fourth, and one Tank reached its fifth.

All five damaged machines were afterwards salved.

This was the last Tank action fought with the Army of Palestine, for, for some reason or other, the repaired and renovated Tanks were never used again.

Later, however, during the Turkish retreat, we had great trouble in rounding up the tattered and wandering Turkish rearguard.

We felt the need of some sort of sheep-dog, so a mission was sent to France to ask for a number of Whippet Tanks.

By an ironical chance, this mission reached Tank Headquarters in France on March 21, the very day the German offensive was launched. It need not be added that no Whippets were sent.

There seemed no work left for the heavies, and the Tank Detachment, therefore, handed over their machines to the Ordnance Department at Alexandria, and returned to England.

CHAPTER XIII

SUSPENSE—THE "SAVAGE RABBITS" EPISODE—THE ENEMY'S INTENTIONS

I

THE story of the Tank Corps from the beginning of February to nearly the end of March 1918 is one of waiting and expectancy, of strategic moves to unexpected places, of diligent rehearsal for first nights upon which the curtain never rose, of endless preparations for events which never happened.

And through all the moves, in all the odd billets, or in the open fields, when—in hourly expectation of the German attack—Tanks and their crews lay ready under the hedges, run the Tank Corps' Pinkerton-like efforts at self-improvement, its determination to finish its winter training.

From before the middle of January we had been perfectly aware that the enemy meant to strike and to strike hard. He held a wasting security. We were waxing and he was waning. He was still our superior, still had more men available, but by Midsummer he knew that the Allies would outnumber him.

He had troubles, we knew, at home too, troubles for which the only salve was victory.

We had besides long known that before the war ended, whenever and however that end might come, we must expect a last desperate struggle. It would be the last spring of the wounded beast in which he might still find our throats, the last staggering blast of the hurricane by which the ship might still be confounded and overwhelmed.

Every sign spoke of the coming storm, but none told from which quarter we must expect it. The Germans were concentrating in such a way—at the base of the great salient formed by their line—that they could plant their blow wherever it might at the last moment seem good to them.

For better or worse, it was decided that our available forces were to be impartially distributed all along the line. Not that we had very much choice, as with our limited resources a concentration at any one strategic point must imply virtual gaps in our defence elsewhere,

For we had in January taken over an additional forty miles of line, and the men for whom the High Command in France had so frequently pleaded had not been sent out to them.

We were in for a lean three months, and to hold the extended line was as much as we could hope to accomplish.

The British and French Spring Campaign must be a defensive one. There was no longer a Russian front, and till the Americans were ready—which could not be till Midsummer at earliest—the Germans would have a numerical preponderance of nearly a quarter of a million men. Besides this, their position on interior lines and their superior lateral railway communications could at any moment give them an overwhelming local superiority.

However, we had faced worse odds before. We would form a strong line and cunning schemes of defence against which the enemy would hammer in vain. Our first defence was a deep forward zone. It consisted first of an outpost line and second of a " line of resistance."

The line of resistance was extremely carefully laid out. About every mile redoubts of special strength were so arranged that on this sector an attack would be entrapped into our wire and held exposed to a cross-fire from our machine-guns.

The line was, in fact, to offer " patches " of resistance, and so break up the ordered advance of the enemy, who was to arrive at the next line, the " battle zone," weakened and disorganised.

Here the main fight was to take place, and upon this zone we lavished all our skill and industry, and, having faith, we prepared no serious positions in rear of it.

The Tanks were spaced out all along a sixty-mile front.

Near Lens in the 1st Army area was the 1st Tank Brigade.

The 2nd Brigade was in 3rd Army Reserve at Haplincourt, near Bapaume.

The 3rd Brigade—which was in process of being equipped with Whippet Tanks—was also in 3rd Army Reserve.

The 4th Brigade was attached to the 5th Army and established itself in camps near Péronne.

The 5th Brigade was in process of forming, and therefore had no definite task allotted to it, though, as we shall see, the 13th (its nucleus) Battalion actually saw a considerable amount of fighting.

Each Tank Brigade got out a defence scheme in conjunction with the Army to which it was attached. As a rule the Tanks—which had been moved up as secretly as possible—were to lie in ambush till the last moment, and then, emerging —as General Elles described it—" like Savage Rabbits from their holes," were to fall upon the Germans in flank or rear.

His phrase struck the fancy of the Tank Corps, and the whole of this period is frequently referred to *tout court* as " Savage Rabbits," somewhat to the bewilderment of the uninitiated.

II

Their schemes prepared, their Tanks in position, after an exhaustive reconnaissance, the Tank Corps waited, a process which all troops find both tedious and demoralising, unless some really profitable means can be found of employing their time.

For the Tank Corps the need of the moment was further training. Several of the Battalions had been dragged untimely from half-finished courses, several were almost fresh from Wool, and had still most of their tactical training to do. Everywhere there were units and individuals who had lost " school attendances " to make up.

The great difficulty was that Battalions and even Companies were so spread out and scattered that it was almost impossible to collect the students for instruction.

The regular curriculums were out of the question, so the directors of Tank training immediately set to work to evolve new courses that would fit the altered circumstances.

In some ways the Reconnaissance Side fared best.

Their chief instructional material—the actual country to be fought over—was there for their students to study, and even when the pupils were so scattered that a sufficient audience could not be collected for a formal lecture, many ingenious little practical schemes could be carried out and written work could always be done.

They had a fairly definite standard to aim at. Had the battalions remained in the training areas, every officer and man would have been put through a five days' course in Reconnaissance. Under normal conditions such courses were arranged more or less as follows:

On the first day, the students heard an introductory lecture, practised chalk layering, heard a short discourse on map reading, did a practical comparison of map and country upon which they had to answer questions.

On the second day, visualising country from a map was taught, and practice indoors was gone through with a model. In the afternoon panorama sketching was practised, a short lecture heard, some visualising was done and the characterisation of landmarks was practised, the day being finished up by night guiding.

On the third morning, close observation of a certain sector, involving sketches and notes, was undertaken, and visibility practices carried out. Later, the students were taken for an " observation march," and having described the features of the country they had traversed, they had to write a report upon the new sector which they had observed in the morning, and upon this report they were later questioned.

On the fourth day, a new sector was visited, upon which they had previously made notes from a map. These notes they had to compare with reality, and to notice whether their imagination had been faulty. A lecture on obstacles commonly found on approach marches followed, and one on aerial photographs with practical work. Night work followed, with special reference to the study of the stars.

On the fifth day, oblique and other aerial photographs were compared with the actual ground, and a lecture was delivered summing up the special points of the course.

Sometimes, however, during the " Savage Rabbit " period, lectures were possible, and for these occasions a rather new type of discourse was evolved, in which the broader aspects of Reconnaissance and of the study of country were dealt with.

Local history was recalled :—how men had lived and fought in the villages and cornfields that lay immediately about them : how that great abbey church that stood alone was erected by a group of pious merchants as a thankoffering for their town's escape from the plague : how to this little town the Revolution had brought a Committee of Public Safety, and how it had held its red assize in the coffee-room of the Hôtel de l'Europe, or how Bonaparte had lain at this or that château on his way to the Camp at Boulogne. Or again, the lecture might be more strictly military and concern the place of Reconnaissance amongst the arts of war, and the action and reaction of one arm of the Service upon another—the ever-present trilogy of wire, trench and machine-gun, new theories of artillery work, the latest fashions in tactics or the effects of the latest poison-gas.

Then, where some isolated Tank Company or even section lay ready day and night by its machines and lectures were impossible, an itinerant instructor would set the exiles little schemes to carry out.

The two following exercises are typical :—

" Exercise I.—Two small parties of officers go at different times to positions from which a good view is obtainable. They pick out landmarks, etc., and their peculiarities, taking notes or making sketches. From these notes or sketches each party writes out three or four questions on landmarks, general observation, routes taken, etc, On their return the two parties exchange their questions, answers are written, and these answers returned to the writers of the questioners to correct.

"Catch questions, such as 'How many windows had such and such a house?' will, of course, be discountenanced, and only useful tests permitted.

"Exercise II.—The student was asked to sketch the outline of a cottage from about 800 yards distant. He then had to consider from the position of the house on the map, and the contour lines of the ground, what the appearance of that cottage would be likely to be from a different point of view. Of this hypothetical elevation he had then to make an outline sketch, and finally to walk over the ground and compare his imaginings with actuality."

Practices for approach marches were also given by means of an exercise on tape-laying and the taking of compass bearings.

III

And still the Germans stayed their hands, and still we waited and speculated upon what the coming campaign might hold for us. For the Tank Corps it seemed certainly to portend a new form of warfare—the Tank duel.

All sorts of things were rumoured concerning the German preparations, and the sheets of the Tank Corps Intelligence Summary for late February are full of little items of information of a perfectly new kind.

Tanks of some sort were certainly being made at Krupp's.

Prisoners had been caught who described them as larger and heavier than the British machines. We had reason to believe that men were being withdrawn from certain other units to form Tank crews.

Then, in the next day's Summary, it would be reported that airmen had found out that in certain Regimental, Brigade, and Divisional training schemes which were being carried out by the enemy, horses and wagons were being used, representing Tanks. Combined infantry and Tank attacks of all sorts appeared to be being rehearsed. Again, some recently captured prisoners said that a few derelict Tanks, which the Germans had taken at Cambrai, were being put into order, they seemed to think, as training rather than as fighting machines.

It is to be imagined that the notion of the new warfare, of meeting their kind in combat for the first time, was exceedingly interesting to all ranks of the Tank Corps; and there was not a single hut in a single camp where wonderful new ideas for tactics and manœuvres wherewith to annihilate the new enemy, were not daily elaborated.

We did not know that the bitterness and anxiety of a long retreat lay before us; a retreat whose gall and wormwood were to enter into our very souls, and of whose confused events it is even now almost impossible to write either with accuracy or impartiality.

CHAPTER XIV

THE MARCH RETREAT

> " A mile around the city,
>   The throng stopped up the ways;
> A fearful sight it was to see
>   Through two long nights and days.
> " For aged folks on crutches,
>   And women great with child,
> And mothers sobbing over babes
>   That clung to them and smiled,
> And sick men borne in litters
>   High on the necks of slaves,
> And troops of sun-burned husbandmen
>   With reaping-hooks and staves,
> " And droves of mules and asses
>   Laden with skins of wine,
> And endless flocks of goats and sheep,
>   And endless herds of kine,
> And endless trains of waggons
>   That creaked beneath the weight
> Of corn-sacks and of household goods,
>   Choked every roaring gate.
> " Now, from the rock Tarpeian,
>   Could the wan burghers spy
> The line of blazing villages
>   Red in the midnight sky.
> The Fathers of the City,
>   They sat all night and day,
> For every hour some horseman came
>   With tidings of dismay."
>   LORD MACAULAY.

I

ABOUT March 14 the 3rd and 5th Armies were warned by their aerial reconnaissance that a new and ominous concentration was taking place behind the enemy's lines.

These two Armies, to which the 2nd, 3rd, and 4th Tank Brigades were, it will be remembered, attached, held the line which lay between Bullecourt to the north and St. Quentin to the south.

Behind them lay the old Somme battlefields, and about them was a dry, rather bare, downland country with few woods and divided up by broad valleys that ran east and west across it. It was a part of the line upon which we had long considered the blow might probably fall.

The 3rd and 5th Armies, now on the alert, immediately set about raiding the enemy and, having captured the desired prisoners and examined them, were consistently told the same story.

Thursday, March 21, was to be the day of attack.

The weather, which had been clear and bright for a week or two, broke on Tuesday, the 19th, and all day it rained heavily. On the night of the 20th a thick mist came up and lay densely over the downs. Such weather conditions only made an attack the more certain, and all along the line Tanks were moved forward into their allotted positions.

At two o'clock in the morning of the 21st the British line was warned to expect an attack. The forward zone was already fully manned, but at 4.30 an order was sent out to man the battle zone. Nor was the order premature. The mist still lay heavily over the lines, and under its cover the Germans had secretly pushed up their troops until all along the front between Bullecourt and La Fère, they had massed thirty-seven divisions on a line little more than a mile from our outposts.

The drama was about to begin. At a quarter to five every German battery from the Marne to Dunkirk opened fire. Such a bombardment had never been known before, and it reached its zenith on the fronts of the 3rd and 5th Armies.

Torrents of gas shells and high explosives were poured out upon our forward and battle lines, upon our Headquarters, upon our artillery positions, and upon all our lines of communication.

The batteries of the 3rd and 5th Armies replied as best they could, but owing to the mist our artillery observers were helpless. It was impossible to see fifty yards ahead, and the German fire seemed to crash upon us out of some alien planet.

By 8 or 9 o'clock the first parties of Germans had begun to advance, to cut our wire here and there along the front of attack, and to filter unobtrusively through our outpost line.

We began to perceive that the enemy was behaving in a most unaccountable way. Even by 10 o'clock—as far as we could learn in the confusion—he seemed in some places to have made no attempt at an infantry attack at all. In others compact but apparently isolated little parties of Guards or Cockchafers, or men from some other picked regiment, had pushed right through our forward zone and were away beyond the places where the cross-fire from our machine-guns was to have checked them, before the men in the redoubts, half-blind amid the clouds of gas, had realised that any Germans had crossed No Man's Land. Again and again the garrisons were overwhelmed from the rear before they could send back any warning to the men behind in the battle zone. When they did endeavour to signal, the S.O.S. would be blanketed in the mist.

Only too often the first news of the attack to reach our batteries was the appearance of German infantry on their flank and rear.

There would be nothing left but to mow down the enemy at point-blank range, till finally the gun crews were overwhelmed by the in-flooding tide.

As at Ypres, we had begun amazedly to feel that we were up against a type of tactics against which we had never fought before. Our conjecture was perfectly right. It was a system of surprise, and of the theory of *Sturmtruppen* carried to its extreme conclusion. Mr. Buchan has likened the new method to the advance of a hand whose finger-tips are shod with steel pushing its way into a soft substance.

In practice the assault was conducted as follows: The infantry attack was preceded by a short but extremely intense bombardment in which a large proportion of gas was used.

This was followed by the advance at irregular intervals of clusters of highly trained assault troops, carrying light trench mortars or machine-guns (each cluster really constituting a kind of human Tank. It was well, indeed, for us that they were no more than mere flesh and blood, and neither armoured nor engined.) These clusters, which were closely followed and supported by the field batteries, made gaps through which the line troops poured, guided by an elaborate system of flares and rockets.

Each section of the defence might thus find itself caught between the " fingers "—outflanked and encircled.

Each body of the advancing enemy was under the command of a specially trained officer, whose leadership generally proved a model of skill and initiative; each detachment was instructed to push on as far as its strength allowed, and every man carried iron rations for several days.

When a regiment had advanced as far as it was able, another took its place, the waves of the advance thus leapfrogging over each other in an endless chain.

The dangers of such tactics are obvious, but on March 21 the system was portentously successful.

II

As in all disasters, events seemed to move with a terrible rapidity.

A moment before the motor accident you are a free man; a moment after and you are involved in an endless line of consequences which have sprung up while you could hold your breath, and amid whose mushroom growth you may wander for the rest of your life.

Five hours after the opening of the German cannonade the world seemed to have changed for the two armies which had stood in the path of the hurricane.

In the course of the next fourteen days the Germans were to sweep forward for forty miles, and their advance was even then to be checked, not by the British Army, but by the gradual attenuation of their supply system.

The whole fourteen days of the retreat were completely confused. Units were inextricably mixed, and communications were impossible.

Some sort of immediate action was always having to be taken by junior Commanders on information which they justly believed to be untrustworthy. There were often more Germans to the flank of any given body than to its front. When we try to form any general conception of the events of this period, we seem to see the actors moving in a kind of mist from which they emerge for a moment, perform some action which may or may not appear relevant, and then disappear again into the confusion, leaving us to guess at the meaning of the play. As far as the events of such a time can be chronicled, we propose for this fortnight to follow separately the doings of the three Tank Battalions chiefly involved, and to make no effort to present a coherent picture of this return to the reign " of Chaos and old Night."

The 4th and 5th Battalions (4th Brigade) lay near Cartigny (south of Péronne).

On the morning of the 21st the two Battalions of Tanks were moved up into the line, two Tanks of the 4th Battalion counter-attacking at Peizière and clearing a railway cutting of the enemy.

On the 22nd all the Tanks were ordered into action. The infantry were retreating, and their chief duty was to gain time and to cover that retreat.

Twelve Tanks of the 5th Battalion attacked the enemy at Hervilly Wood, and several from the 4th Battalion near Epehy. Both detachments suffered rather severely.

At this point the two Battalions seem to have more or less parted company.

Destroying the Tanks

Seventeen Tanks belonging to the 5th Battalion rallied at Cartigny that night, and next day (the 23rd) were ordered to retire over the Somme.

The only available crossing place was the bridge at Brie, a few miles to the south.

They set off immediately, but the enemy advance was too rapid for them. They were unable to cross the bridge, and, lest they should fall into the hands of the enemy, all the machines were destroyed by their crews.

The story of one of these Tanks is told in the 5th Battalion History:

> " Second Lieutenant T. E. Van Zeller's Tank was covering the withdrawal of the infantry across the Somme, moving from Cartigny to Brie on the east side of the river. He inflicted severe casualties on the enemy, and was under heavy and continuous shell-fire. On arriving at Brie late in the afternoon of the 23rd, he found that the bridge was about to be blown up, and that his Tank could not cross. He accordingly destroyed his Tank, and then directed his crew in assisting to carry wounded across the bridge. Finding two men seriously wounded who had been left behind, he decided, with three of his crew, to make an effort to rescue them at the last moment.
>
> " When half-way across, the bridge was blown up in front and behind them. Second Lieutenant Van Zeller, however, succeeded in getting the whole party across the débris under heavy shell-fire, and finally brought them back behind our lines on the west side of the river.
>
> " For this he was awarded the M.C., and the three members of his crew who assisted in the last plucky effort were each awarded the Military Medal."

There were other places where the now " dismounted " Tank crews could cross the river.

But they had no means of transport, and were, therefore, obliged to burn or otherwise destroy most of their stores and kit.

Indeed, as a rule, the Lewis guns from the Tanks were their only salvage.

One Staff Sergeant, however, hid away or buried a number of his tools, and six months later, when the British advance swept back again, they were recovered.

By March 24 the Battalion had lost all its Tanks. But in almost every case the Lewis guns had been salved.

As the crews fell back they were immediately organised as Lewis gun detachments, and distributed along the line wherever their help was most needed.

Colonel O'Kelly, Commanding the 5th Tank Battalion, had to use his own initiative in the matter, as communications were by this time hopelessly disorganised and the need was instant.

Once, too, a detachment had been sent off, it as it were disappeared, and each party had to rely upon its individual Commander.

Tank crews had had no training in this kind of warfare, but the strange dilemmas in which a Tank frequently finds itself had accustomed them to the unexpected, and thus left alone they displayed plenty of initiative.

The chief work which fell to them was that of forming rearguards and of protecting the retreat of the infantry.

Food and ammunition were both short, and they, like the other troops, suffered many hardships.

Each of these Lewis gun detachments was made up of about four officers and forty men, and they ordinarily had twelve Lewis guns with them.

Three such detachments fought near Masvillers and Merlaincourt, others near Villers Bretonneux, Caix, Harbonnières and Marcourt, the general retreat carrying them back almost to Amiens.

Again and again small parties failed to get the order to retire in time, and had to fight their way back after being surrounded and cut off by the enemy.

Sometimes they fought with French infantry, but chiefly with the Sherwoods, Queen's and Royal Fusiliers of the 19th Corps.

Extraordinarily good individual work was done, as the list of honours shows. The story of a 5th Battalion detachment gives a typical picture:

* "The 5th detachment under the command of Lieutenant Pitt, consisted of Second Lieutenants Whyte and Storm, forty-one men and seven guns. On March 28 this detachment was attached to 'Carey's Force' and ordered to hold the line on each side of the Villers Bretonneux—Warfusée-Abancourt Road, a position which was to be held for two days at all costs.

"While placing his guns, Lieutenant Pitt was wounded and Second Lieutenant Whyte took over the command.

"A Vickers gun section was in position north of the road, so Second Lieutenant Whyte posted his guns on the south side. The infantry holding the line at this point were all low-category men and convalescents, and not more than twenty men had any experience of holding a rifle.

* 5th Battalion History.

Lewis Gun Detachments

"At 6 p.m. on the 28th, word was received that the enemy were about to attack and, at close range, machine-gun fire was opened on them.

"The infantry began to fall back, but were rallied by Second Lieutenant Whyte and Captain Bingham, M.C., and taken back to their former position.

"Second Lieutenant Whyte then assumed command of this section. At 10 p.m. the enemy again attacked, but were again driven back by the Lewis gun fire.

"On the following day (29th) the enemy launched an attack on the right, but it was completely broken up by enfilade fire from Second Lieutenant Whyte's guns, the enemy suffering extremely heavy casualties. Some relief was afforded on the night of 29th–30th by cavalry, who came up on the right of this sector.

"Enemy machine-guns and snipers were very active, but two of the former and three snipers were accounted for by Lewis gun fire. Second Lieutenant Whyte held the line until 10.30 p.m. on the 31st, when he was relieved by Australian troops.

"For his gallant defence of this position Second Lieutenant Whyte was awarded the M.C.

"Corporal S. Archbold, working under Second Lieutenant Whyte, showed conspicuous gallantry throughout these trying days. Single-handed he worked his Lewis gun, carrying it and its ammunition to a new position, firing it and loading his magazines without assistance for twenty-four hours. During this period he helped in breaking two enemy attacks.

"On the 30th he was wounded in the head by a sniper, but continued to work his gun all day until he was ordered by his officer to the dressing-station. This devotion to duty gained for him the D.C.M. Another member of this party, Pte. W. Lyon, was awarded the M.M. for carrying important messages in broad daylight across the open under heavy machine-gun and rifle fire at 200 yards range."

Between March 24 and April 2 the 5th Battalion had sent a total of eighty-four Lewis guns and crews into the line.

Every available man had gone, cooks, officers' servants, clerks and orderlies. They had suffered heavy casualties, and on April 4 the Battalion, or what was left of it, was taken to Auchy by lorry.

Here they drew Hotchkiss guns, and began to train again. But they were not to be left long in peace.

On April 12 they had orders to form again as a Lewis gun

Battalion, and next day found them once more in the forward area, this time at Meteren, not far from Hazebrouck, where they relieved an infantry Battalion which had held a switch line through the village and an isolated point near Meteren Church. On April 15 they got news that the enemy had captured high ground between Neuve Eglise and Bailleul, and on the 16th the enemy advanced on Meteren.

> " Breaking through a section of trench which had been left unmanned, they forced back the infantry on the right and also ' B ' Company, and got behind the latter. No. 8 section was entirely cut off and lost.
> " Second Lieutenant Carter showed great presence of mind at this juncture. He was Reconnaissance Officer of his Company. On seeing the position caused by the enemy break-through, he immediately rallied and reorganised the various parties as they fell back and took up a line in rear. He was all the time under heavy shell-fire.
> " The position of ' C ' Company had then become precarious.
> " Second Lieutenant Dawson, assisted by Second Lieutenant Bayliss, immediately placed four of his guns in the open, covered the now exposed flank and held up the attack. During the night of the 27th–28th he dug a trench, connecting these isolated posts with our original line, and posted his guns in this new trench. The enemy mounted two guns behind a hedge about 200 yards in front of the position. These two guns, however, were knocked out before firing a shot. The Germans also tried to assemble behind this same hedge for an attack; but they were driven back with heavy casualties. This well-thought-out defence performed throughout under frontal and enfiladed fire, saved the company from an attack which would have endangered the entire position."

On April 17 the Battalion, except for twenty guns, was relieved by the Argyll and Sutherland Highlanders. After helping to hold back one more serious attack, the remaining gun crews were finally withdrawn and joined the rest of the Battalion at the Mont des Cats.

On April 24 detachments of the 5th Battalion, which were helping to man the line before Kemmel, were heavily in action. The enemy attacked after a fierce bombardment, and Kemmel Hill was taken.

On the 29th the enemy opened a heavy gas and H.E. barrage and attacked Mont Rouge in force. They were driven away, but returned again and again, always being beaten off.

At last in the first days of May the Battalion was relieved, and was sent back to the training and rest area at Blangy, the Divisional General having complimented the gun crews upon their conduct in the field.

The story of the 4th Battalion is very like that of the 5th. All through the last days of March there was the same heartbreaking destruction of machines that had run out of petrol or grease, or were suffering from some slight defect which there was no time to rectify. Again kits and orderly-room material had to be burnt, and again the Lewis guns were salved. The usual Lewis gun detachments were formed, but this time did not have quite so much fighting, their chief battle being on March 26, on the Bray-Albert road, where they did exceedingly well.

The 2nd Battalion was near Maricourt when the crash came, and twenty-five of their Tanks went into action on the afternoon of March 22.

* "The Tanks had to come into view when they crossed the Bapaume-Cambrai road, and as soon as the enemy spotted them coming into action, very heavy machine-gun fire was brought to bear upon them, to be followed in a few minutes by heavy direct artillery fire. Several Tanks were knocked out by shells almost as soon as they arrived amongst the enemy infantry, who were found to be very numerous, as if massing for a further advance.

" The appearance of the Tanks seems to have been a complete surprise to the enemy infantry, who became disorganised and retired some distance in confusion.

" The Tanks carried out the attack without any infantry, and practically no artillery, co-operation.

" The casualties both in Tanks and personnel were heavy, but the attack achieved its object, in that it upset the plans of the enemy and delayed any further attack on their part for nearly twenty-four hours. It was known at the time by the Staff that the enemy was massing for an attack at once, and the appearance of the Tanks rendered this impossible.

" The first Tanks came out of action about 7.30 p.m."

Of the twenty-five Tanks which went into action only six came out undamaged, and the Battalion was not really in a fit state to fight again without reorganisation.

But the enemy were still advancing, and the Albert-Bapaume road had to be defended at all costs.

So on the 24th the surviving Tanks were manned and sent

* 2nd Battalion History.

forward again, and the Tank-less crews were formed into Lewis gun detachments.

They waited all through the night of the 24th expecting to be sent forward.

No orders came till midday on March 25, when they were sent to the 3rd Tank Brigade Camp near Bray, which they later in the day were ordered to burn to prevent it from falling into the hands of the enemy.

All next day the infantry fell back, and with them the Lewis gun teams.

Some idea of the confusion may be gathered from the fact that at this moment the 2nd Battalion was separated into no less than eight parts, none of which could communicate quickly enough with its fellows to make any combined action possible.

The 8th and 10th Battalions still had some Tanks in going order, and, on the day when the 3rd Army was forced across the old Somme battlefield, they fought an exceedingly good rearguard action on either side of the Albert-Bapaume road. The Tanks received a special message of commendation from the General Commanding the 3rd Army.

Another incident—of which the authors have not been able to obtain many particulars—was the action fought by a scratch Tank force formed out of all the fighting Tanks from the driving school, Aveluy.

The 7th Battalion was one of several which were not in the path of the hurricane, and consequently lost no Tanks.

A certain number of its men were, however, organised as Lewis gun detachments, and by mid-April saw a considerable amount of fighting.

One such detachment was attached to the 61st Division near Nieppe Forest, and with them manned a line of fortified shell-holes.

There were no trenches and the country was absolutely flat. The whereabouts of the enemy was extremely uncertain. The Tank Lewis gunners held about a mile and a half of improvised line, their headquarters being a little farmhouse not far from Merville. Hardly had the detachment taken over than the enemy put down a hot barrage. A Reconnaissance Officer who was present described the events that followed in a letter home:

> " I went out of the northern door of the farm. A beastly sniper's bullet whizzed past my head, and then another and another. The bullets were all coming from the north, and it seemed as though Fritz had made his way through the town and would get us from the rear. This is what he did do. A sergeant was killed next to me, and Norton *

* Major Norton, commanding the Lewis gun detachment.

told me to go back to Divisional Headquarters and report the situation. After I had been there about an hour, a runner came back to say Norton had been wounded, and soon after we heard that the enemy had broken through to the north of the Canal. Just at that moment General Elles came up and asked what the situation was, and having heard that there were some Tanks and men of another Battalion on the northern side of the Canal, said he would go up and see for himself. He had his A.D.C. with him, and took me along as well. We motored right up to where we came in touch with our men, who were being pushed back on the north of the Canal. We then got out of the car and went forward on foot. The General had not even his tin hat on, but his red and gold. He went out beyond the withdrawing infantry and taking out his map, held a council of war, a council not uninterrupted by machine-gun bullets.

" He then sent me back a couple of hundred yards and told me to stop every man on a certain cross-road, re-organise them and make them take up fresh positions. This I did, and we thus re-established a line. The General took command and made his Headquarters in a small house until shelled out of it and into a neighbouring ditch. I was sent back to Divisional Headquarters to report and get some more ammunition. When I returned the situation was pretty well the same, and we were holding on all right. The General then suggested that we might see in which houses the enemy really were. During these investigations Ian Stewart went forward by himself on our flank, and had a private battle with a company of Germans, killing, amongst others, one who was on a bicycle, and himself returning on the captured machine, the original rider's papers in his pocket.

" We were relieved about 7 p.m. by a new Division, and I got back to Divisional Headquarters about 9. The next morning the C.O. turned up with the rest of the Battalion."

The 3rd Tank Battalion, whose camp at Bray had been destroyed, were now a fully fledged Whippet unit.

During the first few days the Whippets saw no actual fighting but were subject to plenty of alarms, and made a great number of fruitless excursions from place to place.

At the Bray Camp there had been, unfortunately, a certain number of Whippet machines which were temporarily laid up with engine trouble.

But there were no spare parts and no time for repairs, and a good many machines had to be blown up " unblooded."

On March 26 two Companies of the 3rd Battalion were moved to Mailly-Maillet Wood.

As soon as the machines had arrived the Company Commanders went out to reconnoitre the position near the village (Mailly-Maillet).

The result of their investigations is typical of the whole retreat:

> *" The position on the front between Beaumont-Hamel and Hébuterne proved to be very obscure, a gap in our line appearing to exist between these two places. The only troops of ours to be found consisted of two small posts of about one platoon each on the outskirts of Colincamps, the ground to the front and between them being occupied by enemy patrols and machine-gunners."

About noon the Whippets arrived at the village. The situation was explained to the Section Commanders, and half the Tanks proceeded down the main street while the rest guarded the two flanks.

A small body of our infantry which was holding the village had been on the point of falling back before the rapidly advancing enemy when the Tanks arrived.

The Tanks had gone forward almost beyond the village, when suddenly, round the edge of the wood, they met 300 of the enemy advancing in close formation.

The Germans were too much surprised to attempt to resist, and fled in disorder.

A number of them were shot down by the Whippets' machine-guns, and many surrendered to the infantry who had by now arrived.

The remnant scattered, and were pursued by the Tanks right on to the outskirts of Auchonvillers.

The two Whippets remained out on patrol for about an hour, but no further attack was attempted, and they returned to the village about 3 p.m. Later in the afternoon the gap in our lines was filled by the arrival of a New Zealand Division. This successful little action is interesting as the first ever fought by the Whippets.

There were several other sections of Whippets and heavy Tanks out on patrol on this and the following days.

Several Tanks of the 10th Battalion fought in Rossignol Wood on two occasions, and Whippets of the 2nd Battalion were in action near Bouzencourt in a blinding rainstorm.

Everywhere it was the same story of villages the question of whose ownership was " obscure," of gaps in the line which the

* 3rd Battalion History.

Waste

Tanks had to bridge for a critical hour or two, often firing their machine-guns into the advancing waves of the enemy until the guns grew hot and jammed and the Tanks had to retreat. Often they would go back till their petrol gave out, and the crews had to blow up their machines.

The new Medium A machines (the Whippets) acquitted themselves extremely well, and there were astonishingly few cases of mechanical trouble.

The Battalion histories describe many pitiful scenes which took place during the retreat, the fate of the inhabitants, for whom our withdrawal meant complete ruin, striking the eye-witnesses as the most distressing feature of the whole business.

> *" During the withdrawal the condition of the villagers was pitiful. Women and children and old men crazed with fright and with liveliest memories of the conduct of the Germans in the area occupied by them, were to be seen streaming westwards from their homes, pushing their meagre possessions before them in hand-carts and alternately invoking the aid of their Saints and calling down their wrath upon the hated Boche."

Nor was the retreat only tragic to those of the Tank Corps who had to witness the supreme misery of these processions of the Cross. There was a lesser unhappiness for the tacticians of the Tank Corps in the contemplation of the appalling waste of Tank machines and men.

The Tanks had been far too scattered ever to pull their weight.

> †" To hit with them as they were distributed on March 21 was like hitting out with an open hand instead of with a clenched fist.
>
> " When the German blow fell there was no time to hit and simultaneously to close the fingers."

Out of 870 Tanks which were fit to fight, only 180 saw any action, a great many machines running out of supplies or being incapacitated by some temporary mechanical trouble, and so lost without having fired a shot.

The fault lay in the fact that the infantry Commanders under whom they were acting did not fully understand the functions and limitations of the Tank, or realise that as the final loss of a good many Mark IV. machines in such a retreat was inevitable, it would have been much better to give the Tanks a run for their money.

* 1st Battalion History. † *W.T.N.*

III

Villers Bretonneux

It was not till the German offensive had lasted for more than a month that opposing Tanks at last met in battle.

The enemy had pushed us back to within six or seven miles of Amiens, and he now planned a more or less full-dress attack upon positions on high ground, which were, in fact, the outer defences not only of the town, but of the vital Amiens-Paris railway. A break through on this sector would be a serious disaster, and the situation was an anxious one. The weather was unsettled, and the mornings often still misty in the Somme country.

At 6.30 on April 23 the river fog lay thick, and under cover of this mist the Germans attacked the whole of the line south of the Somme after a short and particularly intense bombardment.

A company of heavy Tanks of the 1st and seven Whippets of the 3rd Battalion had been hastily moved up into the domain of the 3rd Corps, north and south of Villers Bretonneux, where it was rumoured that the Germans were going to use Tanks, and, in fact, when at last the first little knots of German infantry appeared through the fog, three huge forms accompanied them.

It was over Tanks of this type, the "Schultz" and the "Hagan," that the little boys of London scrambled so delightedly on the Horse Guards Parade in the spring of 1919. Now all we could see of them, as they lumbered slowly through the fog, was that they were a good deal larger and heavier than the heavy British Tanks, and that they were rather tortoise shaped, the armoured "shell" everywhere coming down over the tracks like a sort of crinoline.

They broke right through our line, opening a way for the infantry which was following them. But three of our Tanks, under Captain F. C. Brown, M.C., happened to be on their way to the very spot (Cachy) where the German Tanks had attacked. Unfortunately two of the three were females, whose machine-guns were not of much use against the new thick-skinned enemy.

However, they went on, hoping for chinks in their opponents' armour, but in spite of their superior power of manœuvre both the females were soon knocked out by shells from the German Tanks.

The one male Tank, under Lieutenant Mitchell, was now opposed to three undamaged enemy machines, each more heavily armoured than the British Tank. Lieutenant Mitchell, however, immediately engaged them and, after some dodging of the salvos of his three antagonists, who seemed to be trying to close upon him, he managed to obtain a direct hit with one of his six-pounders upon the leading German. Twice again he fired, each time hitting the same machine. The third shot completed its discomfiture; in its efforts to get away it fell into a sandpit, where it lay on its side, its tracks still rattling round ineffectively.

With its first enemy definitely out of action, the British Tank turned upon the other two.

But they had not waited, and had already discreetly turned tail, leaving Lieutenant Mitchell master of the situation.

Such was the rather inglorious end of the Germans' first endeavour to meet the British Tank Corps with its own weapons.

It was not far from the scene of this strange encounter that about half an hour later seven Whippets came into action, debouching from north of Cachy, attacking the enemy on the ridge between Villers Bretonneux and Hangard Wood. The ridge was held by machine-gun groups concealed in shell-holes, while on the eastern slopes two German Battalions were forming up in the open ready to attack. The Whippets moved from shell-hole to shell-hole, destroying the machine-gun groups, and then proceeded to deal with the infantry. Their success was terrible. They got right in among the enemy, who had absolutely no cover, and mowed the unhappy Germans down in ranks as they stood. At least 400 of the enemy are estimated to have been killed, and the rest at last fled in confusion, the threatened attack being completely broken up.

Not only were these two Battalions disposed of, but by nightfall it was clear that for the time being at least some circumstance had definitely held up the German advance. We did not know it, but our defences had withstood and survived the last hungry lickings of the great spring tide.

Its impulse was too far spent to overflow the frail dam of our Villers Bretonneux positions. The German advance had reached slack water.

There had been one incident which had genuinely cheered the hard-pressed men of the Tank Corps. At the very blackest moment of the retreat, when machines were being sacrificed by the dozen, and when the grey waves of the German infantry seemed to pursue our weary men with endless, tireless iteration, General Elles received a telegram from Mr. Docker, the chairman of the Metropolitan Carriage Company of Birmingham:

> "A resolution has been passed unanimously by the Works people of the Metropolitan Carriage Company to forgo any holidays, and to do their utmost to expedite delivery of Tanks to assist their comrades in the Field."

CHAPTER XV

THE EQUILIBRIUM—MINOR ACTIONS—HAMEL THE
BALLON D'ESSAI

I

It is not perhaps too fanciful to envisage the battles of April 24, 25 and 26, though they were by no means uniformly satisfactory little actions, as belonging to a different and a happier era than the action of Villers Bretonneux itself. On the 23rd we had been fighting for our lives. Through the three subsequent days' fighting it began to be more and more obvious that a change had taken place. Either through our desperate efforts to save Amiens, or by the workings of some deeper cause, spent and disorganised as we were, we had begun to pull level with the Germans again. The change was slight, but none the less palpable.

On the 25th, a few Tanks of the 1st and 3rd Battalions fought with the 3rd Corps in a counter-attack against the most advanced of the new German positions in the Bois d'Aquenne. The Tanks did a good deal of execution, and we succeeded in driving in some of the forward German posts.

On the 26th, four Tanks of the 1st Brigade had an interesting experience.

The Allied forces on this part of the line consisted of a most curious mixture of arms and races.

The scene, for example, in a neighbouring wood about ten days before is thus described by the historian of the 1st Battalion:

> "The Bois d'Abbé presented a most picturesque spectacle, and any one taking the trouble to walk through it could have had the unique experience of seeing practically every branch of both the British and French Armies represented. In this wood were to be found Tanks of all descriptions, Mark IV.'s, V.'s, Whippets and French

Rénaults, heavy and light artillery, British infantry, Australians, French cavalry and infantry, Moroccans, and lastly a detachment of the Legion of Frontiersmen mounted on little Arab ponies, which presented a strange contrast to the heavy Percherons of the artillery."

On April 26, it was in company with the Moroccan Division that the 1st Battalion fought.

The enemy had launched a strong attack against the Front held by these troops at 6 a.m. on the morning of the 26th, under cover of the usual heavy mist. Very soon, however, a section of Tanks under Captain Groves got right in amongst the advancing Germans and inflicted heavy casualties upon them. The French Colonial infantry, who had been obliged to fall back, immediately rallied and brought the German assault to a standstill. In the course of the action Second Lieutenant Wilson's Tank found itself among some German heavy guns, which it attacked with case shot * and machine-gun fire, wounding most of their crews and killing the rest. Mr. Wilson then patrolled up and down some trenches held by the enemy and cost them very heavy losses by his enfilading fire. Eventually, having fired every round of ammunition in his Tank, he decided to go back, but while he was on his way his magneto broke down. However, he sent back a messenger to fetch a new magneto, and after this had been fitted, he returned to the rallying point, his Tank having suffered the total casualties of two men slightly wounded.

On the 28th, another Company of the same Battalion again co-operated with the Moroccan Division. This time it was the Allies who were the attackers, their objective being the Hangard Wood. Owing to a mistake, the four Tanks did not get into action until rather late. Second Lieutenant Jones' Tank, however, fought a very good action, clearing out a great number of machine-gun nests in the Wood, and generally giving a great deal of help to the Moroccan infantry in their advance. The Tank stayed in the Wood until all its ammunition had been expended, and then, the infantry deciding not to make a further attack, it was withdrawn and rejoined its Company.

Except a small action of the 1st Battalion on May 2, the Tank Corps saw no fighting for the next six weeks, and it was not till July 4 that they fought again in any considerable action.

* Case shot: bullets not enclosed in a shell, but fired direct from a 6-pounder and scattering like the charge of a shot gun.

II

The general situation in May was still such as to cause our High Command a certain anxiety. It is easy to be wise after the event and say that the Germans must obviously have outrun their transport and overtaxed the limited road capacity of the devastated area which lay behind them. In early May this, though true, was not obvious. Meanwhile we had been too much weakened by the disasters of the last six weeks to be able to counter-attack. Consequently, the enemy had the same opportunities for reconstruction as we had ourselves, and although we felt confident that after such a hurricane of battles there must be a breathing space for both Armies, we were by no means certain what would be the respective rôles of the two opposing sides when the struggle came to be resumed. Our most pressing need was the filling of the gaps in our Divisions and the closing of the huge breaches which the German advance had made in our defensive systems. The greatest need was for men. We had, it is true, to lay out new trench lines and reconstruct such old systems as already existed, but it was not likely that the enemy would afford us time to establish new defences comparable with those which he had already proved his power of overrunning. Therefore it was to procuring new and well-trained troops that our chief efforts must be directed. The men procured, there must be railways upon which to move them.

> * "The depth to which the enemy had penetrated in the Somme and Lys valleys had disrupted important lateral lines of railway, and had created a situation of extreme gravity with regard to the maintenance of communications in Northern France. At Amiens, Béthune, and Hazebrouck, much-used railway junctions had been brought under the effective fire of the enemy's guns, while the railway centre at St. Pol was threatened. To relieve the situation a comprehensive programme of railway construction was undertaken."

Some 200 miles of broad-gauge track was laid between April and July and a complete series of new defences were built, involving, incredible as it may seem, 5000 miles of trench. Nor were Tanks left out of the scheme of reorganisation. But, alas! owing to the extreme need of infantry reinforcements, and the difficulty of immediately re-arming Battalions which had lost their Tanks during the Retreat, this "reconstruction"

* Sir Douglas Haig's Despatch.

all but took the form, not of augmentation, but of diminution. It was proposed to reduce the number of Tank Brigades from six to four. The appearance of enemy Tanks, however, soon quashed this project. Not only had the Corps lost heavily in machines, but the fighting done by the Lewis gun Units had been of a particularly strenuous kind, and several Battalions had sustained such casualties in trained and experienced men as to cause great anxiety at Tank Headquarters. However, the Tank Corps were only in the same predicament as the rest of the British Army, and there was nothing for it but to gather up the bits with as much grace as possible and to start away as quickly as might be on the work of reconstruction. All through May, Mark V. machines were arriving in France at the rate of about sixty a week. Some of the Battalions which had not taken any part in the Retreat had been left in their original areas, in case the Germans should attack, so that we find Battalions (for example of the 1st Brigade) doing " Savage Rabbit " as late as the middle of May. For the most part, however, the Corps was gathered together undergoing intensive training in the Bermicourt area. All Tank Units were to be ready for action—re-armed, re-equipped and re-trained—by August 1.

The Central Workshops set to work in early June to prepare sledges for supply haulage, bridges upon which the Whippets could cross wide obstacles, and " Cribs " for the heavy Tanks. These " Cribs " were big hexagonal oaken crates, reinforced with steel, which were an improved and lighter version of the fascines which were improvised for the Battle of Cambrai. Training grounds and workshops hummed with the preparations, and when, in the last days of July, the call came, it was, as we shall see, found possible to launch 400 Tanks at little over a week's notice.

It was while the Corps was training at Bermicourt that the foundation of the excellent relations which ever afterwards existed between Tanks and the French infantry was laid. A great number of French troops happened to be billeted in and around the Tank Corps area, and their keenness to learn all they could about our machines and their tactics afforded great pleasure to the men of the British Tank Corps. General Le Maistre, commanding the 10th French Army, particularly asked that Tank demonstrations should be held for the Units of his command. This was done, and all through May and June two or three of these demonstrations were given weekly. Besides French troops, representatives from a number of British and Colonial Corps, and the Canadian and Australian Corps, also came to watch, to their great edification.

III

We have said that only a few minor Tank actions were fought during the last part of May and the month of June. Two of these small encounters, however, were rather interesting. To begin with, the 17th Armoured Car Battalion fought its first action in company with the French on June 11. At 9.30 on the morning of June 10 orders were received by Colonel Carter, commanding the Battalion, to report to the 1st French Army at Contay. At Contay instructions were issued for the Battalion to proceed to Ravenel, near St. Just. The Battalion got this order by telephone, and although the night was very dark and wet, and the roads crowded with traffic, it reached Ravenel after a sixty miles' journey by five in the morning of June 11. That same day it went into action with the 10th French Army in its counter-attack at Belloy. Two sections of the Armoured Cars engaged the enemy with machine-gun fire, but unfortunately the roads here were piled high with every sort of débris. This prevented the cars from being as active as they were to prove themselves later.

The second small action was a night raid, interesting as the first in which Tanks had ever been engaged. Here the 10th Battalion fought in conjunction with the 4th Corps. We were endeavouring to capture a series of posts near Bucquoy, only five Platoons of infantry and five female Tanks being employed. The raid began at about half-past eleven at night. We were met with a heavy barrage from trench mortars and machine-guns, and the infantry were held up. The Tanks, however, managed to push forward, and carried on the attack in the pitch dark by themselves. As they advanced they met with a number of large parties of Germans, into the "brown" of which they fired. The Tanks certainly accounted for a great many of the enemy, though it being, as we have said, extremely dark, it was impossible to make a very exact computation of the "bag." Curiously enough, not a single Tank was damaged by the trench mortar barrage, which was extremely heavy. One Tank was swarmed over by a particularly bold party of the enemy and the crew shot them down with their revolvers. Later on this same Tank managed to rescue a wounded infantry officer who had earlier been taken prisoner by the Germans. The raid is interesting as it demonstrated the possibility of manœuvring Tanks in the dark through the enemy's lines— not a single machine lost direction—and also showed how much protection was afforded to the machines by their invisibility.

IV

By the middle of June the British High Command had grown anxious to make some test of the position of things on the enemy's side of the line. This they proposed to do by a more or less limited and tentative attack, an attack which might, if it was successful, be utilised as a dress rehearsal for larger ventures, or which, if it failed, would not commit us too deeply. The Australians had been constantly harassing their *vis-à-vis* on the Villers Bretonneux Front, and the High Command gave out that for this and other reasons they considered that a better place than the sector opposite Villers Bretonneux could hardly be found from which to launch our *ballon d'essai*. What those " other reasons " were did not appear for nearly a month after the battle had been fought. It was proposed that between sixty and seventy Tanks belonging to the 5th Brigade should be employed. Our attack was to have a strictly limited objective, its ostensible purpose being to capture the spur running from the main Villers Bretonneux plateau towards the Somme, on the east side of Hamel, and thus to gain important observation and incidentally a useful jumping-off place for any subsequent advance. " Z " day was to be on July 4.

Directly the attack had been decided upon, Tanks and Australians began their combined training in the area of the 5th Tank Brigade. Tank units were at once permanently affiliated to corresponding Australian infantry units with whom they were to fight, and by this means a very close comradeship was cultivated. It was (tradition relates) most necessary that some special steps should be taken to ensure the confidence of the Australian infantry in the Tank Corps, for, in the absence of artillery preparation, upon the Tanks would almost entirely depend the success and prestige of the Australians in this first Allied offensive since the March disaster.

Now the Australians, though having, as it were, a natural affinity for the activity and surprise of a Tank as against a prepared artillery attack, were not inclined to bestow their approval on the Tanks without due cause being given.

They still had vivid memories of the tragedy of errors of the Bullecourt incident in 1917.

They were, however, very open-minded, and the battle partners had not long been in training together before their relations were particularly cordial.

Coy and hard to please as were the Australians in the beginning, the triumphant success of their partnership in battle left them no memory of their earlier shyness, and made them vociferous in their praises of a combination that the Tanks had long felt would prove notably effective.

The plan of the attack soon took exact shape. It is worth more or less detailed consideration, as it was upon the lines of the Battles of Cambrai and Hamel that all set Tank attacks were afterwards based.

> *" The operation was to be conducted as a direct advance of infantry and Tanks in two waves, under cover of a rolling artillery barrage. From a Brigade point of view, the points of chief interest lay, first, in the preliminary arrangements with the Australian Corps and the infantry concerned; secondly, in the somewhat intricate plans for assembling Tanks at their start lines with due provision for concealment; and, thirdly, in the methods devised for bringing up large quantities of infantry supplies to the final objective. At a conference held by the Australian Corps three days prior to the action the plans were finally settled and no alteration in these was permitted after that date. Thus infantry and Tank officers were able to confer in perfect faith that their mutual arrangements would be carried out without change, and this method was adhered to in all subsequent operations of a prepared type with the Australian Corps. Tanks were employed on a scale that was large in proportion to the front attacked, the saving of casualties to the infantry being made the most important factor in the plan."

The main tactical features of the attack were the strongholds of Vaire Wood, Hamel Wood, Pear-shaped Trench and Hamel Village. There was no defined system of trench, except the old British lines just east of Hamel which the enemy now occupied, and which had, of course, been originally sited to face east. For the rest, the German defensive consisted in machine-gun nests.

The attacking forces were the 4th Australian Division and four companies of American infantry. The Artillery was to provide a rolling barrage, behind which the infantry were to advance, followed by the Tanks, which were only to pass ahead of them when resistance was encountered. This last arrangement did not prove a good one.

The going was good, and the fertile country lay still and smiling in its Midsummer pride. The camp allotted to the Tanks lay five miles behind the line in the angle formed by the meeting of the Somme and the Luce.

* 5th Brigade History.

Hamel

> * " It was an ideal spot in which to spend the summer months. In the cool of the evening, looking toward the west over the uncut cornfields, we could obtain a wonderful view of the old city of Amiens, its large cathedral, with the numbers of smaller church spires and smokeless chimneys clustering around it, being outlined against the setting sun. Toward the east one saw the ruined village of Villers Bretonneux standing on Hill 104, its château dominating the surrounding wreck of houses. It was hard to believe that the line was so close until the view was suddenly obliterated by the familiar sight of bursting shrapnel and the heavy smoke of the gas shells."

The sixty fighting Tanks which were employed in the attack were divided into two waves, the first of forty-eight, and the second of twelve machines. As the advance intended was but a short one, the usual gigantic system of supply dumps was not necessary. On the contrary, each fighting Tank carried forward ammunition and water for the infantry, and the four supply Tanks were detailed to carry up R.E. supplies and other stores.

> † " Each of these four machines eventually delivered a load of about 12,500 lbs. within 500 yards of the final objective and within half an hour of its capture. The total amount of supplies delivered on July 4 at 40 lbs. per man represented the loads of a carrying party 1,250 men strong. The number of men used in the supply Tanks was twenty-four."

No precise information as to time and place had been given to the Tank Corps till just a week before the battle; but as the area had been carefully reconnoitred for the last two months, very little had to be done to complete this side of the preparations.

On the night of July 1–2, the Tanks were moved up to the assembly point, an early move which was the result of the Australians' last lingering doubts as to the capacity of the Tanks for arriving in time at *rendez-vous*. No chance was thus given to any Tank of being late in the starting line.

Machines of " C " flight of No. 8 Squadron of aeroplanes were to make their début as honorary members of the Tank Corps on the morrow, for the wonderful potentialities of aeroplane and Tank co-operation were now fully realised, and the Tank Corps had been allotted a squadron of its own.

* 8th Battalion History. † *W.T.N.*

V

At three o'clock on the morning of July 4, almost before the sky had begun to lighten, the Tank engines were swung up all along our line, and at two minutes past the hour sixty graceful Mark V.'s slid forward after their infantry, two low-flying aeroplanes escorting them. As the Tanks moved along, the crews blessed the sweet running of their new machines, for there had not been a single mechanical hitch of any sort, and they knew that the shrewd eyes of the Australians had been fixed like gimlets upon them.

But the whole day was to be one long triumph for the Mark V.

Here and there as the attack surged forward the Tanks were leading, following close behind the bursting shells. Here and there the Australians were ahead. The enemy's infantry put up little or no fight, but their machine-gunners resisted us with the tenacious courage which we had learned to expect.

But our onrush was inexorable. The new Tanks were possessed, the Germans found, of a deadly power of manœuvre which they used to the full, expending little ammunition upon machine-gun nests, but, even when they had passed an emplacement by in the first rush, swinging swiftly round on the wretched gunners and crushing guns and crews beneath them. As a Tank chronicler somewhat grimly remarks: " This method eliminated all chance of the enemy coming to life again after the attack had passed by."

Over 200 machine-guns were accounted for during the day. There were also other and rarer little groups of picked men which the Tanks here and there routed out of the standing crops.

These little parties, generally consisting of three men, were armed with a special rifle of gigantic size designed to be fired—like our Lewis gun—from a bipod. Its projectile was a heavy steel-cored armour-piercing bullet.

It was a new anti-Tank weapon, a weapon from which the Germans hoped great things.

With the 13th Battalion, a Tank which had advanced ahead of the infantry, came upon some enemy dug-outs, on the far side of a trench too broad for their machine to cross. From these dug-outs the enemy were keeping up a hot fire.

The Tank Commander, Second Lieutenant Edwards, and Private Benns, immediately got out of their Tank and attacked the garrison on foot. Between them the two killed seven of the enemy with their revolvers, and the rest they took prisoners, and handed over to the infantry at the first opportunity.

There were many fine pieces of individual work, especially

instances of Tanks helping each other under heavy fire, and there is little doubt that it was to this friendly co-operation, this towing of lame Tanks out of hot corners, the astonishingly low casualties in machines were partly due.

The despatch tells how the battle fared all along the line.

> "Moving up and down behind the barrage, the Tanks either killed the enemy or forced him to take shelter in dug-outs, where he became an easy prey to the infantry. Hamel was taken by envelopment from the flanks and rear, the enemy was driven from Vaire Wood, and at the end of the day our troops had gained all their objectives and over 1500 prisoners."

Our little success had been complete and triumphant.

No less than fifty-seven of the sixty fighting Tanks came through the day without a scratch, the infantry killed and wounded amounted to less than half the German prisoners who passed through our cages; and as we have seen, the battle between Tanks and machine-guns being *à outrance*, the proportion of Germans killed to those made prisoners had been unusually high.

As for the Tank crews, they suffered only thirteen men wounded. To our great satisfaction also, the five damaged machines were all salved, and thus the armament of the Mark V.'s could not be investigated by the enemy.

But at first almost the most striking characteristic of the victory seemed the perfect co-operation between Tanks and infantry.

The Tanks and the Australians were equally enthusiastic over one another's performances. The Australians were surprised and delighted at the weight and solidity which the sixty Tanks had lent their impact, and at the sense of support and comradeship which their men had experienced.

The Tank Corps were equally impressed by the superb *moral* of the Australians, *"who never considered that the presence of Tanks exonerated them from fighting, and who took instant advantage of any opportunity created by the Tanks."

A generous and lasting friendship had been established. The 5th Tank Brigade and their Australians were destined throughout their coming partnership to prove an almost invincible combination.

But it was not alone the battle partners who were pleased and surprised.

* *W.T.N.*

The whole Allied front rang with the news of victory.

We had sent up our tentative *ballon d'essai,* and behold it had sailed up, high above our highest expectations and now hung, a token in the sky. All men might know that though Apollyon had straddled all across the way, we had beaten him and were at last come out of the Valley of Humiliation.

CHAPTER XVI

WITH THE FRENCH—THE BATTLE OF MOREUIL

I

THE 5th Brigade and the Australians had sworn eternal friendship with a refreshing enthusiasm.

They were like two schoolgirl friends, not to be separated, and at Vaux, whither they had retired for combined training, metaphorically went about all day with their arms round each other's waists.

Therefore, when on July 17 orders reached the 5th Tank Brigade that they were to send a Battalion south to fight with the French, consternation reigned.

If anybody went it would have to be the 2nd Battalion, which had not fought at Hamel at all.

But surely some way out could be found by which the Australians' own Brigade of Tanks should not be thus cruelly dismembered?

And the authorities, with positively avuncular benevolence—after a little humming and hahing—were actually induced to make another arrangement; as the friends firmly believed, solely upon their representations. There were, however, other more military considerations.

The attack was still to be under Brigadier-General Courage, but an extra Battalion, the 9th, should be added to the Brigade for the occasion.

This apparently whimsical outcry of the new-found affinities, and the yielding of the authorities, were to be justified thrice over in the events of the next few months.

For at this early period a little thing might upset the forging of a weapon which was to prove the two-edged sword with which we were to " smite Amalek hip and thigh."

As soon as it had been decided that the 9th Battalion was to go, preparations were at once begun.

The French plans were already well advanced before the Tanks came upon the scene at all. The attacking troops had indeed been in the area since April, but the Tanks felt that they would be eternally disgraced if they were obliged so much as to hint that they would like even a day's postponement of this, their first battle with the French.

Indeed in this battle we see the first instance of the wonderful "speeding up" which the Allied Army underwent almost as soon as the joint command was concentrated in the hands of Marshal Foch.

An officer who was present throughout the battle and its preliminaries writes:

> "On a certain Wednesday General Elles and General Courage had an interview at 3 p.m. with the 4th Army Commander and were consulted as to the project.
>
> "At 4.30 they saw General Debeney (the French Army Commander) and the French Corps Commander, when railheads and a general scheme of movement were decided upon.
>
> "That night the 9th Battalion was warned, and the battle took place at dawn on the following Tuesday."

Practice makes perfect, and we gradually discovered that the kind of full-dress attacks for which we had always, as a matter of course, allowed a month of preparation, could, in fact, be staged in half that time.

We see in the huge Battle of Amiens, of which only ten days' notice was given to the troops who took part, how great a reform we managed to accomplish.

II

The attack was to be at dawn on July 23, and was to be—like Hamel—a more or less limited and experimental battle.

Its immediate object was to seize St. Ribert Wood in order to outflank Mailly-Raineval from the south, to abolish certain highly objectionable German batteries which lay near St. Ribert, and to advance the French field guns eastward in such a way that they would bear upon the high ridges which dominate the right bank of the river Avre.

The country here was undulating and the soil well drained, and, except for a number of large and very dense woods, there were very few Tank obstacles.

There were to be three objectives. The first was a line which ran through the Bois des Sauvillers, Adelpare Farm, and Les-Trois-Boqueleaux. Twelve Tanks and four Battalions of French infantry were detailed for its capture.

The second objective included the clearing of the plateau to the north of the Bois des Sauvillers, and the capture of a corner of the Bois de Harpon. Twenty-four Tanks were allotted to this objective and four infantry Battalions.

The third was a line of German posts, known as the " Blue Line," covering the second objective, and was to be attacked by a strong force of infantry and all the surviving Tanks. The whole attack was to be preceded by a short intense bombardment, including heavy counter-battery work, and the creeping barrage was to consist of a mixture of high explosive and smoke. The Tanks were to attack in sections of three, two in front and one in immediate support, the infantry advancing in small groups close behind the Tanks.

Three days before the battle the officers of the 9th Battalion and some of the Staff of the 5th Brigade came down to the battle site, and, helped by the Staff of the French 3rd Division, made a pretty thorough reconnaissance of the ground. That same evening the Tanks detrained at Contay.

The 9th Battalion had been busy doing such tactical training as was possible with its new colleagues on the 5th Brigade training ground. The time was short and the difficulties of language great, but in spite of this a very friendly understanding had been come to.

Besides this, it had had an unusual amount of trekking to do.

It had had over eight miles to travel across country to its place of entrainment. From Contay, the rail terminus, the Tanks moved in all over another eight miles before they got into action.

At ten o'clock on the night before the battle the Tanks were informed that the attack, which was to have been at dawn, was postponed until 5.30. By this time it would, the Tank crews somewhat ruefully reflected, be broad daylight.

However, there was nothing to be done but to hope that the wind would help our smoke screens.

The weather had for some time been fine, but on the morning of attack heavy rain began to fall, driven up by a south wind.

The prospect of a really effective smoke cloud did not seem very great.

However, it was in the best of fighting spirits that the Tanks and their infantry went forward at zero hour—indeed, though it was no walk-over and all arms suffered fairly heavily, high spirits seem to have particularly characterised both French and British in this battle.

A member of the Tank Corps testifies naïvely to the way in which the Tanks had got their tails up.

" Brigadier-General Courage, who was much in evidence, was continually visiting the Battalion and conversing with the officers. From the nature of his suggestions and advice, a very ordinary thinker could easily come to the conclusion that he did not care for the Germans."

As the first-wave Tanks and infantry advanced, they found that the enemy was putting down a fairly heavy barrage in many places. However, moving ahead of the infantry, the Tanks cleared Arrachis Wood, destroying a number of machine-guns, and after a slight resistance, captured the first objective—Sauvillers Village, Adelpare Farm and Les-Trois-Boqueleaux—fifteen minutes before the infantry arrived. Two Tanks were knocked out by shells.

In the second phase, the Tanks of " B " and " C " Companies moved forward in support of their infantry on either side of Sauvillers Wood. As they swept forward, they outstripped the French patrols, but after a while turned back to maintain touch. It was by now about 9.30 a.m. The Tanks could not immediately find their partners, and unfortunately, as they were thus cruising about, no less than six Tanks were put out of action, one after another, by a single battery, apparently one of those lurking to the south of St. Ribert Wood, and whose destruction was one of the objects of the attack.

In another sector a Battalion Commander in the 51st Regiment of French Infantry, which was moving up in support, determined that if possible he would attack Harpon Wood, and asked the officer commanding " B " Company of Tanks for assistance. The Company Commander immediately entered into the scheme with alacrity, and between them a plan of attack for the French infantry and the seven Tanks was rapidly arranged. This little improvised action was a great success, Tanks and infantry duly capturing the Wood and at least one hostile battery. Only two Tanks were damaged.

It was not far from Harpon that Captain Dalton's Tank, in the confusion due to the smoke, got some distance ahead of its infantry. Near the Wood, Captain Dalton located an enemy battery. After a little manœuvring he managed to get a direct hit upon one of the guns and drove off the crews of the other pieces with machine-gun fire, thus silencing the whole battery. He then manœuvred his Tank into position to tow back one of the enemy guns, but at this moment his machine received a direct hit, and shortly after, a second shell added to the damage. Captain Dalton evacuated his crew, and, having done so, made every effort to get back to the derelict Tank, for it must be remembered that as yet no Mark V. had ever fallen into German hands. He was under intense machine-gun fire and in direct view of the enemy, but, realising the importance of blowing up the remains of his Tank, he still attempted the adventure. But it was in vain, for as he was thus trying to crawl up, he was severely wounded in the thigh. He managed, however, to drag himself back into the French lines.

Nor was Second Lieutenant C. Mecredy, a Section Commander, less anxious that his knocked-out Tank should be completely destroyed rather than fall into the hands of the enemy.

He had been advancing ahead of his infantry, when a shell from a concealed field gun hit the Tank in which he was leading the attack. At once seizing up a number of smoke bombs, he got out of his machine, went back, and, throwing down his bombs, put up a smoke curtain to cover the Tanks that were following him, lest they should share the fate of his own machine. His manœuvre was perfectly successful, for under cover of the smoke the other Tanks changed their direction and escaped the guns. With some difficulty Mr. Mecredy managed to dodge his way back to his Tank, under heavy hostile shelling and machine-gun fire, successfully blew it up, and was preparing to go back when he discovered that one of his crew was lying wounded in the leg in a very exposed place. This man he managed to bring back with him to safety.

By the evening all the three objectives had been gained, and the French Command were very well satisfied with the success of the action.

Especially delighted was the General Commanding the 3rd Division—General Bourgon—who was a great friend of the British Tank Corps, and who had been as anxious as we that no hitch should mar this first combined battle.

Both French and British had suffered rather heavy casualties, the French 3rd Division, with whom we had acted, losing over seven hundred officers and men.

Fifteen Tanks out of thirty-six had been knocked out by direct hits, and of the fifteen rather a large proportion were beyond salving.

However, the enemy's losses were also heavy. The prisoners totalled over eighteen hundred, and we took 5 field guns, 45 trench mortars and 275 machine-guns.

Before the 9th Battalion went back to the training area it had the honour of being inspected by General Debeney, commanding the French 1st Army.

He was kind enough to express extreme pleasure at the way in which the Tanks fought, and in his special Order of the Day gave the Battalion praise of which they will ever be proud.

"Finally, I owe a special tribute of thanks to the Battalion of British Tanks, whose powerful and devoted assistance has aided and assured our success.

"Commanded by an experienced and skilful leader, the Tanks have again added to that rich harvest of laurels which this new arm has not ceased to gather since its first appearance in September 1916. They have given to the Division the finest example of bravery, of energy, of comradeship in action, and of training for war carried to the highest degree of perfection. Their assistance has enabled the infantry to gain a brilliant victory in which they themselves share largely."

Finally, as a token of comradeship between the French troops of the 3rd Division and the 9th Tank Battalion, this Battalion had the honour of being presented with the badge of the French 3rd Division. Since that day they have worn it proudly on their left sleeve.

CHAPTER XVII

THE BATTLE OF AMIENS, OR BATTLE OF AUGUST 8

I

THE ambitious offensive which the Germans had launched on July 15 had collapsed. Our somewhat tentative counter-offensive at Hamel had been surprisingly successful, and there had been a complete change in the general military situation.

The German reserves were, it would seem, nearly used up, while ours—fresh troops which had become available during the spring and early summer—had now been incorporated and trained. Better still, the American Army was growing rapidly.

We were at last ready again to take the offensive on a grand scale.

On July 23, when the success of the battles of the 18th was well assured, a conference was held in which General Foch asked that the British, French, and American Armies should each simultaneously take the offensive.

Their assaults were to be immediate.

On the British front, after some consideration of the rival merits of various battle sites, it was decided that the attack was to be delivered to the east of Amiens on a front extending from Albert to Montdidier, and was to have for its immediate object the freeing of the Paris–Amiens railway, whose proximity to the German lines had proved so exceedingly hampering to our transport arrangements.

If the battle was successful, our advance could be exploited in a second attack directed towards the St. Quentin–Cambrai line. This line was one whose integrity was of vital importance to the enemy, as he had long ago confessed in the labour and money which he had poured out upon the vast elaborations of the Hindenburg defences.

For, twenty miles behind the Hindenburg Line, lay the great railway centres round Maubeuge, the key position of his whole system of lateral communication.

If we could once penetrate so far, we should cut the only

communications by which the German forces to the south in Champagne could be supplied and maintained, and should sever these troops completely from the group of German Armies operating in Flanders.

Of this great enterprise the first step was the ever memorable Battle of Amiens.

II

Preparations for the great attack were instantly begun. The battle plans were first made known in the last days of July to the commanders who were to take part, " Z " day being fixed for August 8.

The three Brigades of Tanks which were to fight (the 5th, 3rd, and 4th) had their first intimation of what was afoot on July 27, and their orders were confirmed on August 4.

Briefly, these were the general lines on which the battle was to be fought.

Preparations were to be rushed through. They were to be as secret as brief.

The battle itself was to be in two phases.

First, an attack without artillery preparation, but under the protection of a creeping barrage. The whole action was to be very much on the lines of the First Battle of Cambrai, save that this time (1) an even larger number of Tanks—about 430 including Whippets—were to head the battle; (2) that light skirmishing lines of infantry were to be used; and (3) that as at Hamel we were this time attacking a more or less improvised defence line. The second phase of the attack, which was to be made by a fresh wave of troops, was to start about four hours after zero, that is, after the first objective had been taken.

During this second phase, the artillery was to be moved up and we were to advance without a barrage.

On the right was to be the Canadian Corps, and with them the 4th Brigade * of Tanks was to fight.

In the centre, with the Australian Corps its usual battle partner, the 5th Tank Brigade,† was again to operate.

On the left, north of the Somme, two Divisions of the 3rd Corps were to have the 10th Tank Battalion attached to them.

Behind these three bodies three cavalry Divisions, the 3rd Brigade of Whippet Tanks, and the 17th Battalion of Armoured Cars, were to be concentrated.

Their work was chiefly the exploitation of the second phase. The Armoured Car Battalion had only just returned from operations with the French.

* The 1st, 4th, 5th, and 14th Battalions.
† The 8th, 13th, 2nd, and 15th Battalions.

* " When the 6th French Cavalry Division was withdrawn to rest, the 17th Battalion proceeded to Senlis, and at 9 a.m., having just entered this town, it received orders to proceed forthwith to Amiens and report to the Headquarters of the Australian Corps. Amiens, which was nearly 100 miles distant, was reached the same night.

" On arriving, Lieut.-Colonel Carter was informed that his unit was to take part in the projected attack east of that town. The chief difficulty foreseen in an armoured car action in this neighbourhood was the crossing of the trenches. Although only one day was available wherein to find a solution to this difficulty, it was accomplished by attaching a small force of Tanks to the Battalion. These Tanks were used to tow the armoured cars over the obstacles, or rather along the tracks the Tanks formed through them. This solution proved eminently successful."

Short as was the time for preparations, an elaborate deceptive scheme was planned and carried out, to make it seem that we intended to fight in Flanders. Canadians were put into the line on the Kemmel front, where in due course the enemy identified them. Ostentatious Headquarters and Casualty Clearing Stations were conspicuously disposed about the area. Throughout the 1st Army sector our wireless stations hummed with messages about the concentration of troops, and arrangements were made to make it seem that a great assembling of Tanks was taking place near St. Pol. Here, indeed, Tanks elaborately trained with infantry on fine days days, that is to say, on which the enemy's long-distance reconnaissance and photographic aeroplanes were likely to be at work behind our lines.

The ruse was perfectly successful and—as we found out afterwards—the news of our " great projected attack in Flanders " soon spread, and by the time we were ready to strike on the Somme the enemy was momentarily expecting to be attacked in force in the north.

III

Meanwhile hectic days and still more hectic nights were being passed near Amiens.

The reader is to imagine that elaborate preparations such as were described as the preliminaries to Cambrai and which took a month to carry out, had now to be executed in a little over a week.

Reconnaissance had to be carried out, details of plans and

* *W.T.N.*

liaison arranged, and dumps had to be made, the last on an unprecedentedly large scale, so great a number of Tanks never having gone into action together before.

In the centre (the Australian sector) certain units in the 5th Brigade had been newly equipped with Mark V. star infantry-carrying Tanks. No one was very familiar with these machines, and so, in addition to other preparations, such units had infantry-carrying to practise with their Australians. One circumstance greatly added to the fraternal feeling of the 5th Brigade towards their familiar battle partners. As soon as the final conference was ended, General Monash laid down the principle that on no consideration should any alteration be allowed in the plans as then approved. It was therefore possible for all the Tank units to work out the details of their schemes in perfect confidence.

The battlefield lay on either bank of the river Somme, which ran to the north of the area of attack, and as far as Péronne, almost at right angles to the lines of the two armies.

South of it, a number of gullies, roughly parallel to the battle front, ran down to the river from high ground which formed the watershed between the Somme and the small river Luce.

Two of these steep gullies, the Cérisy Valley, and another which ran from Morcourt almost to Harbonnières, were to be great features in the battle, forming as they did admirable cover for the concealment of batteries or for the assembling of troops for a counter-attack.

The following notes on the Luce were given to the author by Major Hotblack :—

" The river Luce, though only a small marshy stream, formed *the* great difficulty of the plan of operations.

" Part of it was in the French lines, and as to put up fresh bridges would have attracted the enemy's attention, the attacking troops had to cross it in a few places and deploy afterwards in the dark.

" In that sector where the Luce flowed within the enemy's lines, it ran diagonally across the front of attack of the Canadian Division.

" A great deal of trouble was taken in finding out all possible details of this little river, and it caused anxiety to every one concerned from the Field-Marshal himself downwards.

" The Luce sector of the front lay within the lines then held by the French, and in addition to various Reconnaissance Officers, Major-General Lipsett, commanding the 3rd Canadian Division, and Brig.-General Hankey, commanding the 4th Tank Brigade, carried out personal reconnaissances of the river in general and Domart Bridge in particular.

" Both these General Officers had great reputations for personal gallantry, and always endeavoured to see for themselves what the conditions really were before committing their troops.

"The French troops then holding the line, knowing nothing beyond the fact that they were to be relieved by the British, expressed the greatest astonishment and admiration for our thoroughness and for the remarkable conscientiousness and pertinacity of our Generals and General Staff Officers, in so frequently visiting the forward positions of an unhealthy sector. We had no choice but blandly to assure them that this was their unvarying practice whenever a relief of any sort was contemplated."

As another result of the great secrecy that had been imposed, no officer knew who else was in the secret, and on one occasion Major Hotblack and another British officer met on the banks of the Luce and each made lengthy explanations which explained everything except the real reason why they were there. Two days later these officers met at a conference on the operations, and congratulated each other on the plausibility of their several explanations. It had been no easy matter to pretend that it was quite a normal thing for them to paddle in the Luce in close proximity to the enemy.

On the day all went well, however, and the information about the river proved to be correct to the last detail, and as had been anticipated, though the bridges in the enemy lines had been blown up, the gaps were sufficiently small for Tanks to cross on the abutments.

Generally speaking, the going was good, and the fact that the weather had been reasonably fine for some time before the day of attack made our preparations the easier.

All night, for four or five nights before the battle, the carrying Tanks had plied up and down, forming dumps of tens of thousands of gallons of petrol and water and millions of rounds of ammunition.

At last the time came for the final moving up of both the fighting and supply Tanks to their assembly positions, about two miles behind the lines.

No. 1 Gun Carrier Company of Tanks had been allotted to the 5th Australian Division, and lay up in an orchard north of Villers-Bretonneux.

All went well till the late afternoon of August 7, when a chance shot from the enemy set one of these Tanks blazing.

The enemy promptly began to shell the area heavily, and destroyed nearly the whole Company of Tanks and their loads. It was on this occasion that Second Lieutenant Henderson Smith was awarded the Military Cross.

The following account of his action appears in the list of "Honours and Awards":—

"As soon as the first Tank was hit, Second Lieutenant Smith rushed to the scene and collected men to aid him, and so initiated the work of rescuing the Tanks. He showed the utmost skill in organising the withdrawal of Tanks from the blaze.

"Although several of his helpers were men from other units and inexperienced in Tank work, this gallant officer succeeded in moving two Tanks away from the heart of the fire. This bold action undoubtedly enabled the people on his right to save three Tanks. Unfortunately these two Tanks were hit and set on fire by the explosions on other Tanks. On each occasion Second Lieutenant Smith was the last to leave the blazing machine. The Tanks were loaded with explosives for the infantry, gun-cotton, bombs, trench mortars, etc., besides two fills of petrol each."

The shelling was an uncomfortable incident, not only because of the loss at the last moment of the machines and of the masses of stores which they carried, but because such a bombardment might be an indication that the enemy suspected the presence of Tanks.

However, as at Cambrai, there was nothing to be done, and it remained only to try to hurry forward more stores to replace those which had been burnt. This was successfully accomplished.

Final lying-up places for the 300 heavy Tanks had been arranged all along the front at about 4000 yards from the front line.

At about the time when the Tanks were moving up to these "jumping-off places" the enemy may have been somewhat puzzled to observe that a number of large aeroplanes with exceedingly noisy engines kept flying about between the lines. In any case, what he did *not* observe was the noise made by 300 advancing Tanks.

IV

The night of the 7th–8th was damp and still, and at about four o'clock on the 8th a dense ground mist had begun to drift up the river valley. Soon the whole air was one silent white sea of vapour. So thick was it that the assaulting infantry and Tanks had immediately to prepare to move entirely by compass, for it was impossible to see a yard ahead through the dense silent blanket.

Nothing, it would seem, was further from the Germans' thoughts than that the steaming quiet of the early autumn morning was to be so terribly broken. At a quarter past four his lines were perfectly silent. He was far from being in a truculent mood in this sector, and for a week his attitude had been unobtrusive. Here and there a German sentry, his grey greatcoat silvered like gossamer by the pearls of the mist, would cough, stamping his feet as he peered listlessly through the fog for stray trespassers in No Man's Land.

Suddenly at 4.20 our massed artillery opened an intense fire along the eleven miles of front.

The German front line was drenched in a hurricane of shells, and behind, his unprepared batteries were for some time completely smothered by the violence of our fire.

Before the Germans had had time to recover their wits, all along the line the Tanks emerged by tens and twenties upon them out of the fog.

The forward positions were completely overwhelmed, the Tanks not so much destroying the enemy with their fire as simply running down his machine-gun emplacements and crushing crews and guns beneath them.

Our first wave was soon out beyond the enemy's lightly held front-trench system, and the survivors and the second wave were fighting their way through his scattered machine-gun emplacements towards the first phase objective.

With the Australians in the centre, a Company of the 13th Battalion advanced rapidly over undulating country, apparently " swallowing the ground " of both first and second phases at a run.

> * " The method of attack was adapted to suit the ground ; leaving the infantry established on a crest, Tanks would go forward across the valley, maintaining fire on isolated machine-gun posts, and gain positions on the forward ridge. In all cases this induced the enemy to give themselves up, and enabled the infantry to advance to the next crest. On the right of this sector ' B ' Company quickly placed their infantry in their final first phase objective north of the main road. ' C ' Company on the left had more trouble ; a field gun placed on the high ground across the river near Chipilly was in position to enfilade the advance, and knocked out three Tanks. This for some time caused a withdrawal by the infantry. By noon, however, the remaining Tanks had placed their infantry in the required final positions, and all active opposition had ceased. Throughout the operation there was abundant evidence of the hasty retreat of the enemy. In the gully south-east of Morcourt a transport-park, complete with wagons and

* 13th Battalion History.

harness, was left behind, and at the southern end of the same gully a field canteen was found well stocked with light wines and German beer."

With the Canadians also the advance was rapid, but here the mist was so thick that Tank sections got completely mixed up and fought cheerfully all over each other's areas.

The carefully planned and methodical assault had to give place to a more or less primitive *mêlée* in which each Tank generally sought out and slew Germans wherever they might happen to find them.

Though far from scientific, this method when allied with the *élan* of the Canadian infantry proved highly successful.

With the 3rd Corps the fighting was heavier, and more difficulty was experienced in advancing. The heavy Tanks and infantry, however, soon everywhere held the line whose capture was to mark the end of the first phase (*i.e.*, Marcelcave, and the Cérisy Valley to south of Morlancourt).

V

The second phase of the attack, which started four hours after zero, was very different from the first. The mist which had hampered but concealed our approach had now given place to brilliant sunshine. The enemy had had ample warning and had time to dispose his " stout-hearted artillery and machine-gunners " to meet the advance. In these conditions his resistance stiffened. With the Australians,* " Enemy field batteries firing over open sights engaged and knocked out Tanks, some in the neighbourhood of Bayonvillers and near Cérisy Village. The crews were, however, in many cases able to move forward with their Hotchkiss guns and put the hostile batteries out of action. The surviving Tanks pressed on to the final objective, the Australian infantry being quick to seize the openings that had been made."

The final objective allotted to the 2nd Tank Battalion was Harbonnières Village.

The machine-gun and artillery fire had been heavy. However, the first-wave Tanks rallied at the Cérisy Valley and with the rest of the Battalion launched the attack on the second objective.

Lieut.-Colonel Bryce led his Tanks triumphantly to the successive capture of all the objectives allotted to them—Warfusée, Lamotte, Bayonvillers, and a number of other villages.

At last they reached Harbonnières, their last objective, and,

* 5th Brigade History.

still on foot, Colonel Bryce entered the place with his leading Tanks and ran up an Australian flag over the village.

In the naïve words of " Honours and Awards," " This had a most stimulating effect on every one."

In the same sector, Lieutenant Percy Eade and his Tank (of the 2nd Battalion) appear to have captured a village single-handed, and, best of all, to have solemnly demanded a receipt upon handing it over to the Australians.

> * " During the attack on the 8th inst. this officer showed great initiative, skill and bravery in dealing with unexpected resistance by the enemy.
>
> " On being informed by the infantry that Marcelcave was still holding out and was endangering their right flank, he arranged a scheme of attack with the infantry commander and proceeded to quell the opposition. He destroyed at least six machine-guns with their crews, besides taking many prisoners. He then handed over the village to the infantry, from whom he took a receipt. After regaining his position and during the second phase of the attack, he heard opposition coming from Bayonvillers, so he proceeded towards that village. As he was approaching it from the south-west he discovered a group of three light field guns, two of which were firing at him at short range. These guns had already knocked out several Tanks. With great gallantry and determination he manœuvred his Tank in their direction, and so directed the fire of his own guns that he dispersed the gunners. After running over one of the field guns, he proceeded into the village, where his Tank was directly responsible for capturing at least forty of the enemy.
>
> " Throughout the whole of the operation, this Tank Commander set his crew a magnificent example of courage and determination. (Immediate Reward.) "

The 13th Battalion History is particularly full of allusions to the excellence of their relations with their battle partners, the Australians.

All Tanks of this Battalion displayed on a painted board the colours of their own infantry, of whom one N.C.O. stayed with each crew and rode as an observer in the Tank on the day of battle. It may here be noted that these Australian N.C.O.'s were of the greatest use in keeping touch with the infantry, and incidentally returned to their units with a largely enhanced opinion of the courage and endurance of the Tank Corps personnel.

* Honours and Awards.

In the second phase one Tank was of service in keeping touch between two Companies of infantry, until a gap in the line could be closed.

With the Canadians, the second phase was equally hot. A typical action was fought by a machine belonging to the 14th Battalion.

* " Second Lieutenant Gould's Tank was pushing on towards the Red Line, which overlooked the valley running south. Here the enemy were found to be organising for a counter-attack. Enemy transport with a large number of stragglers, estimated at 1000, was in full retreat up the road, and in the valley itself a force estimated at half a battalion was forming up and being reinforced by other parties coming over the hill in rear. All the time this Tank was under heavy fire from machine-guns and snipers from the left flank and rear. Fire was opened with 6-pounders on the transport and direct hits observed. M.G. fire was also directed with good effect on the excellent targets in the valley, causing confusion and disorganisation in the enemy ranks. With the prolonged running at high speed the interior of the Tank rapidly became unbearable through heat and petrol fumes, and the crew were forced to evacuate it and to take cover underneath. At this moment two of the crew were wounded, one was sick, one fainted and one was delirious. Fortunately, before the enemy could take advantage of the lull, two Whippet Tanks and a body of cavalry came up, and the enemy in the valley began to retreat over the hill."

The 1st Tank Battalion with the Canadians suffered extremely severely.

† " Owing to the French having been held up, the British were subjected to a heavy enfilade fire from the villages of Beaucourt and Le Quesneu, and nine out of the eleven Tanks belonging to ' A ' Company received direct hits from a field battery firing over open sights from Le Quesneu. The majority caught fire and were burnt out, and very severe casualties resulted, three out of the four Section Commanders being killed and the remaining one wounded and captured. This disaster was followed by a particularly heroic action on the part of Second Lieutenant Cassell, who observed the destructive fire of the battery, and, passing through the burning victims of its shells, steered straight

* 14th Battalion History.
† 1st Battalion History.

The Whippets

on to it, in an attempt to avenge the destruction of his comrades. His heroism was in vain, for before he had proceeded many yards he received a shell through the front of his Tank which put it out of action and killed Second Lieutenant Cassell and most of his crew."

Meanwhile the Whippets and the cavalry had pushed forward.

They and the armoured cars were to press on beyond the limits of the infantry and heavy Tank attack.

Generally the Whippets were to precede the cavalry, in order to silence machine-guns, deal with wire, if any, and generally to pave the way.

In practice, however :

* " Difficulty was found in maintaining touch with cavalry owing to the impossibility of keeping up with galloping horsemen on the one hand, and to the impossibility of a mounted advance in the face of heavy machine-gun fire on the other hand. Thus, two sections of ' C ' Company 3rd Battalion lost touch with their cavalry in climbing a steep hill out of Ignaucourt Valley."

There were, in fact, innumerable instances of liaison difficulties.

* " Another Company was ordered to obtain touch with 3rd Cavalry Brigade, but on reporting to the rendezvous, no cavalry was seen.

" Zero hour had been postponed three hours, but this was not known till later.

" Being unable to obtain touch with the cavalry, assistance was rendered about noon to Canadian infantry attacking Beaufort and Warvillers. This attack was successful and Whippets rendered great assistance."

Far happier was the lot of certain Whippets which played an independent part. The following is a first-hand account of the adventures of one such machine, the ever-to-be-remembered Whippet, " Musical Box."

As the story will show, for many months no news was obtained of the fate of the machine or of her crew of one officer, Lieutenant C. B. Arnold, and two men, Gunner Ribbans and Driver Carney, and it was not till January 1919 that the following amazing tale appeared in *Weekly Tank Notes* :—

" On August 8, 1918, I commanded Whippet ' Musical Box ' in ' B ' Company, 6th Battalion. We left the lying-up point at zero (4.20 p.m.) and proceeded across country

* 3rd Battalion History.

to the south side of the railway at Villers-Bretonneux. We crossed the railway, in column of sections, by the bridge on the eastern outskirts of the town. I reached the British front line and passed through the Australian infantry and some of our heavy Tanks (Mark V.), in company with the remainder of the Whippets of 'B' Company. Four sections of 'B' Company proceeded parallel with the railway (Amiens-Ham) across country due east. After proceeding about 2000 yards in this direction I found myself to be the leading machine, owing to the others having become ditched, etc. To my immediate front I could see more Mark V. Tanks being followed very closely by Australian infantry. About this time we came under direct shell-fire from a 4-gun field battery, of which I could see the flashes, between Abancourt and Bayonvillers. Two Mark V. Tanks, on my right front, were knocked out. I saw clouds of smoke coming out of these machines and the crews evacuate them. The infantry following the heavy machines were suffering casualties from this battery. I turned half-left and ran diagonally across the front of the battery, at a distance of about 600 yards. Both my guns were able to fire on the battery, in spite of which they got off about eight rounds at me without damage, but sufficiently close to be audible inside the cab, and I could see the flash of each gun as it fired. By this time I had passed behind a belt of trees running along a roadside. I ran along this belt until level with the battery, when I turned full-right and engaged the battery in rear. On observing our appearance from the belt of trees, the gunners, some thirty in number, abandoned their guns and tried to get away. Gunner Ribbans and I accounted for the whole lot. I cruised forward, making a detour to the left, and shot a number of the enemy, who appeared to be demoralised, and were moving about the country in all directions. This detour brought me back to the railway siding N.N.W. of Guillaucourt. I could now see other Whippets coming up and a few Mark V.'s also. The Australian infantry, who followed magnificently, had now passed through the battery position which we had accounted for and were lying in a sunken road about 400 yards past the battery and slightly to the left of it. I got out of my machine and went to an Australian full Lieutenant and asked if he wanted any help. Whilst talking to him, he received a bullet which struck the metal shoulder title, a piece of the bullet-casing entering his shoulder. While he was being dressed, Major Rycroft

The Story of "Musical Box"

(horse) and Lieutenant Waterhouse (Tanks) and Captain Strachan of 'B' Company, 6th Battalion, arrived and received confirmation from the Australian officer of our having knocked out the field battery. I told Major Rycroft what we had done, and then moved off again at once, as it appeared to be unwise for four machines (Lieutenant Watkins had also arrived) to remain stationary at one spot. I proceeded parallel with the railway embankment in an easterly direction, passing through two calvary patrols of about twelve men each. The first patrol was receiving casualties from a party of enemy in a field of corn. I dealt with this, killing three or four, the remainder escaping out of sight into the corn. Proceeding further east, I saw the second patrol pursuing six enemy. The leading horse was so tired that he was not gaining appreciably on the rearmost Hun. Some of the leading fugitives turned about and fired at the cavalryman when his sword was stretched out and practically touching the back of the last Hun. Horse and rider were brought down on the left of the road. The remainder of the cavalrymen deployed to right, coming in close under the railway embankment, where they dismounted and came under fire from the enemy, who had now taken up a position on the railway bridge, and were firing over the parapet, inflicting one or two casualties. I ran the machine up until we had a clear view of the bridge, and killed four of the enemy with one long burst, the other two running across the bridge and on down the opposite slope out of sight. On our left I could see, about three-quarters of a mile away, a train on fire being towed by an engine. I proceeded further east, still parallel to the railway, and approached carefully a small valley marked on my map as containing Boche hutments. As I entered the valley (between Bayonvillers and Harbonnières) at right angles, many enemy were visible packing kits and others retiring. On our opening fire on the nearest, many others appeared from huts, making for the end of the valley, their object being to get over the embankment and so out of our sight. We accounted for many of these. I cruised round, Ribbans went into one of the huts and returned, and we counted about sixty dead and wounded. There were evidences of shell-fire amongst the huts, but we certainly accounted for most of the casualties counted there. I turned left from the railway and cruised across country, as lines of enemy infantry could be seen retiring. We fired at these many times at ranges of 200 to 600 yards. These targets were fleeting, owing to the enemy getting down into the corn when fired on. In spite of this, many casualties must have been inflicted, as we cruised up and down for at least an hour. I did not see any more of our troops or machines after leaving the cavalry patrols already referred to. During the cruising, being the only machine to get through, we invariably received intense rifle and machine-gun fire. I would here beg to suggest that no petrol be carried on the outside of the machine, as under orders we were carrying nine tins of petrol on the roof, for refilling purposes when well into the enemy lines (should opportunity occur). The perforated tins allowed the petrol to run all over the cab. These fumes, combined with the intense bullet splash and the great heat after being in action (by this time) nine to ten hours, made it necessary at this point to breathe through the mouthpiece of the box respirator, without actually wearing the mask.

"At 2 p.m. or thereabouts I again proceeded east, parallel to the railway and about 100 yards north of it. I could see a large aerodrome and also an observation balloon at a height of about 200 ft. I could also see great quantities of motor and horse transport moving in all directions. Over the top of another bridge on my left I could see the cover of a lorry coming in my direction; I moved up out of sight and waited until he topped the bridge, when I shot the driver. The lorry ran into a right-hand ditch. The railway had now come out of the cutting in which it had rested all the while, and I could see both sides of it. I could see a long line of men retiring on both sides of the railway, and fired at these at ranges of 400 to 500 yards, inflicting heavy casualties. I passed through these and also accounted for one horse and the driver of a two-horse canvas-covered wagon on the far side of the railway. We now crossed a small road which crossed the main railway, and came in view of large horse and wagon lines—which ran across the railway and close to it. Gunner Ribbans (R.H. gun) here had a view of south side of railway and fired continuously into motor and horse transport moving on three roads (one north and south, one almost parallel to the railway, and one diagonally between these two). I fired many bursts at 600 to 800 yards at transport blocking roads on my left, causing great confusion. Rifle and machine-gun fire was not heavy at this time, owing to our sudden appearance, as the roads were all banked up in order to cross the railway. There were about twelve men in the middle aisle of these lines. I fired a long burst at these. Some went down and others got in amongst the wheels and undergrowth. I turned quarter-left towards a small copse, where there were more horses and men, about 200 yards away. On the way across we met the most intense rifle and machine-gun fire imaginable from all sides. When at all possible, we returned the fire, until the L.H. revolver port cover was shot away. I withdrew the forward gun, locked the mounting and held the body of the gun against the hole. Petrol was still running down the inside of the back door. Fumes and heat combined were very bad. We were still moving forward and I was shouting to Driver Carney to turn about, as it was impossible to continue the action, when two heavy concussions closely followed one another and the cab burst into flames. Carney and Ribbans got to the door and collapsed. I was almost overcome, but managed to get the door open and fell out on to the ground, and was able to drag out the other two men. Burning petrol was running on to the ground where we were lying. The fresh air revived us, and we all got up and made a short rush to get away from the burning petrol. We were all on fire. In this rush Carney was shot in the stomach and killed. We rolled over and over to try to extinguish the fumes. I saw numbers of the enemy approaching from all round. The first arrival came for me with a rifle and bayonet. I got hold of this, and the point of the bayonet entered my right forearm. The second man struck at my head with the butt end of his rifle, hit my shoulder and neck, and knocked me down. When I came to, there were dozens all round me, and any one who could reach me did so and I was well kicked. They were furious. Ribbans and I were taken away and stood by ourselves about twenty yards clear of the crowd. An argument ensued, and we were eventually marched to a dug-out where paper bandages were put on our hands. Our faces were left as they were. We were then marched down the road to the main railway. There we joined a party of about eight enemy, and marched past a field kitchen, where I made signs for food. We had had nothing since 8.30 p.m. on the night previous to the action, and it was 3.30 p.m. when we were set on fire. We went on to a village where, on my intelligence map, a Divisional Headquarters had been marked. An elderly stout officer interrogated me, asking if I was an officer. I said 'Yes.' He then asked various other questions, to which I replied, 'I do not know.' He said, 'Do you mean you do not know or you will not tell me?' I said, 'You can take it whichever way you wish.' He then struck me in the face, and went away. We went on to Chaulone to a canvas hospital, on the right side of the railway, where I was injected with anti-tetanus. Later I was again interrogated, with the same result as above, except that instead of being struck, I received five days' solitary confinement in a room with no window, and only a small piece of bread and a bowl of soup each day. On the fifth day I was again interrogated, and said the same as before. I said that he had no right to give me solitary confinement, and that unless I were released, I should, at first opportunity, report him to the highest possible authority. The next day I was sent away, and eventually reached the camp at Freiburg, where I found my brother, Captain A. E. Arnold, M.C., Tank Corps. The conduct of Gunner Ribbans and Driver Carney was beyond all praise throughout. Driver Carney drove from Villers-Bretonneux onwards.

"(*Signed*) C. B. ARNOLD, Lieut.,
" 6th Tank Battalion.

"*January* 1, 1919."

The Tank was found close to the small railway on the eastern side of the Harbonnières–Rosières Road.

The final stage of the day's battle had been reached by early afternoon.

The armoured cars, moving rapidly east along the main roads, did much to complete the demoralisation of the enemy.

*" The enemy, once in retreat, became completely demoralised. One heard from the commanders of the armoured cars which were returning on the main Villers-Bretonneux road, how they chased excited German Staff cars and officers through the ruined village of Faucourt, and eventually had been held up, because the enemy's traffic was so congested on the roads behind his lines that they could penetrate no further. The Air Force were then reported to have completed this confusion, by obtaining some excellent results in flying low over these roads. . . .

" The cars which had turned northwards entered Proyart and Chuignolles, two moving up to the river Somme. At Proyart the cars found the German troops at dinner; these they shot down and scattered in all directions, and then moving westwards met masses of

* 8th Battalion History.

The End of the Day

the enemy driven from their trenches by the Australians. In order to surprise these men who were moving eastwards, the cars hid in the outskirts of Proyart and only advanced when the enemy was between fifty and one hundred yards distant, when they moved forward, rapidly shooting down great numbers. Scattering from before the cars at Proyart, the enemy made across country towards Chuignolles, only to be met by the cars which had proceeded to this village, and they were once again fired on and dispersed. Near Chuignolles one armoured car obtained 'running practice' with its machine-guns at a lorry full of troops, and kept up fire until the lorry ran into the ditch. There were also several cases of armoured cars following German transport vehicles, without anything unusual being suspected, until fire was opened at point-blank range.

"Although more than half the cars were out of action by the evening of the 8th, there were no casualties amongst their personnel sufficiently serious to require evacuation."

The Mark V. star Tanks successfully reached the day's final objective and delivered their infantry machine-gunners on the line which was to be the limit of our advance.

That they were duly "delivered" is, however, about as much as can be said of many of these unfortunates.

The motion, the heat, and the fumes of the inside of a Tank closed for action, almost invariably proved too much for all but the Tank's own well-salted crew.

Consequently where little fire had been met with, the machine-gunners had come up either riding or walking behind it.

Where the fire had been heavy and they had been sternly ordered in and the Tank closed up, they had been delivered flushed, feverish, and either vomiting or extremely faint and quite unfit for duty until they had been given at least a couple of hours' rest.

The Australian Corps and their Tanks had alone taken about 7900 prisoners, and our total captures amounted to over 13,000 prisoners and more than 300 guns, besides all kinds of stores and ammunition. Along the eleven miles of attack we had advanced to a depth of nearly seven miles, and (except Le Quesnoy, which we captured before dawn on the 9th) the whole of the outer defences of Amiens had been taken. The armoured cars and some of the cavalry had, as we have seen, been in action far beyond. It was north of the Somme that our advance had been most hotly contested, but even here we had pushed forward considerably and the enemy's casualties had been particularly heavy.

The Paris–Amiens railway was completely disengaged, and the Despatch characterises the first day's fighting as a "sweeping success."

VI

All night, to the east beyond the limit of our advance, we could hear the enemy blowing up his ammunition dumps.

All night his transport and limbers streamed eastwards, and all night our airmen hung upon his retreating columns.

Next morning we attacked again along the whole line, no less than 155 Tanks being actually engaged.

The Australians advanced upon Lihons, Framerville and Vauvillers, while on their right the Canadians continued the attack south of the Amiens–Chaulnes railway.

In the attack on Framerville, out of thirteen Tanks engaged, only one was hit.

This fact was attributable to the admirable co-operation between the infantry and Tanks,

> * "Riflemen working hand in hand with the machines picking off the enemy's field gunners, as soon as the Tanks came into observation. At Vauvillers, seven Tanks went into action just before noon, unaccompanied by infantry and without artillery support. After the Tanks had gone forward a little way, the 5th Australian Division followed up and not only captured the high ground, but the village itself, which was not included in their original objective."

Near Rosières the opposition stiffened, and here no less than eight Tanks were knocked out by a German battery which came into action near Lihons. It was not until 5 p.m. that this battery was silenced, and we did not reach Lihons that night.

> * "The day's operations were especially interesting through the rapidity with which the enemy got his field batteries into action from commanding positions against Tanks advancing in broad daylight. He also employed a number of low-flying aeroplanes against the infantry, but as these did not carry bombs their fire had no effect upon the Tanks. The resistance put up by his riflemen and machine-gunners was feeble, and showed clearly the moral effect of the victorious advance of the previous day."

* From a Battalion History.

With the Canadians as many Tanks as possible were rallied and about fifty-five went into action. They went forward, as before, in waves, the same Tank Battalions working with the same Infantry Divisions as on the previous day.

North of the Somme, with the 3rd Corps (which included the 33rd American Division) the 10th Tank Battalion put sixteen Tanks into action.

They had a hard task round Chipilly, where the enemy had a large number of machine-guns cleverly concealed in woods and gullies. By the early evening, however, all the objectives were taken, and our positions advanced in line with those which we held south of the river, an advance achieved at a cost of five casualties to the sixteen machines engaged.

The Whippets' action, in as far as they were billed to act with the cavalry, was disappointing. By some fault of liaison they were kept too long at Brigade Headquarters.

At Beaufort and Warvillers, however, they were able to give great help to the infantry by chasing hostile machine-gunners out of the standing corn and shooting them down as they fled.

On the whole, August 9th was a successful day, for we continued to push forward steadily all along our line.

VII

We had, in fact, pushed forward so far that all along the line during the next day's fighting we reached the old trench systems of the First Battle of the Somme. And it was this fact, combined with the usual and inevitable petering out of all attacks which are not supported by immense reserves, that now slowed our rate of advance down to nothing. Two days later we left off hammering.

The 10th proved an unfortunate day for the Tanks, for though we advanced, the eighty-five Tanks engaged suffered heavily in every sector.

With the Canadians, owing to orders having been issued late, the hour of attack had to be altered, and it finally took place in daylight without smoke.

A stubborn resistance was encountered, and of the forty-three Tanks engaged no less than twenty-three received direct hits.

Before Warvillers the cavalry and Whippets had a particularly poor time of it, the old trench systems and the old shelled area, of which the enemy had taken ingenious and thorough advantage, proving too much for both arms.

With the Australians a rather remarkable night attack was arranged.

During the three previous days' fighting it had been found

very inconvenient to have the Somme Valley as an inter-corps boundary, and General Monash was allowed to extend his territory northward in such a way that the Australians should hold both sides of the valley.

An encircling movement was, therefore, undertaken, of which Captain Denny, M.C., M.P., gives the following account in his article on the work of the Australians which appeared in the *Daily Telegraph* of April 1919 :

> " The 3rd and 4th Australian Divisions were ordered to carry out an encircling operation on the night of August 10–11 in order to cut off the Etinehem spur north of the Somme and the ridge east of Proyart, south of the Somme. The general lines of the operation both to the north and the south of the river were similar. Columns were to move along defined roads leaving the objectives well to the flanks, and then encircle the enemy positions. Each column was accompanied by Tanks, and was to move in an easterly direction, and then to wheel inwards towards the Somme. It was recognised that this action involved certain risks, as Tanks had never been tried by night in this way, but in view of the condition of the enemy's *moral* at this stage it was considered that the effect of the advance of the Tanks and infantry would lead immediately to the collapse of the defence.
>
> " The action north of the river was entirely successful. South of the river the enemy bombed the forward area heavily early in the night, causing considerable delay in the preparations for the attack. Progress was at first slow owing to heavy enemy artillery and machine-gun fire and the disorganisation caused by the bombing. Two of the Tanks allotted for the operations were destroyed or put out of action very soon after zero hour."

Almost from the outset of the attack heavy enemy machine-gun fire was encountered from the large enemy dump by the side of the main road. Tanks were unable in the dark to locate these machine-guns, and could not do much to assist the infantry. It was therefore decided to abandon the operation and withdraw the infantry under cover of unaimed fire from the Tanks, who were themselves recalled when the infantry had got clear away.

It was not till the evening of August 12 that Tanks and infantry were able to advance in this sector, and that we gained the positions east of Proyart.

By August 11 the Tank Corps reserves were used up, and the Tanks and their crews were almost fought to a standstill.

THE ARMOURED CARS GOING UP.

A TANKODROME.

SMOKE SCREEN AND SEMAPHORE.

MOVING UP—BATTLE OF AMIENS.

They had had three days of continuous fighting and marching, and of the thirty-eight Tanks which went into action on the 11th there was not one but badly needed overhauling. The crews were completely exhausted. We have already described the conditions under which the men fought in the Mark V. Tank, and how after an average of three hours in a closed Tank whose guns are in action, all men begin to suffer from severe headache and giddiness, and most from sickness, a high temperature and heart disturbance.

After the Battle of Amiens the crews of most of the surviving Tanks had fought for three days, not three hours, and 50 per cent. of them were on the verge of collapse. However, as we have said, thirty-eight machines and crews were scraped together, and on August 11 ten Tanks of the 2nd Battalion helped in the taking of Lihons by the Australians. These Tanks had an approach march of eight miles before they reached their jumping-off places.

With the Canadians, Tanks attacked Domeny and twice entered the village, but the 4th Canadian Division could not get forward to consolidate, owing to lack of support on the right.

On the 12th, while six Tanks were still thrashing out the Proyart affair north of the Somme, the 4th and 5th Brigades were withdrawn, to be followed next day by the remainder of the Tanks.

VIII

We called a halt, and the Battle of Amiens was at an end, for it was again at last the Allies who chose the time and the place where they would offer battle.

Commanders who had the bitter taste of the forced actions of the March retreat in their mouths, must have savoured this easy choice extraordinarily. There is something thrilling in the assured words of the Despatch. We did not care for the new battle site! We would change it and fight elsewhere!

> "The derelict battle area which now lay before our troops, seared by old trench lines, pitted with shell-holes, and crossed in all directions with tangled belts of wire, the whole covered by the wild vegetation of two years, presented unrivalled opportunities for stubborn machine-gun defences. . . .
>
> "I therefore determined to break off the battle on this front, and transferred the front of attack from the 4th Army to the sector north of the Somme, where an attack seemed unexpected by the enemy. My intention was for the 3rd Army to operate in the direction of Bapaume so

as to turn the line of the old Somme defences from the north."

We struck at once. Only four days were given to the Tanks for overhauling machines and patching up the crews, for on August 21 we opened the new battle.

Meanwhile it was hard to realise how great was the moral and physical blow which we had dealt the Germans. The July attacks had been tentative, but the Battle of Amiens was the decisive victory, the sure proof that the Germans had lost all hope of winning the War by force of arms.

But at the time we could not read the thundering sign of our deliverance with certainty. We could see only what were the more immediate results of the battle.

> * "Within the space of five days the town of Amiens and the railway centring upon it had been disengaged. Twenty German Divisions had been heavily defeated by thirteen British Infantry Divisions and three Cavalry Divisions, assisted by a regiment of the 33rd American Division and supported by some 400 Tanks. Nearly 22,000 prisoners and over 400 guns had been taken by us, and our line had been pushed forward to a depth of some twelve miles in a vital sector. Further, our deep advance, combined with the attacks of the French Armies on our right, had compelled the enemy to evacuate hurriedly a wide extent of territory to the south of us.
>
> "The effect of this victory—following so closely after the Allied victory on the Marne—upon the *moral* both of the German and British troops was very great. Buoyed up by the hope of immediate and decisive victory, to be followed by an early and favourable peace, constantly assured that the Allied reserves were exhausted, the German soldiery suddenly found themselves attacked on two fronts and thrown back with heavy losses from large and important portions of their earlier gains. The reaction was inevitable and of a deep and lasting character.
>
> "On the other hand, our own troops felt that at last their opportunity had come, and that, supported by a superior artillery and numerous Tanks, they could now press forward resolutely to reap the reward of their patient, dauntless, and successful defence in March and April."

We knew, however, that we had still hard fighting before us, and we were careful to analyse every phase of the action to

* Sir Douglas Haig's Despatch.

"Lessons Learnt"

see if we could not learn some practical lesson from it that should help us in the coming months.

The Tank Command noted several points "for reference." In the first place, the battle would have been ended the quicker if the Tanks had had a larger general reserve.

Then neither the Mark V. nor the Whippet was fast enough for open warfare.

Had we then possessed machines such as we have now,* of double the speed of the Mark V., and having a radius of action of 100 miles and more, we should, at a modest estimate, have finished the battle on the first day.

Last, we had not used our Whippets to the best advantage. The 3rd (Light) Brigade Commander, Brig.-General Hardress-Lloyd, thus admirably summarised the lessons of the battle, and laid down alternative principles upon which the light machines might be used:

> "I do not think it advisable to attempt to use the present Whippet in conjunction with cavalry. Better results would have been obtained during these operations if Whippets had been working in close liaison with Mark V. Tanks and infantry.
>
> "The Whippet is not fast enough to conform to cavalry tactics in the early stages of a battle. . . .
>
> "The Whippets' rôle should be to push on amongst the retreating enemy and prevent him from reorganising, engage reinforcements coming up, eventually enabling the infantry to make a further advance, capture prisoners, guns, etc.
>
> ". . . They must move forward in close touch with the heavy Tanks so as to be near enough up to go through when required. If kept back with the cavalry the speed of the Whippet is not sufficient to enable the machine to be in the forward position at the required moment, and its offensive power will be seriously diminished."

But it was not for us that the battle of August 8 had its chief lessons.

The German High Command waxed eloquent with indignant exhortation, and demanded passionately that the experiences of the German Army should be utilised, and that such things as had occurred on the 8th should never happen again.

On August 11 General Ludendorff issued a secret Order:

> "Troops allowed themselves to be surprised by a mass attack of Tanks, and lost all cohesion when the Tanks

---

* Summer, 1919.

suddenly appeared behind them, having broken through under cover of a mist, natural and artificial. The defensive organisation, both of the first line and in the rear, was insufficient to permit of a systematic defence. . . . As a weapon against Tanks, the prepared defence of the ground must play a larger part than ever, and the aversion of the men to the pick and shovel must be overcome at all hazards. . . . Especially there must be defences against Tanks. It was absolutely inadmissible that the Tanks, having penetrated into our advance line without meeting with obstacles or anything, should be able to push on along the roads or beside them for miles. . . . The principle that a body of troops even when surrounded must defend their ground, unless otherwise ordered, to the last man and the last cartridge, seems to have fallen into oblivion . . . a large proportion of our ranks fight unskilfully against Tanks. A Tank is an easy prey for artillery of all calibres. . . ."

An account follows of measures for the proper disposition of artillery against Tanks, and the rest of the Order is occupied with directions to the infantry concerning the question at what range the anti-Tank rifle and gun are most effective. The consideration of these points is long and exhaustive. Ludendorff further hopes much from " the active and inventive genius of the lower ranks of the non-commissioned officers to arrange Tank traps, and demands that every encouragement should be shown to those who show any inventive talent."

These were but peddling remedies. When, as at Amiens, the understanding between infantry and Tanks is almost perfect, and when the magnificent *élan* of an assault by Australians and Canadians is supported by the weight of 400 Tanks, not even the troops of what was the best-trained Army in the world can stand the concerted shock of their attack.

A Special Order was issued on August 16 by General Sir Henry Rawlinson, the 4th Army Commander:

" *Tank Corps.*—The success of the operations of August 8 and succeeding days was largely due to the conspicuous part played by the 3rd, 4th and 5th Brigades of the Tank Corps, and I desire to place on record my sincere appreciation of the invaluable services rendered both by the Mark V. and the Mark V. star and the Whippets.

" The task of secretly assembling so large a number of Tanks entailed very hard and continuous work by all concerned for four or five nights previous to the battle.

" The tactical handling of the Tanks in action made calls on the skill and physical endurance of the detachments which were met with a gallantry and devotion beyond all praise.

"I desire to place on record my appreciation of the splendid success that they achieved, and to heartily congratulate the Tank Corps as a whole on the completeness of their arrangements and the admirable prowess exhibited by all ranks actually engaged on this occasion. There are many vitally important lessons to be learned from their experiences. These will, I trust, be taken to heart by all concerned and made full use of when next the Tank Corps is called upon to go into battle.

"The part played by the Tanks and Whippets in the battle on August 8 was in all respects a very fine performance.

"(*Signed*)   H. RAWLINSON, General,
"Commanding 4th Army.
"Headquarters, 4th Army,
"*August* 16, 1918."

Nor were the Australians less generous.

The following message is typical of many. It was sent to Brig.-General Courage (commanding 5th Tank Brigade) by the 4th Australian Divisional Commander:

"G.O.C. 5th Tank Brigade.

"I wish to express to you and the command associated with us on August 8 and following days, on behalf of the 4th Australian Division, our deep appreciation of the most gallant service rendered during our offensive operations by the Tank Corps. The consistent skill and gallantry with which the Tanks, individually and collectively, were handled during the battle, was the admiration of all ranks of the infantry with whom they were so intimately associated, and our success was due in a very large measure to your efforts.

"We hope sincerely, that in future offensive operations in which we may take part, we shall have the honour to be associated with the same units of the Tank Corps as during the operations on August 8 and following days.

"(*Signed*)   E. G. SINCLAIR MCLAGAN,
"Major-General,
"Commanding 4th Australian Division."

Finally, in a congratulatory telegram after the battle, the Commander-in-Chief paid a high tribute to the skill and bravery displayed by the Tank Corps in the gaining of this signal victory.

CHAPTER XVIII

THE GERMAN ATTITUDE—"MAN-TRAPS AND GINS"—THE BATTLE OF BAPAUME

I

WE had, as we have said, called a halt to the Battle of Amiens.

But the pause was to be only one of a few days.

The new battle was to be fought in the area which lay between the rivers Somme and Scarpe, and for his selection of this particular place Sir Douglas Haig in his Despatch gives two reasons.

> "The enemy did not seem prepared to meet an attack in this direction, and, owing to the success of the Fourth Army, he occupied a salient, the left flank of which was already threatened from the south. A further reason for my decision was that the ground north of the Ancre River was not greatly damaged by shell-fire, and was suitable for the use of Tanks. A successful attack between Albert and Arras in a south-easterly direction would turn the line of the Somme south of Péronne, and gave every promise of producing far-reaching results. It would be a step forward towards the strategic objective St. Quentin-Cambrai."

It is interesting to see how high a place Tanks now held in the estimation of the General Staff, and how carefully their peculiarities were considered.

But it was not only the British High Command which had begun to busy itself with the natural history of the Tank.

Since the lesser battles of July and the greater battle of August 8, the attitude of the German G.H.Q. had entirely changed.

When we first began to use Tanks it will be remembered that the Germans, though perfunctorily alluding to them as "cruel and detestable," had in effect sneered at them as makeshifts by which we hoped to supplement our scanty supply of more legitimate munitions of war.

Besides, their contempt for all we did being sincere, the Tanks' British parentage damned them without further investigation.

" Search and see, for out of Galilee cometh no good thing."

The Germans themselves made their attitude perfectly clear.

> " The use of 300 British Tanks at Cambrai (1917) was a ' battle of material,' and the German Higher Command decided from the very outset *not* to fight a ' battle of material.' "

Their policy was masses of men rather than mechanism, quantity rather than quality.

The best men went to machine-gun units and to assault troops. In many cases the remainder of the infantry were of little fighting value, though many of the men might have been otherwise usefully employed in a war which, if not one of material, was at least one in which economic factors played a large part.

The German Higher Command was able, however, to look at an order of battle, showing some 250 Divisions on paper.

But the Germans were thus naturally not in a position to find the labour for the construction of additional material, such as Tanks; they were, besides, concentrating any labour and any suitable material they possessed upon the work of submarine making.

It seems clear that the whole policy, at least as far as Tanks were concerned, was regretted before the end of the War.

The following now well-known extracts from German documents indicate the effect of our Tanks on the German Army:

" Staff officers sent from G.H.Q. report that the reasons for the defeat of the Second Army* are as follows :

" 1. The fact that the troops were surprised by the massed attack of Tanks, and lost their heads when the Tanks suddenly appeared behind them, having broken through under cover of natural and artificial fog.

" 2. Lack of organised defences.

" 3. The fact that the artillery allotted to reserve infantry units at the disposal of the Higher Command was wholly insufficient to establish fresh resistance with artillery support against the enemy who had broken through and against his Tanks.

" LUDENDORFF, 11.8.18."

* *i.e.*, in the Battle of Amiens, 8.8.18.

"*Crown Prince's Group of Armies.*
"12.8.18.

" G.H.Q. reports that during the recent fighting on the fronts of the 2nd and 18th Armies, large numbers of Tanks broke through on narrow fronts and pushing straight forward, rapidly attacked battery positions and the headquarters of divisions.

" In many cases no defence could be made in time against the Tanks, which attacked them from all sides.

" Anti-Tank defence must now be developed to deal with such situations."

Signal Communication—

" Messages concerning Tanks will have priority over all other messages or calls whatsoever."

" Order dated 8.9.18."

II

The first efforts at combating Tanks made by the German High Command were half-contemptuously instituted chiefly to reassure their infantry, who seemed to them, for no particular reason, liable to extraordinary fits of nerves and panic upon the approach of their new assailants.

The measures of defence were ill devised and carelessly used.

In the autumn of 1917, it will be remembered that the Germans had captured a number of our Mark IV. machines.

These they used for the purposes of propaganda, parading them in the streets of Berlin and showing them to the Army, as a man might demonstrate the harmless nature of snakes by the aid of a tame cobra.

The infantry were lectured to about the miseries endured by the crews who manned Tanks, as to their mechanical defects, their vulnerability and general worthlessness. For example, the following passage appeared in an Order issued to the 7th German Cavalry Division. It will be gathered from the text that the Order was illustrated by detailed drawings.

"7th Cavalry ' Schützen ' Div.   Div. H.Q. 26.9.18.
" Subject :—Anti-Tank Defence.

"*Divisional Order*

" 1. *General.*

" The infantry must not let itself be frightened by Tanks. The fighting capacity of the Tank is small owing to the bad visibility, and the shooting of the machine-guns and guns is cramped and inaccurate as the result of the motion.

"It has been proved that the Tank crews are nervous and are inclined to turn back, or leave the Tank, even in the case of limited fire effects, such as a light T.M. (Trench Mortar) barrage at 800–1000 yards. In order to make it more difficult for the artillery, the Tanks pursue a zigzag course towards their objective.

"The hostile infantry follows Tanks only half-heartedly. Experience shows that hostile attacks are soon checked by aimed machine-gun and artillery fire. Co-operation between the Tanks and their infantry detachments must be hindered as much as possible. The arms should be separated and destroyed in detail. All projectiles which do not hit the armour-plating at right angles ricochet off instead of penetrating. Artillery, light trench mortar and anti-Tank rifle fire is effective against all portions of the Tank, especially against the broadside and the cab (framed in red in the illustrations). Machine-gun and rifle fire with A.P. bullets, on the other hand, should be aimed especially at the observation and machine-gun loopholes (framed in green and blue in the illustrations)."

But the enemy was not content with a merely dialectical defence. Among other practical measures the Germans, with curious inconsequence, decided to form a small Tank Corps of their own, partly armed with new Tanks of German manufacture and partly with captured British machines.

But here a little unexpected awkwardness arose. The infantry, from whom they now wished to recruit their Tank crews, had unfortunately been completely convinced by the unanswerable arguments which they had just heard, and now thoroughly believed in the perfect uselessness, and extreme vulnerability, of Tanks.

Thus it came about that the German Tank Corps was made up of a quite astonishingly reluctant and half-hearted body of men. Altogether, only fifteen German Tanks were ever manufactured, and only twenty-five captured British Mark IV. Tanks were repaired, so that the whole affair amounted to but little.

The German Tanks were, as we have said, much heavier and larger than the British or French heavy Tanks, though, as we have noted, they rather resembled the French St. Chamond. They could not cross large trenches or heavily shelled ground, owing to their shape, and the lack of clearance between the ground and the body. On smooth ground their speed was good—being about eight miles an hour.

Their armour was thick and tough, capable of withstanding

armour-piercing bullets, and, at a long range, even direct hits from field guns not firing armour-piercing shells. Only the front of the Tank was, however, sufficiently strong for this, and the roof was scarcely armoured at all.

They were very vulnerable to the splash of ordinary small arms ammunition, owing to the numerous crevices and joints left in the armour-plate.

The most interesting feature of these otherwise exceedingly bad machines was the fact that they ran on a spring track. The use of springs for so heavy a Tank was the one progressive departure in the German design.

Their crew consisted of an officer and no less than fifteen other ranks. This huge crew, twice that of a heavy British Tank, actually went into action in a Tank 24 feet long by 10 feet wide. However, the close association of the crew was merely physical, for they were composed of no less than three distinct arms, and appear to have done little or no training together as a crew.

There were the drivers who were mechanics, there were the gunners who were artillerymen, and the machine-gunners who were infantrymen. Members of the British Tank Corps were at one time much puzzled by German Tank prisoners' statements, that on such or such an occasion the infantry had spoiled their shooting, or that the artillery had not backed them up, in circumstances when there was no particular question of co-operation with other arms. They came afterwards to understand that the anathema'd representatives of rival arms were inside the machine, not out.

But in reality rival machines constituted but a small part of the German anti-Tank measures, for, as we have said, after the victories of July and early August, these begin to be panic-stricken in their elaboration, and after the Battle of Amiens, we find Ludendorff himself pouring out his soul on the subject.

He obviously realised that anti-Tank defences had been neglected, and he probably saw also that this neglect was going to be difficult to explain to an Army and a public which, as the result of failures, were about to become extremely critical of their leaders.

After the Battle of Amiens, therefore, the Germans began feverishly to set their house in order, and we find special Staff officers appointed at the Army, Corps, Divisional and Brigade Headquarters, whose sole duty it was to organise the anti-Tank defences within their formation.

A special artillery was told off and divided into two sections. The first was to provide a few forward silent guns in each divisional sector. They were to remain hidden till the moment of our attack, and then to concentrate upon our Tanks. These guns, however, proved apt to be smothered by our barrage, or not to be able to distinguish their prey in the half-light of our dawn attacks. Secondly, there were to be reserve guns whose duty it was to go forward and take up previously reconnoitred positions after the Tank attack had been launched. It was generally from these pieces that the Tanks had most to fear. Finally, all German batteries, including howitzers, had general instructions to plan their positions in such a way that advancing Tanks would be subject to a direct fire at about 500 or 600 yards' range. In the event of a Tank attack, the engagement of our machines was now to be the first call upon the artillery, to the exclusion of counter-battery or any other work. As for the infantry, the chief rôle allotted to them was " to keep their heads," and " to keep calm." Other Orders instructed them to move to a flank in the event of a Tank attack. "No advice was given, however, as to how this was to be done when Tanks were attacking on a frontage of twenty or thirty miles."

A large armoury of special anti-Tank weapons arose, and of these the most important was the anti-Tank rifle, of which we have spoken before.

> * "The weapon weighed 36 lb. and was $5\frac{1}{2}$ feet long. It had no magazine and fired single shots, using A.P. ammunition of ·530 calibre. It was obviously too conspicuous and too slow a weapon to be really effective against Tanks, though the steel core could penetrate the armour of British Tanks at several hundred yards' range.
>
> "The chief disadvantage of the anti-Tank rifle, however, was that the German soldier would not use it. He was untrained in its use, afraid of its kick, and still more afraid of the Tanks themselves. It is doubtful if one per cent. of the A.T. rifles captured in our Tank attacks had ever been fired."

Road obstacles, such as carts full of stones, linked up with wire cables, concrete stockades and mines, provided a good deal of the rest of the enemy anti-Tank stock-in-trade. Of mines there was a considerable variety. They ranged from elaborate specially made pieces of apparatus to high explosive shells, buried and hastily fitted with a device by which the weight of the Tank exploded them.

They were sometimes buried in lines across roads, and sometimes extensive minefields were laid. Their singular ineffectiveness always seemed somewhat mysterious to members of the Tank Corps, the proportion of effort to result seeming always many tons of mine to each Tank damaged.

* *W.T.N.*

However, we always thought we might some day encounter a really effective type of mine, and possibly the Germans were satisfied if their efforts so much as made our monsters walk delicately, for in an elaborate document, giving every kind of anti-Tank defence instructions, they somewhat pathetically conclude: "Every obstacle, even if it only checks the hostile Tank temporarily, is of value."

But there was one form of weapon which was, we felt sure, bound to be evolved by the Germans. It was one which we were not at all anxious to encounter. We imagined a weapon which should practically be the machine-gun version of the anti-Tank rifle; that is to say, a weapon which could pour out a stream of high-velocity, large-calibre bullets at the rate of two hundred a minute. Actually it was almost precisely such an engine that the Germans had got in their "Tuf" machine-gun, of which an interesting account is given in *Weekly Tank Notes*.

The name was an abbreviation for "*Tank und Flieger*" (tank and aeroplane), for it was against these enemies that this machine-gun was intended. It was to consist of no less than 250 pieces, which were made by sixty different factories, of which the *Maschinen Fabrik Augsburg, Nürnberg*, was the only one entrusted with the assembling and mounting. The projectile fired was to be 13 millimetres in diameter. From experiments made with captured Tanks, the Germans ascertained that these bullets could pierce steel plates of 30 millimetres in thickness. No less than six thousand of these guns were to be in the field by April 1919, and delivery was to begin early in the previous December—just a month too late. However, when the Armistice was signed, the firms were already in possession of the greater part of the stores and raw material for the manufacture of the guns, a quantity of which were by then well on the way to completion. Immediately after the signing of the Armistice, all the factories were instructed by telephone to continue manufacturing the "Tuf," and about November 20 they received confirmation in writing of this order, and were instructed to keep on their workmen at all costs. Our occupation of the left bank of the Rhine proved a serious drawback to a continuation of the manufacture, as it completely interrupted communication between several of the factories. The Pfaff Works of Kaiserslautern (Palatinate) and the great Becker steel works of Frefeld, which played an important part in the manufacture of the guns, had to close down, both being on the left bank of the Rhine.

The Minister of War throughout the period of its manufacture asked for daily and minute reports as to the progress of the "Tuf," and it was given priority over both submarines and

GERMAN ANTI-TANK GUNNERS.
(From a photograph found on a prisoner.)

A GERMAN ANTI-TANK RIFLE.

A CAPTURED GERMAN TANK.

AN ANTI-TANK GUN IN A STEEL CUPOLA (YPRES).

aeroplanes. But once more, as ever in all that concerned Tanks, the Germans were several months too late. We were never destined to face this particular weapon with the Mark V. The modern Tank fears it not at all.

III

Our chronicle has now reached the three last, and the three decisive months of the war.

It was a period of continuous fighting, in which a battle begun in any particular sector would spread along the front on either hand, until at last, by the middle of October, the whole line was in roaring conflagration; and by the second week in November the blaze had swept on almost to the borders of Germany, and the forces of the enemy had withered and shrivelled before it.

At first we made a series of more or less set attacks. Then came the break through the Hindenburg Line after the Second Battle of Cambrai, and the hastily-organised running fights of October, which culminated in the complete overthrow of German arms.

The whole period is at the moment of writing exceedingly difficult to dissect and to classify into definite battles, it being usually a matter of opinion when one engagement can be said to have ended and another to have begun. The nomenclature even is still fluid. Take, for example, the vast inchoate battle which raged from August 21 and 23 and culminated on September 2. It was fought by three separate armies. There were at least three principal " Z " days, and the battle seems to be indifferently known as the Battle of Bapaume, the Second Battle of Arras, or even as the Battle of Amiens. Nor if the historian were to attempt to name it by date would it be clearly more proper to call it the Battle of August 23 or 21. There is a good deal to be said for the German plan of christening their battles by some fancy name, of dubbing them " Kaiserschlacht " or " Clarence," according to one's taste. A campaign of nameless battles is apt to defy Clio's efforts at dissection and tidy arrangement, and to defeat her longing to see a neat row of actions dried, classified, and labelled in her *Hortus Siccus*.

We have indicated the changes which had taken place in the attitude of our own and the German High Commands toward Tanks. Much had been learnt by the Tank Corps themselves, and much had been regularised and systematised in their methods. We find that by August, Tank Corps preparation for a battle had been so completely reduced to a routine that to attempt to chronicle the preparation for any of our set attacks would be to make a mere *cento*, whose pieces might be culled from particulars already recorded for Cambrai, for Hamel and for Amiens. We therefore trust that the reader, without hearing any enumeration of gallons of petrol, tons of grease, or acres of maps, will understand that each of these " formal " battles was preceded by the usual herculean tasks of preparation.

IV

The Battle of Bapaume was, as we have already said, to constitute a sequel to the Battle of Amiens (August 8). On August 21 the 3rd Army was to launch an attack to the north of the Ancre with the general object of pushing the enemy back towards Bapaume. Meanwhile the 4th Army was to continue its pressure on the enemy south of the river. August 22 was to be a " slack " day and was to be used to get troops and guns into position on the 3rd Army front. The principal attack was to be delivered on the 23rd by the 3rd Army, and those divisions of the 4th Army which lay to the north of the Somme, the rest of the 4th Army fighting a covering action on the flank of the main operation. Afterwards, if our efforts were successful, the whole of both Armies were to press forward with their utmost vigour and exploit any advantage we might have gained. If our success was such as to force the enemy back from the high ground he held, thus securing our southern flank, the 1st Army was further to make another attack immediately to the north. This gradual extension of the front of assault was intended to mislead the enemy as to where the main blow would fall and cause him to throw in his reserves piecemeal.

A large number of Tanks were to be concentrated in the 3rd Army area. They were to attack between Moyenneville and Bucquoy with the 4th and 6th Corps. With them the 1st and 2nd Brigades were to operate.

With the 4th Army the 3rd Corps was to attack on August 23, between Bray and Albert, and the 4th Tank Brigade was to assist in this assault. Then, with the portion of the 4th Army which operated south of the Somme, namely, the Australians, the 5th Tank Brigade was as usual to co-operate, their action also taking place on the 23rd. In the course of the two days' operations the 3rd, 6th, 7th, 14th, 15th, 11th, 12th, 10th and 17th Battalions were to be employed.

The total of 280 machines seems at first sight a curiously small one, considering the number of battalions involved, but it must be remembered that most units had been hotly in action at Amiens ten days before, and that some battalions could not muster more than sixteen fighting Tanks, pending repairs and a fresh issue of machines.

Supply Tanks and aeroplanes were to co-operate as usual, the latter in greater strength than before; for just before the battle No. 73 Squadron, armed with Sopwith Camels, was attached to the Tank Corps, in addition to No. 8 Squadron for counter-gun work.

One of the most prominent features of the whole sector of attack was the Albert-Arras railway, which lay some distance behind the enemy's front line. It proved to have been carefully prepared for defence by the enemy, being commanded at point-blank range by a large number of field guns, which had been specially and secretly withdrawn from more forward positions, and all the sections of the line where it would be possible for the Tanks to cross—that is to say, the " neutral " portions where the line was neither embanked nor in a cutting—were not only carefully registered, but were blocked by concrete and iron anti-Tank stockades.

The attack was to be opened at 4.55 a.m. on the 21st by the 4th and 6th Corps and their Tanks.

V

The morning dawned in the inevitable white blanket of mist which now always seemed to accompany our attacks. Till nearly 11 a.m. it was impossible to see more than a few yards ahead, and it was with the greatest difficulty that the Tanks kept their direction. If, however, the mist was confusing to us, it was doubly so to the enemy. The Germans were completely taken by surprise; we even found candles still burning in the trenches when we crossed them, and papers and equipments were scattered broadcast, bearing witness to a hurried flight.

We carried the front line so easily that we soon realised we must be up against a system of defence rather like that which the Germans had adopted at Ypres. He was keeping his reserves well in rear of a lightly-held outpost line, and, as we have said, unknown to us, his guns had been withdrawn in such a way as to cover the railway.

The Armoured Cars and the Whippets both took an active part in the attack on Bucquoy. At the entrance of the village a large crater had been blown in the road over which the armoured cars were hauled, after a smooth path had been beaten down across it by a Whippet. The cars then sped on through the enemy's lines, reaching Achiet-le-Petit ahead of our infantry, and silenced a number of machine-guns. Two of

Q

the cars received direct hits, one of them being burnt and completely destroyed.

During the attack on Courcelles, Captain Richard Annesley West of the 6th Battalion took charge of some infantry who had lost their bearings in the dense fog. He gathered up all the scattered men he could find. He was mounted, and in the course of the morning he had two horses shot under him; but after the second horse had been shot he went on with his work on foot. Having rallied the infantry, he continued his original task of leading forward his Tanks, and our capture of Courcelles was chiefly due to his individual initiative and gallantry. He was awarded a bar to his D.S.O.

About eleven o'clock the greater number both of Mark V. Tanks and Whippets had reached the line of the railway. A few leading Tanks had even crossed it, when all in a moment the mist lifted with the suddenness of a withdrawn curtain. A blazing sun appeared, and each advancing Tank stood out clearly under its bright light. The German artillery, which was covering the railway, immediately directed a deadly fire on the Tanks, and each individual machine became the centre of a zone of bullets and bursting shells. The infantry as they advanced had to avoid these little whirlwinds of fire. It was at this time that most of the thirty-seven Tanks which were hit by shells during the day were accounted for.

It was a good day for the enemy from an anti-Tank point of view, such a day indeed as they were never to repeat.

Second Lieutenant Hickson of the 3rd Tank Battalion was one of the few who had got his Tank across the line just before the mist lifted. As the sun came out he found himself right in front of the enemy's batteries at point-blank range. His Whippet was immediately hit, but he managed to get his two men away in safety. The artillery and machine-gun fire was extremely heavy, but without any thought of his own safety, he at once went back on foot to warn a number of other Tanks which were about to cross the railway at the same place. In this he was successful and undoubtedly saved a large number of machines from being knocked out. Later, though the spot was still under heavy fire, he made several ineffectual efforts to salve his Tank.

The weather could hardly have done us a worse turn. Had the mist lasted for half an hour longer the Tanks would have been able to overrun the artillery positions without being seen. However, the lifting of the fog at least enabled the aeroplanes attached to the Tanks to go up. The counter-gun machines at once flew out to attack the hostile batteries, and a good deal of execution was done.

All the rest of the day we fought under a blazing sun.

The German resistance was curiously patchy; here and there we found every inch of our advance disputed, the machine-gunners and artillerymen fighting their weapons till the last moment, and the reserves launching small counter-attacks whenever opportunity offered.

Here and there large parties, a hundred and more strong, would surrender before the Tanks had time to open fire.

The Tank crews—especially of the Mark V.'s and the Whippets, whose ventilation was less adequate than the old Mark IV.'s—suffered greatly from the terrific heat.

In one or two instances the whole crew of a Mark V. seem to have become unconscious through the appalling heat, the fumes from their own engines, and the gas used by the enemy, the unconsciousness being followed by temporarily complete loss of memory and extreme prostration.

Inside the Whippets, though the men fared slightly better, the lack of ventilation was equally fatal to efficiency.

> * " The heat temporarily put several Whippets out of action as fighting weapons.
>
> " On a hot summer's day one hour's running with door closed renders a Whippet weaponless except for revolver fire.
>
> " The heat generated is so intense that it not only causes ammunition to swell so that it jams the gun, but actually in several cases caused rounds to explode inside the Tank.
>
> " Guns became too hot to hold, and in one case the temperature of the steering wheel became unbearable."

But evening came at last, and with the darkness the two armies disengaged.

We had suffered more casualties than we had quite bargained for—chiefly owing to the accident of the mist—but upon the whole we were well satisfied with the events of the day.

We had reached the general line of the railway practically along the whole front of attack. We had captured Achiet-le-Petit and Logeast Wood, Courcelles and Moyenneville. Most important of all, the position we needed for the launching of our principal attack had been successfully gained, and we had taken over 2000 prisoners.

* 3rd Battalion History.

CHAPTER XIX

BREAKING THE DROCOURT-QUÉANT LINE—THE BATTLE OF EPEHY

I

WE have said that August 22 had, in the original plan, been devoted to consolidation and to the moving up of guns. Only the 3rd Corps in the 4th Army area, with its twenty-four Tanks of the 4th and 5th Battalions, launched an interim attack on the Bray-Albert front.

We gained all our objectives. The 18th Division crossed the river Ancre, captured Albert by an enveloping movement from the south-east, and our line between the Somme and the Ancre was now advanced well to the east of the Bray-Albert road.

The left of the 4th Army was taken forward in conformity with the rest of our line.

The way had now been cleared for what was really the main attack, though it was not the attack in which the greatest number of Tanks were employed.

The assault opened on August 23 by a series of attacks on the whole of a thirty-three-mile front, that is to say, from our junction with the French, north of Lihons, to the spot near Mercatel where the Hindenburg Line from Quéant and Bullecourt joined the old Arras-Vimy defence of 1916.

The hundred Tanks which went into action on this day were nearly all fresh machines which had not fought on the 21st.

They were distributed in groups along the fronts of both the 3rd and 4th Armies.

South of the Somme, with the Australians near Chuignolles, the largest group of nearly sixty Tanks went into action. They were machines belonging to the 2nd, 8th and 13th Battalions.

The enemy had withdrawn their anti-Tank guns to the top of the ridge, which it was impossible for Tanks to climb except at one spot. Upon this one crossing-place they had trained their guns, and here several Tanks suffered direct hits.

We attacked as usual without a preliminary bombardment and met with a desperate resistance, the German machine-gunners defending their posts with extraordinary heroism, and often firing their guns till the very moment when they and their weapons were crushed to the earth by an attacking Tank.

A particularly interesting account of the action is given in the 13th Battalion History:

> " It was soon evident that the enemy were prepared to make a stout resistance; there was no definite trench system, but nests of machine-guns were encountered in organised shell-holes almost from the start; while Saint Martin's Wood and the gully to the east of this, Herleville Wood, and the quarry at its southern end, were all strongly held by machine-guns in prepared emplacements. As before, the German gunners fought with magnificent pertinacity and courage; one Tank Commander claimed to have knocked out over thirty machine-guns, and this claim was supported by the infantry with him; the estimates of several other Tanks were almost as high. These machine-guns were provided with armour-piercing bullets, and Tanks were pitted all over and in many places penetrated by these. There is no doubt that by themselves becoming the targets for these batteries, the Tanks saved many casualties among the infantry. With the machine-guns well in hand, the Australian infantry were quick to seize the chances of advance, and by 6.30 a.m. were all established in their final objectives. After sunrise the heat of the day became oppressive in the open air, and in the Tanks intolerable. Several cases were reported of men becoming delirious during the action. The cause appears to be threefold: the weather conditions were trying even to fresh men; in many cases the composite crew had recently endured the strain of action without a complete rest to follow; and a third disadvantage, which was inherent in the design of the Mark V. Tank, was now for the first time becoming evident. In these engines the heat generated by the explosion of the propelling gases is very great, and the exhaust pipes speedily become red, and even white hot. In a new engine this is merely an inconvenience, but after a certain period of use the joints of the exhaust pipes tend to warp, and thus to release into the inner air the carbon gases of the explosion. These gases, if breathed continuously, even in small quantities, produce exhaustion, mental confusion and finally uncon-

sciousness. Further, the effect is cumulative, and a man once poisoned by the fumes becomes more quickly affected by further exposure to them. The study of these conditions and the remedy for them became henceforward a matter of the first importance.

"Of the twelve Tanks of the 13th Battalion which started in this action, seven reached their final objectives. Five Tanks received direct hits from enemy field guns, the crews in these cases going on with their Hotchkiss guns and assisting the infantry forward. . . .

"Eventually nine Tanks rallied to Company Headquarters, two of these being towed out of action by their friends."

Altogether in this part of the battle 2000 prisoners and the important villages of Chuignolles, Herleville and Chuignes had fallen to us before nightfall.

It was the same story all along the line.

In the 3rd Army area, where altogether sixty-five Tanks fought in several fairly widely separated groups, the battle was opened rather earlier by a moonlight attack, which began just before 4 a.m. against the village of Gomiécourt. In the 6th Corps' domain, the 3rd Division was supported by ten Mark IV. Tanks of the 12th Battalion. They attacked Gomiécourt, carried it triumphantly and captured 500 prisoners. To the north of them, in the second phase, the Guards Division, with four Mark IV.'s, captured the village of Hamelincourt. At Bihucourt, just beyond Achiet-le-Grand, 300 of the enemy were forced by Tanks to surrender to the infantry. In one Whippet Tank, the officer and the sergeant were both killed, and the private drove his Tank into action by himself, when a target presented itself, locking his back axle and firing his Hotchkiss gun.

Later in the morning, some of the Whippets of the 6th Battalion were operating with the infantry of the 4th Corps to the east of Courcelles. It was suddenly noticed that the artillery barrage table had been altered, and that the rate of progress of the barrage was now 100 yards in four minutes, that is to say, considerably slower than it had been originally intended. The Tanks were therefore obliged to manœuvre and wheel about, in order to let the barrage keep ahead. They were constantly under anti-Tank gun fire at this time. Seven of the Whippets, however, did not wait, but passed through our barrage, and getting beyond it, surprised and scattered large numbers of the enemy who had taken cover. As the Germans ran, the Whippet machine-gunners were able to inflict heavy casualties upon them. Meanwhile these seven Tanks were played upon by a perfect hail of machine-gun fire, especially from the direction of Achiet-le-Grand. Changing their direction, they advanced upon the troublesome machine-guns and succeeded in cutting off several hundred of the enemy north of the village, who had been holding up an attack by our infantry. The Whippets headed and drove them neatly towards our lines, where the King's Royal Rifles immediately took them prisoners. Achiet-le-Grand was captured with extraordinarily small losses.

Owing to the better weather conditions, aeroplane co-operation was much more successful throughout the day than it had been on August 21.

Messages dropped by aeroplanes were invaluable in keeping the whole straggling action in hand, and in giving information, by means of which commanders could send up reserves where they were wanted.

The following will give the reader an idea of the sort of information that the aeroplanes were constantly furnishing:

"*Messages dropped on H.Q., 1st Brigade.*

"Lieutenant Wittal (pilot). Lieutenant Mitchell (observer).
12 *noon.*

"Four Whippets seen in G. 21, two Mark IV. and several Whippets seen in G. 15d, all moving S.E.

"Several Whippets and Mark V. seen in G. 16a, G. 10 and 11d, proceeding S.E.

"We do not hold Bihucourt."

The counter-Tank gun work done on this day was also exceedingly successful. The following is the report of an action fought by a counter Gun Machine:

"*No. 73 Squadron.*

"At 1.15 p.m. batteries were observed unlimbering and coming into action near Béhagnies. Twenty-four bombs were dropped and nearly 2000 rounds fired at these batteries, causing the greatest confusion. Several limbers were overturned, and horses stampeded, and the personnel scattered in all directions."

Altogether we had every reason to be satisfied by the events of the day, and we prepared to continue the action with all possible vigour on the morrow.

II

But by August 24 there were only fifty-three Tanks of the 1st, 3rd and 4th Brigades fit for action, and nearly all the units which went in on this day were motley collections from various Battalions. One composite unit of the 11th Battalion fought a very successful action in conjunction with the 4th Corps, in spite of the fact that their orders reached them late and that they had an approach march of six or seven miles. They managed to catch up the infantry and all their objectives were taken.

In the course of the afternoon, Tanks belonging to the 9th Battalion attacked and met with very stubborn resistance opposite Mory Copse, where the Hindenburg Line was strongly held. Here more than one enemy garrison refused to surrender and had all to be killed. One party of about sixty was accounted for by four rounds of 6-pounder case shot.

One machine, which was doing a piece of reconnaissance work near Croisilles later in the day, had a particularly exciting experience. The crew was forced to evacuate the Tank on account of the phosphorus bombs with which the enemy had drenched it. Before leaving it, the officer in command turned the head of his machine towards home and started the Tank on its lonely way; then, almost choked with the fumes, he got out and walked between the front horns of the moving machine till the inside of the Tank was clear of phosphorus. All the while, he and the machine were completely surrounded by the enemy. In the end, he got his Tank home in safety.

On the 4th Army front, five Tanks of the 1st Battalion attacked at dawn with the 47th Division in an effort to recapture Happy Valley, which had been lost by us on the previous afternoon. The attack was exceedingly successful, and besides our original objective, the large village of Bray was added to our gains.

For the next week, the fighting consisted of a series of small local engagements for the most part improvised on the spot by the Divisions concerned.

Tanks fought every day in one part of the line or another, and every day we forced a stubbornly resisting enemy further and further back.

We propose only to give a short account of most of the actions of this period.

On August 25, about forty-two Tanks were again in action in little " blobs," strung out on the fronts of the 4th and 6th Corps. Tanks from the 3rd, 7th, and 10th Battalions went into action, the 9th Battalion attacking with the Guards Division, north of Mory. Owing to the dense mist, co-operation between Tanks and infantry was phenomenally difficult and the attack was not very successful. During the engagement one Tank had five of its crew wounded by anti-Tank rifle bullets.

On the Canadian Corps front an attack was carried out on August 26, near Fampoux and Neuville-Vitasse, with the help of Tanks of the 9th and 11th Battalions.

Near Monchy several Tanks were knocked out, the crews joining the infantry to repel a local counter-attack. The sergeant of one crew hearing that the enemy had captured his Tank, collected his men and charged forward to recover it, arriving at one sponson door of the machine as the enemy were scrambling out of the opposite one.

The Tank Corps records characterise August 27 as " an uneventful day." Fourteen Tanks of the 9th and 11th Battalions were used for mopping up points of resistance.

On the 28th no Tanks went into action at all.

But the 29th was more memorable, for on this day the enemy evacuated Bapaume, and in a minor attack on Frémicourt Lieutenant C. H. Sewell won the V.C.

It was a very small engagement south-west of Beugnâtre, in which only four Whippet Tanks took part.

The following is extracted from the report of the engagement sent in by Lieutenant Sewell's Commanding Officer :

> " At about 2.0 p.m. on the afternoon of August 29, 'Whippets' of the 3rd (Light) Tank Battalion reached the Quarry near the 'Monument Commémoratif,' south-west of Favreuil. Acting under instructions received from the New Zealand Division, one Section of 'Whippets' under Lieutenant C. H. Sewell was ordered forward to clear up the situation on the front of the 3rd New Zealand Rifle Brigade before Frémicourt and the Bapaume-Cambrai road, where the infantry were reported to be held up by machine-gun fire.
>
> " On reaching the railway line south-east of Beugnâtre in advance of our infantry, enemy batteries and machine-guns opened heavy fire on the Section of 'Whippets.' In manœuvring to avoid the fire and to retain formation, Car No. A.233, commanded by Lieutenant O. L. Rees-Williams, side-slipped in a deep shell crater and turned completely upside down, catching fire at the same time.
>
> " Lieutenant Sewell, in the leading ' Whippet,' on seeing the plight of Lieutenant Rees-Williams' car, immediately got out of his own 'Whippet' and came to the rescue; with a shovel he dug an entrance to the door of the cab, which was firmly jammed and embedded in the side of

the shell-hole, forced the door open and liberated the crew.

"Had it not been for Lieutenant Sewell's prompt and gallant action, the imprisoned crew might have been burnt to death, as they were helpless to extricate themselves without outside assistance.

"During the whole of this time ' Whippets ' were being very heavily shelled and the ground swept by machine-gun fire at close range. On endeavouring to return to his own car, Lieutenant Sewell was unfortunately hit several times, his body being subsequently found lying beside that of his driver, Gunner Knox, W., also killed, just outside the Tank, which at that time was within short range of several machine-guns and infantry gun-pits."

The rescued men were emphatic in their praise of the gallant manner in which Lieutenant Sewell had saved them from a peculiarly horrible form of death.

On the 30th, the 3rd Division was to undertake operations designing to seize the villages of Ecoust and Longâtte with the trench system beyond. Six Tanks of the 12th Battalion were to operate, and in anticipation of their orders had already moved forward to the head of the Sensée Valley. Unfortunately their orders did not reach the Battalion till 9 p.m. on the night before the battle. The night was intensely dark, and as luck would have it, the Reconnaissance Officer who alone knew the ground had been recalled to England that day, and there still remained nearly four miles by the shortest route before the Tanks reached the jumping-off place. It was clear the machines would have their work cut out if they were to reach the place in time. The whole operation was dogged by misfortune. The taping party took the wrong direction in the pitch dark, and when at last the Tanks reached the point where the infantry guides were to lead them the rest of the way, the guide for the left-hand section lost himself and the Tanks completely before they had gone half the distance. For an hour the Tanks and their conductor wandered about the devastated wastes about Ecoust. The guide could not even point out on the map where the infantry were formed up. At last the Section Commander went forward by himself and managed to discover the whereabouts of the front line and his own position, but only to find he was nearly a mile away and it wanted five minutes to "zero." It was impossible that he should reach the battle in time, and he withdrew his Section according to instructions, as he was in an exposed position. Thus the unfortunate infantry went over the top unaccompanied by a single Tank. The assault was a complete failure and the infantry suffered heavy casualties.

*" On August 31 a further action took place, 'C' Company of the 15th Battalion under Captain G. A. Smith assisting the 185th Brigade in attacking Vaulx-Vraucourt from the south. . . .

" Five Tanks reached their objectives, one failing owing to mechanical trouble; these Tanks did considerable execution and rendered great assistance to the infantry. Again heavy machine-gun and anti-Tank rifle fire were encountered. After the show the Tanks themselves bore mute witness to what they had been through. In particular the Tank 'Opossum,' commanded by Lieutenant C. F. Uzielli, had very little paint left on its sides because of bullet marks. The infantry suffered heavily. In one case the strength of a platoon on reaching its objective was only three men."

III

But we had reached a stage of the battle when it was clear that another considerable effort on our part would be well worth the making.

The enemy's resistance showed him passionately anxious to gain time. He retreated with extreme reluctance.

It was the moment to redouble our blows.

The actual small operations carried out by the Tanks during these last few days were only a minor consideration. Tanks and infantry were busy preparing for a considerable attack which was to take place on September 2. On this day, the whole vast battle reached its zenith and we broke the famous Drocourt-Quéant Line which we had failed to reach in April 1917. This line was a switch which joined on to the Hindenburg system. Though we had had scant time for elaborate preparation, the attack was to be practically a full-dress affair, eighty-one Tanks being put in on a comparatively small area. We were expecting a heavy resistance and our dispositions were very carefully made. The order of our attack was as follows, starting from the south:

With the 4th Corps near Villers-au-Flos the 7th Tank Battalion.

With the 6th Corps near Lagnicourt and Moreuil the 12th and 6th Battalions of the 1st Brigade, and against the actual Drocourt-Quéant Line with the Canadians and the 17th Corps as many Tanks as the 9th, 11th and 14th Battalions of the 3rd Brigade could muster (about forty in all).

The battle was to be fought in the intricate country of the

* 15th Battalion History.

Sensée Valley, and active operations were taking place throughout the time of preparation for the renewed battle. It was, therefore, under conditions of exceptional difficulty that the Tanks assembled, some of them being obliged to travel along our front across areas which were far from healthy. The enemy's defences had been built in the Spring of 1917. They were remarkable for extremely strong belts of wire, and we expected that every effort would be made by the Germans to hold these defences at all cost.

Zero was at 5.30 a.m. and a clear dawn was just breaking when we launched our attack.

On the Lagnicourt sector, Tanks of the 12th Battalion immediately came under tremendous fire from field guns and anti-Tank rifles.

As it grew lighter, we discovered that a number of the heavy rifles were being fired with great effect from a derelict Whippet. This nest was soon dealt with by a male Tank.

One female Tank in this sector fired over 4000 rounds of S.A.A., until, having all its Lewis guns except one disabled, and five of its crew severely wounded, it endeavoured to return, its Commander, Lieutenant Saunders, alternately driving, working the brakes and firing the remaining gun. As the Tank was thus being successfully withdrawn, a direct hit set it on fire and the wounded men were rescued with great difficulty.

It was not far from Lagnicourt that the Whippets of the 6th Battalion operated.

They were commanded by Lieut.-Colonel West, of whose action on August 21 we have already told the story:

> * "On the night of September 1–2, nine Whippets, under Captain C. H. Strachan, left Gomiécourt to attack in the direction of Lagnicourt. Owing to the pressure at which the Tanks had been working for the last five weeks, little time had been available for overhauling, and as the Tanks were running badly, it was impossible to get them up in time for zero hour. The Commanding Officer, Lieut.-Colonel R. A. West, D.S.O., M.C., left camp early on the morning of September 2, with two mounted orderlies. It was his intention to get up with the Whippets before they went into action, by Lagnicourt. He went as far as the infantry on horseback, in order to watch the progress of the battle, and to ascertain when to send the Whippets forward. He arrived at the front line when the enemy were in process of delivering a strong local counter-attack. The infantry battalion had suffered heavy officer casualties,

* 6th Battalion History and "Honours and Awards."

and its flanks were exposed. Realising that there was a danger of the Battalion giving way, he at once rode in front of them, under extremely heavy machine-gun and rifle fire, and rallied the men. In spite of the fact that the enemy were now close upon him, he took charge of the situation, and detailed N.C.O.'s to replace officer casualties. He then rode up and down in front of the men, in face of certain death, encouraging all, and calling upon them to ' Stick it, men, and show them fight.' His last words were ' For God's sake put up a good fight.' He fell, riddled by machine-gun bullets."

The infantry had been inspired to redoubled efforts by Colonel West's example and the hostile attack was defeated. He had originally come to the Battalion as a Company Commander, and had been awarded the D.S.O. for his work in the Arras battle. Between August 8 and September 2 he was awarded the M.C., a bar to his D.S.O., and, for his last action, the V.C.

Elsewhere the fighting was not so heavy, and on the whole we met with less opposition than we had expected.

In the Canadian sector, the armoured cars were working in close conjunction with Tank Corps aeroplanes. At one moment a number of cars were going along a road, when four machines were hit by shells from hidden batteries. Their accompanying aeroplanes, however, immediately attacked the German guns so vigorously that the crews of the disabled cars, though completely surrounded by the enemy, were able to escape capture.

By noon, on the Canadian section, the whole elaborate maze of wire, trenches and strong points, which constituted the Drocourt-Quéant Line, was in our hands, but elsewhere there was hard fighting until dusk, especially on the reverse slopes of Dury Ridge. Dury itself we took, capturing the Town Major. Our task had not, however, we considered, been quite completed that day, and next morning Tanks and infantry prepared to " tidy up " the line, especially Maricourt Wood.

But long before zero hour, at 5.20, a glare of burning dumps in the east seemed to show that the enemy were already withdrawing, and, in fact, when the Tanks went over just after dawn, they encountered scarcely any opposition at all, save a perfunctory fire from rearguard machine-gunners. Small parties of the enemy were found in dug-outs, waiting to be captured. His infantry and guns were already well on their way back to the Canal du Nord.

IV

The Second Battle of Arras was over, and we had pierced the renowned Drocourt-Quéant Line and had delivered a blow from which the enemy's *moral* never quite recovered.

Since August 21, in all, some 500 Tanks had been in action, and except for one or two minor failures every attack had culminated in a cheap success. We had pushed forward for fifteen or twenty miles along about thirty miles of front.

* " During the night of September 2–3, the enemy fell back rapidly on the whole front of the 3rd Army and the right of the 1st Army. By the end of the day, he had taken up positions along the general line of the Canal du Nord, from Péronne to Ytres, and thence east of Hermies, Inchy-en-Artois and Ecoust St. Quentin to the Sensée, east of Lecluse. On the following day he commenced to withdraw also from the east bank of the Somme, south of Péronne, and by the night of September 8 was holding the general line Vermand—Epehy—Havrincourt, and thence along the east bank of the Canal du Nord.

" The withdrawal was continued on the front of the French forces on our right.

" Throughout this hasty retreat our troops followed up the enemy closely. Many of his rearguards were cut off and taken prisoner; on numerous occasions our forward guns did great execution among his retiring columns, while our airmen took full advantage of the remarkable targets offered them. Great quantities of material and many guns fell into our hands."

But the Tank Brigades were, all of them, in such urgent need of refitting, of new machines and of fresh crews, that after the 3rd they had to be withdrawn into G.H.Q. reserve, and, " faint with pursuing," were unable to take any further part in the battle for just over a fortnight.

Even so, that fortnight was spent, not in rest, but in feverish preparation of the most arduous kind. We had begun to practise the fitting of Cribs, for we were getting back to the Hindenburg Line.

The other dogs of war were in full cry. The Tanks did not propose to waste time.

By September 18, the 5th Brigade was able to put a few machines into the field. They belonged to the 2nd Battalion, which had not fought since the earlier stages of the last battle.

* Despatch.

V

This time the Tanks were to be put in the south, in the 4th Army area.

There were to be about twenty Tanks, and they were to work with the Australians and the 9th and 3rd Corps on a wide front between Epehy and Villeret.

> *" The operations about to be undertaken by the 4th Army aimed at the capture of the Hindenburg Outpost Line in order (1) to secure direct observation over the main Hindenburg Line, and (2) to allow our artillery positions to be advanced in preparation for the assault on the main positions."

The area attacked had a front of about fourteen miles; thus a Battalion of twenty Tanks could merely be employed against certain known strong points.

Eight Tanks were allotted to the 3rd Corps on the left, eight Tanks in the centre were to work with the 1st and 4th Divisions of the Australian Corps.

On the 9th Corps sector on the right, four Tanks were allotted to the 6th Division.

The night had been fine, but when zero hour came (5.20) it was raining heavily, and all day the weather was dull and cloudy, visibility being often bad enough to make the Tank Commanders glad of their compasses.

> †" The company operating with the 3rd Corps had for their two main objectives the villages of Epehy and Ronssoy. The former place was taken with no great resistance, the enemy surrendering in numbers on the appearance of the Tanks. Ronssoy was more stoutly defended; here machine-gun fire with armour-piercing bullets was very heavy, and anti-Tank rifles were also freely used. Two Tanks had for their objective the very strong organisation of trenches and fortified cottages known as the Quadrilateral, which formed the key to the German Defensive System between Fresnoy and Selency."

During the attack two Tanks belonging to " C " Company fought an extremely gallant action.

> †" Fresnoy was the line of the first objective, but in going forward, the infantry came under heavy machine-gun fire

---

* A Brigade History.   † Unit History.

from the Quadrilateral on their right flank. Both officers, unseen by one another in the mist and smoke, headed their Tanks straight for the thickest of the fire. Second Lieutenant G. F. Smallwood arrived first and encountered terrific resistance, with which he was successfully dealing when his Tank became ditched while crossing a sunken road, all guns but one being covered. It was impossible to use the unditching beam owing to the intense fire from short range. At this moment Second Lieutenant W. R. Hedges, driving his own Tank, as the driver had been killed and the second driver badly wounded, appeared from the mist heading for the Quadrilateral with all guns firing. Captain Hamlet, the Section Commander, was also inside this Tank. Just as Second Lieutenant Hedges was appearing to get the upper hand of the enemy his Tank burst into flames. Desperate efforts were apparently made to put these out, but after five minutes Captain Hamlet and the crew jumped out of the Tank on the right-hand side straight into the arms of the Huns, who had surrounded the Tank. Second Lieutenant Hedges, however, sprang out from the other side and darted through them though subject to a heavy fire. Though hit two or three times he reached the shelter of the sunken road about fifty yards from Second Lieutenant Smallwood's Tank. The latter left the Tank and brought Second Lieutenant Hedges back with him. Heavy shelling all round the Tank compelled its evacuation, and Second Lieutenant Smallwood and crew took up a position with their machine-guns and successfully held off the enemy. Later on, the infantry, who had been held up some 200 yards behind, were able to come up and take over the post. Meanwhile Second Lieutenant Hedges had been sent to a Dressing Station, but he never arrived there. This very gallant officer's fate is still unknown."

On the 9th Corps front progress was slow, but by the end of the day we held Ronssoy and Hargicourt.

A good idea is given of the minor mechanical difficulties of this part of the campaign in the 2nd Battalion History:

" Liaison, reconnaissance and Tank maintenance were rendered far more difficult than usual owing to the lack of transport, which was in such a state that no car, box-body, lorry or motor-cycle could be relied upon. The nearest M.T. Park for repairs was twenty-five miles away. Long treks by night meant work on Tanks by day. Reconnaissance and liaison had often to be carried out on foot with consequent loss of time. There was very little rest or sleep for any one between September 13 and 18."

We did not renew the advance till the 21st, when nine Tanks helped the attack on the 3rd Corps front against the Knoll and Guillemont and Quennemont Farms. Two of these Tanks were of the Mark V. Star pattern and carried forward infantry machine-gunners.

But we were up against a desperate enemy resistance, machine-guns firing armour-piercing bullets, anti-Tank rifles, field guns and land mines all being used against us.

The attack did not succeed in gaining us the coveted positions, and we were to pay dearly for this failure.

Again two days elapsed, and meanwhile (on the 20th) the 8th, 16th and 13th Battalions, and the 5th Supply Co. had been brought forward.

There was a big enterprise in view.

This hitherto more or less isolated sector of attack was to be " federated " with the new vast projected attack which was to be made by no fewer than three Armies, their blows timed to fall in rapid succession.

Meanwhile a piece of ground which we coveted remained in enemy hands.

We were anxious to hold the high ground north of Selency and to clear up the formidable Quadrilateral south of Fresnoy.

The 9th Corps, therefore, was to attack on a two-division front with the aid of twenty Tanks of the newly arrived 13th Battalion.

The plans were discussed at a conference held on September 22, and the Tanks brought up to the assembly points by skeleton crews that same night.

The fighting crews were brought up by lorry the following afternoon, according to the wise practice which was now beginning to be generally employed, whenever there was enough personnel to make it possible. The final approach-march was begun at 8.30 p.m. the night of the 23rd.

* " After clearing St. Quentin Wood, in which some delay was caused by overhead signal wires, which had to be passed from hand to hand to avoid catching the semaphore standards, Tanks had to pass through a heavy harassing fire in which gas shell was largely employed. Thus the latter part of the march was made with Tanks closed and gas masks often worn; in consequence the crews, especially of the company working on the left suffered greatly from

* Unit History.

gas and petrol fumes. While waiting on the Start Lines, Tanks were heavily shelled, and enemy 'planes twice during the night dropped flares exactly over the sections with the 6th Division on the right."

Anti-Tank guns were extremely active throughout the operation.

Three Tanks, which with their infantry penetrated right into the Quadrilateral, were all put out of action by a single gun.

Altogether, the Tanks suffered a 50 per cent. loss of machines in this action.

However, we won some of the points of observation that were needed for the next attack, and though we failed to hold the Quadrilateral we had practically outflanked and sterilised it by the end of the day.

So ended the little Battle of Epehy.

Our advance had not been a long one, for the enemy had contested every yard with a desperate valour.

His losses had been enormous, and this minor battle added no less than 12,000 prisoners and 100 guns to the Allied "bag."

CHAPTER XX

THE SECOND BATTLE OF CAMBRAI, OR THE BATTLE OF CAMBRAI-ST. QUENTIN

THE enemy was in full retreat, but we had every reason to suppose that once he had got " home," back to the Hindenburg Line, he would resist our further attempts to advance with all his strength.

If we attacked the line and our assault was successful, and we could break his defences, the way, as we have said, lay clear to the heart of his great system of lateral railway communications. We could cut his forces completely in two. But besides this, if we could beat him here on his chosen battleground, if we could wound him, even behind the rampart upon which he had for years spent such an infinity of toil, where, in the open unprepared country behind, could he hope to withstand us? The lists were set for a struggle *à outrance*, the two forces faced each other grimly, for upon the fortunes of the champions in this combat hung the fate of the German nation. It was to be a Tank attack. We were to make the assault on a very wide front, and were to continue our system of hitting in rapid succession in alternate Army areas. The last blow had been delivered by the 4th Army on September 18. The new battle was to be begun by the 1st and 3rd Armies.

> * "On the 1st and 3rd Army fronts, strong positions covering the approaches to Cambrai between the Nord and Schelde Canals, including the section of the Hindenburg Line itself north of Gouzeaucourt, were still in the enemy's possession. His trenches in this sector faced south-west, and it was desirable that they should be taken in the early stages of the operation, so as to render it easier for the artillery of the 4th Army to get into position."
>
> * Sir Douglas Haig's Despatch.

To the south, as soon as certain points of vantage, Quennemont Farm, the Knoll and Bellicourt, were in our hands, there was to be a lull, and the 4th Army was to attack in strength on the 29th, two days later—as soon, that is, as the Germans had had time thoroughly to involve their reserves in the first mêlée.

Meanwhile the Tank Brigades had to be rapidly reorganised and redistributed, the Battalions being almost all reshuffled. About one-third of the available machines were to be put in on the northern part of the front, and the other two-thirds were to fight with the 4th Army on the 29th.

For the sake of clarity, it is simpler to treat the two halves of the battle separately, for though they were completely interdependent and formed part of one strategic conception, each offered very distinct tactical problems of its own. In each the ground had very marked topographical features, features that gave to each half a special character.

PART I

I

We have said that the 1st and 3rd Armies were to strike first. Tanks belonging to the 7th and 11th Battalions of the 1st Brigade were to fight with the Canadians and the 4th Corps opposite Bourlon and Gouzeaucourt, and the 2nd Brigade was to contribute the 15th Battalion, which was to co-operate with the 17th Corps opposite Graincourt and Flesquières.

Altogether fifty-three fighting Tanks were to be employed.

As in the 4th Army sector, the peculiar lie of the country was the chief influence which shaped our battle tactics; as in the 4th Army area, a canal was the central feature of the attack.

In the First Battle of Cambrai the Tanks had all attacked from south of the northward bend of the Canal du Nord near Havrincourt, and so worked up the enemy's side of this great obstacle.

Now we were in a better position to force a direct crossing, both strategically and mechanically, and the hazardous venture was to be attempted. Direct ground reconnaissance of the Canal itself was impossible, as the enemy held the hither bank in strength, but every conceivable source of information was exhaustively exploited in the endeavour to find crossing-places for the Tanks, that might offer at least a possibility of success.

Daring flights were made by special observers in low-flying aeroplanes, and a wonderful mosaic was pieced together from successive sets of air-photographs.

This was annotated, re-photographed, enlarged, and circulated to all concerned for further amplification and annotation as additional information was collected; Major Macavity of the Canadian Corps Intelligence, and Captain Oswald Birly of 1st Army Headquarters, being largely responsible for the thoroughness of this, as well as of several previous " over-the-line " surveys.

In addition, the *Garde Champêtre*, the *Ponts et Chaussées* service, and the engineers' working drawings for the Canal, were all laid under contribution, as well as the evidence of a number of prisoners, refugees and *repatriés*.

From such sources and on such evidence the requisite number of crossings were at length determined on, and the Tanks definitely and severally allotted to them, for good or ill.

But when all had been done, there were one or two points about which there still remained a disquieting element of doubt.

At one of these, where aerial photographs showed a breach through the retaining banks of the dry Canal that just might, or that just might not, allow sufficient width for Tanks to cross, a crossing was imperative for the local success of the attack. Somehow, a passage had to be positively assured—and there seemed but one sure way of keeping our contract with the infantry, who were to storm the Canal at that place.

A bridge was to be formed of three old and obsolete Tanks, upon the broad backs of which their juniors and betters might scramble across and get to close quarters with the enemy. Four elderly machines, warranted unsound, were accordingly sought out, specially stiffened up with internal timber struts, and allotted the self-sacrificing task of slithering down into the Canal bed, and there swinging and shunting until they lay side by side ready for the fighters to crawl over them.

Under the heading " A BRIDGE OF TANKS," the actual crossing was very vividly described in the Press.

" *Paris, September 28.*

" A French correspondent relates the following interesting episode which happened in the battle yesterday.

" It had been decided that a Tank detachment of the older types should lead the attack, expose themselves to the enemy fire, and, on arriving at the brink of the Canal, drop themselves into the bed so as to form an improvised bridge from one Tank to the other. The fast Tanks were to follow, and this new rapid type was to pass over the backs of their older comrades, opening out a path for the infantry. Volunteers were asked for this post of danger, and for one crew wanted ten crews offered themselves. Lots had to be drawn finally to choose the heroic winners of this contest of honour. The wonderful feat was accomplished. The old scarred Tanks, covered with ancient gashes and wounds proudly gained in the fighting on the Somme, and in the fighting of over a year ago before Cambrai, took for the last time their slow and massive way, and plunged with noble abnegation over the edge. Over their bodies the new strong Tanks passed with giant strides, our soldiers followed them to victory, and shortly after eight o'clock they penetrated Flesquières."

As a matter of fact, the actuality fell somewhat short of this description. The veteran machines found themselves quite unequal to the long trek, and even the least decrepit of the four finally doddered to a standstill whilst yet miles away from the Canal.

So there was no " Bridge of Tanks " after all, though, as things turned out, its absence embarrassed no one, with the possible though unlikely exception of the " close-up " correspondent.

Most fortunately the doubtful crossing proved practicable, and all machines, save one that struck a land-mine, passed safely over.

II

The attack was, as usual, at dawn, and, as the first-wave Tanks and infantry went over the top, they met with fierce resistance. On the right we encountered particularly strong opposition near Beaucamp Ridge.

The 11th Battalion History remarks upon the extraordinarily gallant fighting of the enemy on this sector.

> " In some cases they even attempted to pull the machine-guns and 6-pounders out of the Tanks. We inflicted many casualties by actually running over machine-guns and infantry, as well as by our fire."

Indeed, the Germans here constantly counter-attacked throughout the day, so important did they deem the position. In spite of them, however, we successfully established our right flank.

Just to the north of them the Guards and the 3rd Division forced a crossing of the Canal in face of their heavy machine and field gun fire, captured Ribecourt and Flesquières, the Guards taking Arival Wood and pushing north of Premy Chapel, where the 2nd Division took up the advance.

The 15th Battalion History tells the story of four Tanks

which were co-operating with the Guards Division. It is typical of this part of the battle. On the northern outskirts of Flesquières they awaited the arrival of the 1st Grenadiers, filling in the interval by helping the Gordons in their occupation of the village.

When the Guards arrived the situation was still somewhat obscure, and Major Skeggs, commanding the Tanks, made a daring forward reconnaissance from Flesquières towards Premy Chapel.

The Tanks were brought round north of the village immediately, engaging a number of machine and field guns, which were firing from Arival Wood. In order to cover the advance of the infantry, the Tanks had to come up over a bare stretch of country, exposed to direct fire from a number of field pieces.

Two Tanks, " Orchid " and " Othello," were soon knocked out, and 2nd Lieutenant Riddle's " Orestes " and Sergeant Whatley's " Oribi " only were left.

But it was in the centre that the Tanks fought their chief battle. Under cover of darkness, the Canadians and the 63rd Division had moved down the west bank of the Canal near Mœuvres and Sains-lez-Marquion. In the half light of dawn they stormed the Canal itself. The resistance here was far from well organised.

> * " Silkem Chapel and Wood Switch were packed with enemy infantry, who were in great confusion, unable to move one way or the other. The Tank ' Odetta,' commanded by Second Lieutenant C. W. Luck, did great execution there, bringing all his guns to bear on the enemy, and using case shot at point-blank range."

All day the 15th Battalion fought.

> " About 4.30 p.m. the G.S.O.3, 63rd Division, brought up a Brigadier-General (brigade not ascertained), who asked if Tanks could go forward with his Brigade, who were then about to resume the advance. He was informed that they had very little petrol left, but would go on if he (the Brigadier-General) would accept responsibility for Tanks being stranded right forward without petrol. The Brigadier-General agreed to this, and said he wanted to get his Brigade on to the Marquion Line.
>
> " The two Tanks went forward and picked up the infantry north of Graincourt. From this point they preceded the infantry, encountering practically no opposition.

* 15th Battalion Tank History.

"Beyond Anneux, the Tanks came under a lot of machine-gun fire from the direction of Fontaine-Notre-Dame. Both Tanks were turned broadside on, and fire was brought to bear on the German machine-guns in order to support the infantry advancing on the left. Parties of the enemy, who were seen coming over the crest towards the Marquion Line, were engaged by all Tank guns which could be brought to bear. The enemy ran away and many casualties were caused.

"Soon after this some heavy shells, believed to have been fired from trench mortars, fell very close to the Tanks. These two Tanks reached a point about 1000 yards from Cantaing before completing their work.

"Petrol was then almost finished, crews were much exhausted, having left the final lying-up place at about twelve midnight, on September 26–27. The work required of the Tanks was completed, so they were withdrawn to a point well east of the Canal."

Meanwhile our line had been pushed on east of Anneux to Fontaine-Notre-Dame. Bourlon Village had been carried by the 7th Tank Battalion and the Canadians. We had passed through Bourlon Wood, which was now wholly in our possession.

On the extreme left a Division of the 22nd Corps had also crossed the Canal, cleared Sauchy-Lestrée and had moved on northward.

The air co-operation had been particularly effective throughout the day. The work of the 8th Squadron had, however, been a good deal hampered, as they had concentrated on the 4th Army front for the recent fighting there, and therefore had a long flight and difficult signal communications when ordered to work with the 3rd and 1st Armies. However, their arrangements with their Tank partners were, as usual, admirable. With the 7th Battalion, who, with the Canadians, had been set the task of crossing the Canal du Nord opposite Inchy, and then taking Bourlon Village, co-operation was particularly good: not only were vital messages dropped at Battalion Headquarters, but a gun which was firing on three of our Tanks from Bourlon Wood was effectively bombed, and twice the airman chased its crew away with his machine-gun.

On September 28 Tanks of the 7th and 11th Battalions fought again at Baillencourt. Seven Tanks of the 11th Battalion with the 5th Corps captured Villers Guislain and Gonnelieu.

By the evening of the 28th we had taken all our objectives, and had advanced beyond our old high-water line of the First Battle of Cambrai. Fontaine-Notre-Dame, Bourlon Village, Epinoy and Haynecourt were all ours, and we had captured

THE BELLICOURT CANAL TUNNEL.

CARRIER-PIGEON BEING RELEASED.

INFANTRY ADVANCING BEHIND TANKS. A PRACTICE ATTACK AT BERMICOURT.

over 10,000 prisoners and 200 guns. The Tanks had suffered heavy casualties, but they had not suffered them in vain.

Part II

I

We have said that in the original battle scheme, certain points of vantage, Quennemont, the Knoll, and Bellicourt, were assumed to be in our hands a day or so before the main attack on the 4th Army front was launched.

These fortified heights were of importance owing to the singular geography of this sector of the line.

All along this piece of the front, more or less parallel to the lines of the armies, runs—deep and broad—the St. Quentin Canal.

For three and a half miles, however, between Bellicourt and Vendhuille it runs underground through a tunnel.

We have seen how, in the northern part of the line, the enemy had relied upon the Canal du Nord to form the principal obstacle to an attack.

In August we had captured a document which proved that he realised that if we attacked at all in the south, and whether we attacked with Tanks or not, it would be in that three-and-a-half-mile gap that our heaviest blow would fall.

The photograph facing p. 248 gives an excellent notion why we had to avoid certain sectors of the Canal at all costs, and Sir Douglas Haig, in his Despatch, gives an admirable idea of some of the complex features which the topography here possessed.

> "The general configuration of the ground through which this sector of the Canal runs, produces deep cuttings of a depth in places of some sixty feet; while between Bellicourt and the neighbourhood of Vendhuille the Canal passes through a tunnel for a distance of 6000 yards. In the sides of the cuttings the enemy had constructed numerous tunnelled dug-outs and concrete shelters. Along the top edge of them he had concealed well-sited concrete or armoured machine-gun emplacements. The tunnel itself was used to provide living accommodation for troops, and was connected by shafts with the trenches above. South of Bellicourt the Canal cutting gradually becomes shallow, till at Bellenglise the Canal lies almost at ground level. South of Bellenglise the Canal is dry.
>
> "On the western side of the Canal, south of Bellicourt, two thoroughly organised and extremely heavily wired lines of continuous trench run roughly parallel to the Canal, at

average distances from it of 2000 and 1000 yards respectively. . . . The whole series of defences, with the numerous defended villages contained in it, formed a belt of country varying from 7000 to 10,000 yards in depth, organised by the employment of every available means into a most powerful system, well meriting the great reputation attached to it."

On the three and a half miles of front, where alone Tanks and artillery could cross the line of the Canal, the outpost system, which everywhere protected the Hindenburg Line, was doubly reinforced, and gained a natural strength from its position on the heights, beneath which the Canal had burrowed.

Only a very "full-dress" attack on so highly organised a system as the Hindenburg Line was likely to be successful, and in order to launch such an attack it was essential that we should already hold the Knoll and Guillemont and Quennemont Farms.

We have seen how in the last day or two of the Battle of Epehy we assaulted the line again and again, and duly captured the sector opposite Bellicourt, but how, two days before the main attack was to be launched, the Knoll and Quennemont were still in the hands of the enemy.

This state of affairs caused grave anxiety, as the whole set-piece attack was based on the idea of using this line as a "jumping-off" position.

It had been intended that the two American Divisions, which were to fight on this sector, should only be put in when this line had been secured.

It was now decided that they must themselves make a final effort to capture the outpost line before the main assault, which was due for dawn on September 29.

Therefore, at dawn on the 27th, the 27th American Division, assisted by twelve Tanks of the 4th Battalion, again attacked under cover of a creeping barrage.

* "The attack met with strong opposition, and the final position reached was the subject of conflicting reports from the troops engaged and from the air observers. Subsequent events showed that small parties of Americans and Tanks had reached the vicinity of their objective, and had very gallantly maintained themselves there; but the line as a whole was not materially advanced by the day's operations. . . . The barrage could not now be brought back on this flank owing to the knowledge that parties of American troops, as well as a number of American wounded, would be exposed to our own fire. Also any alteration in the

* Captain Denny, *Daily Telegraph*, April 1, 1919.

barrage plans, which had already been issued, would inevitably lead to confusion."

Either, therefore, the whole main attack must be delayed, or the American Divisions and some of the British troops north of them must start some 1000 yards behind their barrage, and from a very indefinite jumping-off line.

The latter course was decided upon.

> * " The artillery start line, as originally planned, was to hold good, and the troops of the 27th American Division would form up for the attack on a line as far forward as possible, and would be assisted by an additional number of Tanks. The strength in Tanks was augmented to such an extent as should easily overwhelm the enemy resistance west of the start line. It was thought that this, with the slow rate of barrage, would enable the Americans to carry out their task."

But there was yet one more difficulty, a serious obstacle of which we were serenely unaware. A British anti-Tank minefield, consisting of rows of buried heavy trench-mortar bombs, each holding 50 lb. of ammonal, had been put down just prior to our loss of the area in March 1918, and of this minefield no information had reached the Tanks.

It will thus be seen that the dice were very heavily loaded against success on this part of the front before day dawned on the eventful 29th of September, 1918.

The whole attack was to be on a twelve-mile front. The infantry were to take advantage of a number of foot-bridges, which our bombardment had prevented the enemy from getting out to destroy, and in some places our men were prepared to wade or swim through the water.

It was expected, however, that the chief resistance would be offered on the famous three and a half miles.

Altogether about 175 Tanks, including the new American Battalion, were to be launched, and four Corps were to be involved.

To the 9th Corps on the right, the 5th, 6th and 7th Tank Battalions of the 3rd Brigade were allotted.

In the centre, with the Australian and American Corps, the 1st, 4th and 301st American Battalions of the 4th Brigade were to fight.†

The 8th, 13th and 16th Battalions of the 5th Tank Brigade were to be held in 4th Army Reserve.

* Captain Denny, *Daily Telegraph*, April 1, 1919.
† The 301st was attached to the 27th American Division.

Almost up to zero hour on the 29th we still hoped to get news that we held the Knoll and Quennemont. But no reassuring message came through.

It was thus in a very singular world that the 301st American Tank Battalion was destined to make its début.

* " The 301st's reconnaissance before the battle was very efficiently carried out in spite of many disadvantages. The taping especially was a classic example of pluck and efficiency. It must be borne in mind that this was no quiet front, and that the attempts to take his outpost line had made the Boche exceedingly nervous and alert. In consequence, the nights preceding the battle were some of the dirtiest I've experienced. The Battalion R.O. (I've forgotten his name), one Company R.O. (Lieutenant T. C. Naedale) and a sergeant were knocked out whilst supervising the taping. Lieutenant Naedale got his wounds dressed and continued his work up till zero hour. It is worthy of mention, in connection with this incident, that each American Tank had its own tape laid out over our front line towards the Boche by the Company R.O.'s. Tank Commanders told me afterwards that they had to start fighting before the end of their tape was reached."

II

When the dawn broke the usual mist lay thick and added its quota of confusion to the uncertainties of the morning.

All along the line, the battle swayed confusedly, developing into what was perhaps the most complete " mix-up " of any battle of the War.

To the north, the fighting was extremely heavy.

Owing to the employment of an effective barrage having been impossible, the American 27th Division suffered severely from the fire of massed hostile machine-guns from the moment the attack began.

Just as the Tanks of the 301st were moving up in support, ready to deal with the machine-guns which were, as an eye-witness describes it, by now " mowing down the other Americans in swathes," no less than ten machines struck upon the forgotten minefield.

The American Tanks experienced the bitterest of war's accidents, useless destruction at the hands of their own colleagues.

The explosions were terrific, the whole bottom of many

* From information specially given to the author by Captain Hatton-Hall, Reconnaissance Officer of the Brigade.

Major Hotblack's Exploit 253

machines being torn out and a large proportion of the crews being killed.

A little further to the south our attack was progressing well. Tanks of the 4th and 5th Battalions and their infantry had pushed forward. The intricate trench system and the confusion of wire and dug-outs, however, were responsible for a certain loss of cohesion, so that by the time the village of Bellicourt had been reached the attacking troops were some distance behind the barrage, and a good deal of the weight had gone out of the assault.

But though several large parties of the enemy still held out, we had, on this sector, actually penetrated the Hindenburg Line before noon.

But now the mist began to lift. The enemy still held Quennemont Farm and the land to the north of it in great strength, and from that high ground they were now beginning to be able to see well enough to pour a devastating fire into the backs of the troops who were advancing in the Bellicourt Sector. The situation was critical and called for immediate action.

Major Hotblack, the Head of the Tank Corps Intelligence, who was watching the progress of the battle near this point, luckily realised the situation before the enemy and rushed to try to improvise a diversion. He fortunately found two Tanks* which were waiting, ready to take part in a later stage of the attack. With the permission of the Battalion Commander, the two machines were hastily set going, and Major Hotblack jumped into the leading Tank. The machines were driven rapidly towards Quennemont Ridge. There was no body of infantry immediately available, and with the weather in its present mood, there was no time to wait; so the two Tanks without artillery or infantry support attacked what afterwards proved to be an unbroken sector of the enemy's front.

But if confusion reigned in the British line, there is no doubt that the Germans, though fighting exceedingly well, were far from clear about the actual position. In the confusion, they appear to have mistaken the two isolated machines for a considerable force. The two Tanks successfully made their way on to the heretofore impregnable Ridge, and actually succeeded in driving the enemy off it, killing large numbers of the defenders and capturing a quantity of machine-guns. Then at last the German field gunners awoke to the situation, and being otherwise unharassed, opened a devastating fire upon the two presumptuous machines. They succeeded in hitting and setting fire to both of them, the crews being obliged to evacuate, having suffered considerable casualties.

* 16th Battalion.

Major Hotblack, though partially blinded, was able to carry on, but the only other officer was severely wounded, and a derisory little force—one officer and five or six men—was thus left to hold the Ridge. Quite undaunted, they immediately set to work to prepare for the German counter-attack which, now that the Tanks were out of action and ablaze, seemed imminent. There was an abundance of enemy machine-guns lying about, and some of these were got ready for action, for the Tanks' own guns had been destroyed when the machines were knocked out.

While these guns were being turned round ready for their late owners, the tiny garrison was joined, first by an Australian and then by an American officer, each with an orderly, who had each separately come out to try and find out the position of affairs. The situation was rapidly explained to them, and was soon made clearer still by the expected counter-attack from the Germans. Twice during the previous week's fighting, the enemy had regained this Ridge when it was held in force. This time less than a dozen men successfully held it against them, and although almost every one of the defenders was wounded, they held out until relief came, several hours later.

For his part in this action Major Hotblack was awarded a bar to his Military Cross. This was his last action in the war, as the wounds he received on this occasion incapacitated him till the Armistice had been signed.

It is rather interesting to note that this officer was wounded five times during the course of the war—on four occasions in the head; but so admirable is our hospital system that he is now practically none the worse for his experiences.

On the extreme right of the battle the attack of the 9th Corps was a complete success, the 46th Division particularly distinguishing itself in the capture of Bellenglise.

> * " Equipped with lifebelts, and carrying mats and rafts, the 46th Division stormed the western arm of the Canal at Bellenglise and to the north of it, some crossing the Canal on foot-bridges, which the enemy was given no time to destroy, others dropping down the sheer sides of the Canal wall, and, having swum or waded to the far side, climbing up the farther wall to the German trench lines on the eastern bank."

The Tanks were, of course, unable to cross with their infantry. They moved on Bellicourt, crossed over the tunnel at the nearest point, and swung south, working down the further bank of the Canal and arriving just in time to take part in the attack on Monchy.

* Sir Douglas Haig's Despatch.

Montbrehain and Beaurevoir

Our success here was so complete that one division alone captured 4000 prisoners and seventy guns.

Many of these batteries were taken from the rear by Tanks and infantry while they were still in action, the enemy not realising in the least that they had been outflanked.

III

At the end of the day it was pretty clear what must be the ultimate result of the battle. But our front was extremely ragged and the breaches we had driven in the Hindenburg Line but narrow.

So for some days our attacks continued on all fronts; from north of Cambrai, where the 7th Battalion Tanks and the Canadians met with a desperate resistance, right down to our junction with the French 1st Army south of St. Quentin.

With the exception of a party of six machines belonging to the 1st Brigade, who helped in an attack just north of Cambrai, all the Tank actions of this period were fought in the 4th Army area, where we were busied in driving in the wedge whose thin end we had inserted with so much effort on September 29.

On the 30th, twenty Tanks belonging to the 5th, 6th, 13th and 7th Battalions fought in different groups, none with striking success, in one or two cases owing to the fact that the fresh infantry who had been brought up were unaccustomed to Tanks, and that liaison was therefore defective.

The village of Bony, which had just been entered by the Armoured Cars on the 29th, still held out stubbornly.

On October 1, Tanks of the 9th Battalion were engaged with the 32nd Division in an attack on a part of the line near Joncourt. In this action the Tanks made very successful use of smoke screens.

On the 2nd no Tanks fought, but on October 3 about forty machines went into action.

As on the previous days, we met with stubborn resistance, and as on the previous days, foot by foot, inch by inch, we pushed our line forward, always patiently enlarging the width of the holes we had pierced.

A new attack on a large scale was now contemplated, and for this assault the Tank Corps had to furnish between eighty and ninety machines, some on the 3rd, some on the 4th Army front. Preparations were immediately begun, and no Tanks fought on the 4th.

Our line, however, had just reached the outskirts of two large villages, Montbrehain and Beaurevoir, and we were anxious not to begin the day of our new attack with street fighting—of all forms of warfare the most incalculable.

Therefore, the Australians and the 16th Tank Battalion attacked Montbrehain, and after fighting a strenuous but brilliant little action, captured it.

The last phase of the Cambrai-St. Quentin battle was at hand; nay more, the last phase of the warfare we had known for nearly four years.

The next day we were to match our strength against that torn and breached, but still formidable ruin, that had once been the Hindenburg Line.

CHAPTER XXI

THE SECOND BATTLE OF LE CATEAU—THE RUNNING FIGHT

I

" TANK CORPS INTELLIGENCE SUMMARY, OCT. 8 "

" An attack was launched this morning between Cambrai and St. Quentin on a front of eighteen miles, which was entirely successful—all objectives being gained—in spite of obstinate machine-gun defence.

" Heavy Tanks and Whippets co-operated.

" The line now runs N. and E. of Niergnies—E. of Seranvillers and La Targette—Esnes Mill—E. edge of Esnes — through Briseux Wood — Walincourt-Audigny trench line to Walincourt Wood—W. of Walincourt—N. and E. of Serain—E. of Prémont—E. of Brancourt—E. of Beauregard.

" Depth of penetration varies, the maximum being 6000 yards.

" The French continued the attack on the southern portion of the battle front and made progress in the vicinity of Fontaine Utertre and Essigny le Petit.

" A large number of prisoners have been taken, but the actual numbers are not yet known.

" The enemy made a heavy counter-attack from the direction of Awoingt against our line between Niergnies and Seranvillers, and the situation at Forenville is not quite clear.

" In this counter-attack the enemy used captured British Tanks. Seven appeared in the sunken road N.E. of Niergnies without any infantry support. Our infantry used enemy anti-Tank rifles, and four or five enemy Tanks are reported to have been put out of action."

This was the form in which the news of what proved the

s

last set action of the war reached resting Tank Battalions, and the great Tank organisation behind the lines.

The whole action had somehow seemed unusually dramatic. There was now everywhere a sense of the momentousness of events. We knew in our hearts that the hour had come. Still, the enemy had so often revealed unexpected strengths, we had so often been tricked into optimism, and now we fought with a sort of surprised joy in thrusting home, of feeling the German resistance really crumble under our blows.

Every time we struck we were feverishly impatient at our own weariness, a weariness which delayed the next blow. We longed to be sure, to strike again and again, no matter how, and so end the long nightmare.

All through that last month we hurried on, blind with fatigue, too eager for the next battle to have been fought, too deeply concerned with the culmination of the great drama, to care what had been the details of our achievements in the last action.

It is difficult in attempting any chronicle of this period not to feel again the impatience of the hour, or to achieve enough detachment to describe the individual threads out of which the great pattern of victory was woven.

II

To return to the attack of October 8.

Besides the very good action fought by Whippets of the 3rd and 6th Battalions near Serain and Prémont, there were two particularly interesting features in the attack: first, the action fought by the 301st American and 1st Tank Battalions; and, second, the German counter-attack with Tanks which is mentioned in the Summary.

Nineteen Tanks of the 301st went into action opposite Serain, doing great execution.

> *" In one railway cutting near Brancourt, which was a mass of machine-guns, I counted nearly fifty mangled Boches who had been caught in enfilade with case shot as the Tanks crossed the line. The infantry casualties were very low, and all agreed on the masterly way the American Tank gunners had dealt with M.G. opposition.
>
> " The *pièce de résistance* of the battle was the performance of Major Sasse, D.S.O., for which he received his decoration.
>
> " As on a former occasion, he went into action in the

* Captain Hatton-Hall.

Wireless Tank. After the capture of Brancourt he left his Tank this side of the village and went forward to reconnoitre. He eventually ascended the church tower in order to get a forward view of the battle. While doing this a very heavy bombardment of the village commenced, and Major Sasse noticed that the infantry had begun to retire. He accordingly descended and tried to find the officer in charge of the troops on the spot. Not being able to do this he assumed command himself, stopped the retirement and organised the troops as a defensive force round the outskirts of the village. Lewis guns were posted and the men ordered to resist any attempt on the part of the Boche to retake the village, should this be made. As was expected, a determined counter-attack developed, which was successfully beaten off by Major Sasse's detachment. This occurred a second time, and Major Sasse sent off a wireless message for help. He was rescued some hours later from a somewhat precarious position by American reinforcements."

It was to Tanks of the 12th Battalion that the interesting lot fell of meeting captured British Mark IV. Tanks in action.

Four Tanks belonging to " A " Company were in the neighbourhood of Niergnies when the enemy launched a strong counter-attack. The battlefield was thick with smoke and it was not yet fully light, and when in the half-dark the Tank crews and infantry saw four Tanks advancing to meet them, they supposed that the strangers belonged to " C " Company, who had been sent to execute an encircling movement, and who had, they imagined, somehow been able to outflank the enemy with extraordinary speed. " L 16," commanded by Captain Rowe, was near a farm named Mont St. Meuve when the Tanks appeared in sight, and the foremost was within fifty yards before Captain Rowe realised that it was an enemy machine. He immediately fired a 6-pounder shot at it which disabled it, but almost at the same time " L 16 " was hit by two shells, one of which came through the cab, wounding Captain Rowe and killing his driver. The Tank Commander immediately got his crew out and crossed over to " L 19," which was near at hand, and led it forward towards the German machines, of whose presence it was still unaware. " L 19 " had already had five men wounded, had been on fire, and having no gunners left, could not use its 6-pounders. Its Commander, Second Lieutenant Worsap, however, nothing daunted, immediately engaged the enemy with his Lewis guns until the Tank received a direct hit which set it on fire a second time. There was nothing now to be done but to evacuate the machine, and as the German counter-attack seemed to be succeeding, Mr. Worsap blew up the wreck of his Tank.

"L 12," the third Tank, a male, was hit and finally disabled before its Commander and crew had discovered that the strange Tanks did not belong to "C" Company. There remained "L 8" under Lieutenant Martell, but this Tank had a leaky radiator and was almost out of water. It, too, had been hit, and three of its Lewis guns put out of action. Lieutenant Martell, however, sent his crew back, and he and an artillery officer managed to get up to a captured German field gun, which the two turned round and used against the enemy's Tanks, almost immediately obtaining a direct hit on one of them. Two of the German machines were now accounted for. And now at last a genuine "C" Company Tank—a female—appeared and finally drove or scared away the two remaining German machines. The situation was restored, and the infantry, who had retired before the counter-attack, went forward again and reoccupied the ridge beyond Niergnies. A comparison of the British and German accounts of this action is not unentertaining.

German Wireless News

"During the heavy fighting south of Cambrai on October 8, German . . . Tanks and a column of infantry advanced . . . behind a wall of artificial fog. The German Tanks, which were feeling their way forward, surprised a large number of Englishmen who were standing in disordered groups. By means of machine-gun fire and Tank gunfire the English were driven back. The English troops on the eastern outskirts of Niergnies took to flight and evacuated. On the Cambrai-Crèvecœur Road there were five English Tanks advancing in support of their own infantry. As they came into sight of the German Tanks the English Tanks stopped, and they were set on fire by their own crews."

By the end of the day we had advanced and widened our line along the whole front of the attack, and the next day was devoted to exploitation.

The enemy was in full retreat and a rapid advance met with the feeblest opposition. The contemporary record in the Tank Corps Intelligence Summary remarks upon this feature.

" October 9.

"A penetration of over six miles has been made towards Le Cateau, and in the area gained, twenty-six villages have been occupied.

HIS MAJESTY THE COLONEL-IN-CHIEF AND GENERAL ELLES.

SPECIAL ORDER NO. 18.

By Major-General H. J. ELLES, C.B., D.S.O.
Commanding TANK CORPS in the Field.

18th October, 1918.

1. His Majesty the King was graciously pleased to become COLONEL-IN-CHIEF of the Tank Corps on the 17th instant.
2. The following telegram was sent on behalf of the TANK CORPS.

"To H.M. THE KING.

"The news that your Majesty has graciously consented to become Colonel-in-Chief of the Tank Corps has just been received here. All ranks are deeply sensible of this signal honour conferred upon the Corps and are determined to continue worthy of it.

"GENERAL ELLES.

Advanced H.Q. Tank Corps.
In the Field. 17th October."

3. The following reply has been received.

"To MAJOR-GENERAL H. J. ELLES,
H.Q. Tank Corps. In the Field.

"I sincerely thank you for the message which you have conveyed to me in the name of all ranks of the Tank Corps.

"I am indeed proud to be Colonel-in-Chief of this great British organization invented by us which has played so prominent a part in our recent victories.

"I wish you all every possible good luck.

"GEORGE R.I.
"Colonel-in-Chief."

Buckingham Palace,
London, 18th October."

MANUFACTURE.

"Tanks again co-operated.

"Shortly after midnight our troops commenced the attack N. of Cambrai, capturing Ramillies and securing a bridgehead over the Escaut Canal at Pont D'Aire.

"The whole of Cambrai was occupied this morning. . . .

"Air reports state that there is great confusion on roads N.E. and S.E. of Le Cateau, and that our low-flying scouts have been shooting at record targets. . . .

"The number of prisoners taken in yesterday's attack by the British Armies amounted to 6300, and by the French in the St. Quentin area 1200. No detail yet received of captures to-day."

The Battle of Cambrai-St. Quentin was at an end, and the Hindenburg Line had now to all intents and purposes ceased to exist, broken as it was on a front of nearly thirty miles.

Before the whole British forces in France, from north of Menin to Bohain, seven miles north-west of Guise, open country stretched, uncut by trench, unhung by wire. The time for exploitation had arrived.

Considering our comparative numerical weakness, the lateness of the season and the nature of the country, to have fought their way so far had been a notable performance. Now to carry out a rapid pursuit was beyond even the endeavours of the infantry. For the German Army, though beaten, was not yet broken.

> * "A pursuit by cavalry was unthinkable, for the German rearguards possessed many thousands of machine-guns, and as long as these weapons existed, pursuit, as cavalry dream it to be, was utterly impossible. One arm alone could have turned the present defeat into a rout—the Tank, but few of these remained, for since August 8 no less than 819 machines had been handed over to salvage by the Tank Battalions, and these Battalions themselves had lost in personnel 550 officers and 2557 other ranks, out of a fighting state of some 9500."

The 3rd, 4th, 5th, 7th and 15th Battalions—or what was left of them—had all to be withdrawn into G.H.Q. reserve on October 12.

* *W.T.N.*

III

THE BATTLE OF THE SELLE

As fast, however, as the weariness of our infantry and the fewness of our Tanks allowed, we pursued the flying but still coherent German Divisions.

Again and again the enemy tried to turn, to stand just so long behind some natural defence as should enable him to organise his retreat. He still had a hope that a shortened line might enable him to make a final rally, if only, meantime, too headlong a flight had not reduced his army to a mob, and if the advance of the Allies could be stemmed for a little before the vital centre of Maubeuge.

Seven Tanks of the 5th Battalion had advanced with the French and the 9th Corps near Riquerval Wood; but the first action of this new type, in which any considerable number of machines took part, was the Battle of the Selle River, which began in the 4th Army area on October 17.

> *"Our operations were opened on October 17 by an attack by the 4th Army on a front of about ten miles from Le Cateau southwards, in conjunction with the French 1st Army operating west of the Sambre and Oise Canal. The assault, launched at 5.20 a.m., was delivered by the 9th, 2nd American and 13th Corps. . . . The enemy was holding the difficult wooded country east of Bohain, and the line of the Selle north of it, in great strength, his infantry being well supported by artillery."

The 4th was the Tank Brigade concerned.

The 1st Battalion was allotted to the 9th Corps on the right.

The 2nd American Corps in the centre fought as usual with the 301st American Battalion.

On the left the 13th Corps had the 16th Battalion, while the 6th Tank Battalion was in Army reserve.

The Germans had chosen their battle ground with great skill. They held the right bank of the Selle, and the river itself, therefore, threaded No Man's Land. This particular choice of a defence was undoubtedly dictated by a fear of Tanks. There had been heavy rain, and the river was in flood.

* Sir Douglas Haig's Despatch.

The Crossing of the Selle

* " Very little was known of the stream, except that it varied every few yards in nature, breadth and depth; and the only way of establishing safe crossing-places for the Tanks, was by personal reconnaissance.

" This work was done successfully by the R.O.'s of the 1st and 301st Battalions, which were fighting alongside each other.

" The reconnaissance necessary on the front of the 301st promised to be extremely dangerous and the success rather doubtful, owing to the presence of several unlocated Boche posts on our side of the stream. It was a question of slipping through these unobserved, gaining the necessary information, and coming back again through their lines.

" Lieutenant T. C. Naedale, Battalion R.O., undertook to do this in the company of an infantry guide from the sector. This officer walked down the stream 500 yards, literally under the noses of the Boche posts, and returned to our lines with the requisite intelligence. He was thus able to pick safe crossings for all his Tanks."

At 5.30 a.m. on October 17, the fog was so thick that Tanks had to move forward on compass bearings. The infantry could see nothing, and had, in many cases, to rely almost entirely on the Tanks as guides. Every Tank of the forty-eight carried a crib, and with their help, north of St. Souplet and of Molain, both Tank Battalions crossed the river in safety at the previously selected fords.

The Germans had clearly relied almost entirely upon the flooded river for their defence, and it was only here and there that we met with any opposition. Isolated posts would, however, occasionally hold out with great vigour, and what with the fog and the irregular speed of our advance, the whole battle was an exceedingly confused one. The enemy was well supplied with artillery, and wherever the fog permitted made good use of it.

At about 10 a.m. the infantry, who were badly held up by machine-guns near Demilieue, summoned Whippets of the 6th Battalion to their help. A number of machines immediately hurried up, but even then, so heavy was the machine-gun fire, that it was only with great difficulty that the infantry could advance even under cover of the Whippets. Just as they were approaching the village, three Whippets were knocked out in rapid succession by a single field gun. Deprived of the cover of these machines, the infantry had to retire again. It was not till considerably later that the village was taken.

* Captain Hatton-Hall.

On the 18th and 19th the infantry managed to make good progress, and at 2 p.m. on the 20th we made another attack, still on the line of the Selle, north of Le Cateau.

Only four Tanks of the 11th Battalion were employed. The enemy's resistance was serious, for he had been able to erect strong wire entanglements along the greater part of the line. This time, there being no available fords, the Tanks successfully crossed the river by means of an under-water sleeper bridge, which the Sappers had secretly constructed at night, the enemy being quite unaware of its existence, until, to their dismay, they saw the Tanks crossing over it.

There was severe fighting round Neuvilly, Solesmes and Haspres, but we gained all our objectives on the high ground east of the Selle, all the four Tanks successfully reaching their final goal.

Our capture of these positions on the river Selle was immediately followed up by a larger bid, this time for the general line running from the Sambre Canal along the edge of Mormal Forest to the neighbourhood of Valenciennes. We were to make a night attack on a fifteen-mile line in the 4th Army area, the 9th, 5th and 13th Corps being supported by thirty-seven Tanks from the 10th, 11th, 12th and 301st (American) Battalions.

Zero hour was 1.30 a.m. Unfortunately the hoped-for moonlight was shrouded, and the night misty and dark. To add to our difficulties, the enemy was shelling freely with gas. Gasmasks had to be worn, and through them it was impossible to see anything. Consequently we did not make much progress until dawn. But directly it was light we went ahead, the Tanks had fine shooting at " ground game," and a great amount of case shot was fired, and both Tanks and infantry ultimately won through to their objectives.

Next day the 17th Corps took up the attack in the 1st Army area, so extending our line of assault a further five miles north to the Schelde. No Tanks, however, operated at this stage of the 1st Army's offensive, but six machines belonging to the 10th Battalion attacked near Robersart. One of these Tanks managed to explode a German ammunition dump with a lucky shot from one of its 6-pounders. This threw the enemy into great confusion, whilst the explosion of his own shells helped us considerably with the killing.

IV

We had now reached another—the last—stage of the battle. The nature of the terrain had begun to change, for we were travelling at last.

* " Despite the unfavourable weather and the determined opposition at many points from the German machine-gunners, in two days our infantry and Tanks had realised an advance of five or six miles over difficult country."

We had now reached the half-wooded, half-pasture and orchard country which lay on the outskirts of the Forest of Mormal, " like fringe upon a petticoat," and the last of our battles had been fought amid the trees of the Bois L'Evêque and of Pommereuil.

We were within a mile of Le Quesnoy, which lay in a clearing in the Forest.

There was no chance of giving our machines an overhaul. It was therefore in a state of mechanical " efficiency," which a little while before we should have said made any sort of fighting out of the question, that most of the remaining Tanks gaily tackled this difficult piece of the advance.

* Sir Douglas Haig's Despatch.

CHAPTER XXII

THE ROUT—MORMAL FOREST—THE BATTLE OF THE SAMBRE—
THE ARMISTICE

I

"Some greater issue was at stake, some mightier cause, than ever before the sword had pleaded or the trumpet had proclaimed."
DE QUINCEY.

ON November 4, the 1st, 3rd and 4th Armies were to deliver an attack on a combined front of about thirty miles, from the Sambre to the north of Oisy and Valenciennes. The country across which our advance was to be made was exceedingly difficult: in the south, the river Sambre had to be crossed almost at the outset. In the centre the great Forest of Mormal, though here and there thinned by German foresters, still presented a formidable obstacle. In the north lay the strongly fortified town of Le Quesnoy, which was defended naturally by several streams which ran parallel to the line of our advance, offering the enemy repeated opportunities for a successful defence.

On November 2 we fought a small action west of Landrecies. We were anxious to improve our position near Happegarbes before the big attack on the 4th.

Only three Tanks of the 10th Battalion took part.

Unfortunately, although we took all our objectives, the Germans suddenly plucked up heart, launched a surprise attack, and we lost them again before nightfall.

The Battle of Mormal Forest was the last set Tank attack of the War, and for it we could only scrape together just thirty-seven machines.

Tank units were bled almost white. Sections took the place of companies, companies of battalions, and Tanks were parcelled out in such a way that the very most might be made of their scanty numbers.

At dawn, after an intense bombardment, Tanks and infantry

moved forward to the assault under a heavy barrage, and it was not long before they had penetrated the enemy's positions on the whole battle front.

On the right of the attack, zero was at 5.45. The 9th Corps, which, it will be remembered, was supported by four sections of the 10th Tank Battalion, pushed forward and captured Catillon, where the Tanks fought a particularly good action. The infantry were able to cross the Sambre at this place, capturing a lock some two miles to the south of it. By two hours after zero two battalions of infantry were east of the river.

The Tanks with the 13th Corps were also extremely successful, especially in the neighbourhood of Hecq, Preux and the north-western edge of the Forest of Mormal.

An account of the fighting on this central part of the line is given in the Tank Corps Intelligence Summary.

> " The early morning was fine and clear, but a dense mist came up with the dawn and persisted until about 8.30. In addition, the country S.W. of Mormal Forest is peculiarly enclosed with thick orchards, quick-set fences and hedgerow trees, confining visibility to no more than fifty yards or so, under the best conditions. The infantry largely depended on the Tanks to give them their direction, and many of the latter had to steer exclusively by compass. By this means they were able to keep approximately to their allotted routes, and were of considerable help to the infantry in breaking through the dense hedges (some wired) and in dealing with machine-guns. In places the enemy barrage came down heavily with a high proportion of gas, whilst elsewhere it was inconsiderable. Resistance also was unusually 'patchy,' some few M.G. posts holding out well, whilst many others, though well sited and camouflaged, were found not to have fired a round. A show of resistance was put up at Landrecies bridge by some 300 German infantry and machine-gunners, but they gave in when outflanked by the crossing of the canal on rafts further to the south. The enemy had lined some of the hedges with deep and very well camouflaged rifle-pits, which here and there were held in strength. The main body of the enemy, however, appears to have been withdrawn a kilometre or so in rear of his forward positions just prior to our attack. French inhabitants of the most forward villages state that he started withdrawing at five o'clock this morning. In a number of instances the enemy was found hiding, unarmed, awaiting an opportunity to surrender. In one village over fifty Germans

emerged from the house cellars, where they had been hiding together with the inhabitants. Other Germans attempted to hide themselves in trees and were dealt with with case shot. A number of anti-Tank rifles were found in rifle-pits, etc., but appear to have been made little or no use of. There were instances of detached field guns being sited to enfilade hedges and cover crests, but so far no reports have come in as to their effect—if any. One Brigade operating with Tanks is reported to have had over 350 prisoners through its cage before 11 a.m., including a Regimental Commander and part of his Staff, whilst one Division reported over 1000 prisoners by 12.30. A German pigeon loft (complete with birds) was captured in Landrecies. Air visibility was nil until after 9 a.m., and communication therefore difficult.

" *Later.*—Prisoners now reported 10,000 with 200 guns."

It was at Landrecies that three supply Tanks managed, despite their almost complete lack of arms or armour, to take a most gallant and effective part in the battle.

These three Tanks were working for the 25th Division, and were carrying up material to rebuild one of the numerous bridges that the Germans had destroyed; as they drew near their rendezvous they found that the enemy was still holding the place in some strength, and had succeeded in stopping the advance of our infantry. As the Tanks approached they began to draw fire and their situation became precarious. With great pluck and resource the Tanks decided to go on, and rely on their appearance (which was similar to that of the fighting Tanks) to drive the enemy from his position. One Tank became a casualty, but the other two went straight for the enemy. Even when the Tanks got close up, the Germans were still under the impression that they were being faced by fighters, and part of the garrison put up their hands, whilst the remainder fled.

With the 5th Corps, the 1st Company of the 9th Battalion encountered stiff resistance, but nevertheless they pushed forward far into the Forest of Mormal.

The Tanks were particularly active in the attack on Jolimetz, just south of Le Quesnoy, when they and the 37th Division took upwards of 1000 prisoners, and later in the afternoon and evening pushed on into the heart of the Forest. North of them the New Zealanders had surrounded Le Quesnoy by 8 a.m. Here also Tanks were operating.

By the end of the day we had made a five-mile advance, reaching the general line Fesny-Landrecies—the centre of Mormal Forest—and five miles beyond Valenciennes.

THE WESTERN EDGE OF MORMAL FOREST.

* " In these operations and their developments twenty British Divisions utterly defeated thirty-two German Divisions, and captured 19,000 prisoners and more than 450 guns. On our right the French 1st Army, which had continued the line of attack southwards to the neighbourhood of Guise, kept pace with our advance, taking 5000 prisoners and a number of guns.

" By this great victory the enemy's resistance was definitely broken. On the night of November 4–5 his troops began to fall back on practically the whole battle front."

II

But the Tank Corps was at last at an end of its resources both in machines and in men.

Pending reinforcements from England, they could at the moment muster but eight machines that could be sent after the flying enemy, and therefore, though the Armoured Cars went on, it was on November 5 that the last Tank action of the War was fought, when eight Whippets of the 6th Battalion took part in an attack of the 3rd Guards Brigade, on the northern outskirts of the Forest of Mormal.

The weather was atrocious and the country most difficult for a combined operation, for it was intersected by numerous ditches and fences, which rendered it ideal for the rearguard actions which the Germans were now fighting all along their front.

† " At 10 a.m. on the morning of November 5 the 3rd Guards Brigade, having pushed through the 1st and 2nd Brigades, were ordered to continue the advance by bounds."

No definite orders had reached the Whippets' Company Commander as to what part—if any—his machines were to play.

He and the General commanding the 3rd Guards Brigade, however, came to the conclusion that in view of the nature of the ground and the fact that the Bultiaux River would have to be crossed in the first stage of the battle, the Whippets should lead the attack upon the second, third and final objectives only.

Two Tanks proved unfit for action owing to mechanical trouble. The three Tanks which covered the advance of the

* Sir Douglas Haig's Despatch.
† 6th Battalion History.

Grenadiers found themselves in a country of small orchards divided by extremely high hedges, where it was most difficult to locate the enemy machine-guns, whose fire was here considerable.

The Whippets therefore worked up and down the hedges like ratting terriers, being ordered to * " fire short bursts along them for moral effect even when no enemy were visible. This they did, and found a few fleeting targets before returning to get in touch with the infantry."

Two Whippets which were co-operating with the Scots Guards met with a good deal of opposition. Twice had they and the infantry attempted to capture and consolidate high ground beyond the village of Buvignies.

The driver of the first Tank was hit as he was endeavouring to put right a minor mechanical trouble, and the second Tank went on alone.

In attempting to run over an enemy rifle-pit, it ran on to a jagged tree stump and was damaged, finally breaking down in the enemy's lines beyond Buvignies.

* From accounts of civilians, who were behind the enemy's lines, it appears that the crew held out till midnight, the Tank being then blown up.

> "They also reported that after the Tanks had been through Buvignies the enemy hurriedly departed, and also vacated the railway, which had been holding up the Grenadiers."

The 3rd Guards Brigade pushed forward unopposed for a mile and a half during the night, but when darkness came the four remaining Whippets were ordered to rally.

> "It was decided not to use these four on the following day, and work was concentrated on getting fit the six Whippets which might be made available to trek or fight."

For, though through all this period we knew well enough that the end had come, in these last few days of the War we acquired a new tradition. It became the magnificent custom of the British Army to act as though the War would go on for ever.

The spirit that says, " I've been lucky so far. Why tempt Providence with the War won, anyway? " must have reared its head in every man. But it was rigorously kept down, and never among the attacking troops in these last tense days

* 6th Battalion History.

was there found any inclination to spare themselves or to spoil our victory by undue chariness of life and limb. Not only in the racking circumstances of the battlefield, but also behind the lines, this new tradition was manifest, and after the 5th the Tank crews were everywhere feverishly engaged, day and night, in refitting and furbishing up their machines on the complete assumption that they would surely be called upon to fight again. Everywhere, too, the Staffs were busy endeavouring to build up an organised fighting force from the scarred, battle-weary remnants of the Corps.

The Tank Corps' record since August 8 was indeed a remarkable one. There had been ninety-six days of almost continuous battle since that great Tank attack, and in these ninety-six days about two thousand Tanks and Armoured Cars had been engaged.

Nearly half this number of machines had been handed over to salvage. Of these, 313 had been sufficiently badly damaged to be sent to Central Workshops, which had repaired no less than 204 of them and reissued them to battalions. Of the whole 887, only fifteen machines had been struck off the strength as beyond repair.

The personnel, too, had been lamentably reduced. However, the total strength of the Tank Corps on August 7, 1918, had been considerably under that of a single infantry division, and in the old days of the artillery battles, such as the First Battle of the Somme, an infantry division often sustained 4000 casualties in twelve hours. In comparison, the Tanks' losses of just over 3000 in three months, out of a fighting strength of under 10,000, seem comparatively light. They were heavy enough, however, effectually to cripple the Corps for several weeks.

III

Meanwhile the last act of the great drama was being played out.

Though there were for the moment no Tanks to share in the culminating glories, our forces were pushing forward along the whole front. On November 6 and 7 the enemy's resistance had very much weakened. Early on the morning of the 7th the Guards entered Bavay; next day Avesnes fell. Six cars of the Tank 17th Armoured Car Battalion here did excellent service in conjunction with "Bethell's Force," the cars, "full out," putting roadside machine-guns out of action and in many cases preventing the flying enemy from blowing up the cross-roads behind his rearguards. Hautmont was captured, and our troops reached the outskirts of Maubeuge, the goal upon which our eyes had for so long been fixed. To the north of Mons the enemy was now rapidly withdrawing. All through the night of November 7–8 we could see the glare of burning dumps behind the German lines, and could hear the irregular clamour of their detonations. At Tournai the enemy abandoned his bridgehead without a fight.

On the 9th the enemy was in full retreat on the whole front; the Guards entered Maubeuge at the moment when the Canadians were approaching Mons. The whole of our 2nd Army crossed the Schelde, and next day all five British Armies advanced in line, preceded by cavalry, cyclists and Armoured Cars.

Only round Mons was any opposition met with, and at dawn on November 11 the Third Canadian Division captured the town, killing or taking prisoner the whole of the German garrison.

It was the last of the tasks of slaughter to which our hands were to be forced.

For four days there had been a coming and going of envoys and of messages. For four days men and women in England had listened and waited, restless and sick with expectancy, with a sudden realisation of their longing to emerge from the long nightmare.

On November 11, just after eleven in the morning, the church bells were rung in every town and village at home; and in France the expected message was quietly passed from mouth to mouth. There is no need to describe a moment which no reader of this book will ever forget.

EPILOGUE

I

AND what, the reader will ask, is the conclusion of the whole matter?

First, how far did Tanks really contribute to our overthrow of the Germans?

Secondly, what would be the place of the Tank if another war broke out within the next generation; and, thirdly, what place are Tanks going to be given in the reconstituted British Army?

As far as they can be answered, we will reply to these questions in order. For upon the performances of the Tanks in this war, will be—or should be—based the answers to the other questions, and on this point we propose to call the evidence of three or four expert witnesses.

For the rest, the reader has had an opportunity of studying a large mass of evidence for himself.

He has seen how, when the line from Switzerland to the sea had been formed, both armies sought some means of putting an end to the stalemate.

How to both the Allies and the Germans the solution by artillery was the first to occur. How, secondly, we and the Germans, each according to our national habits of mind, thought of another solution. The Germans—who were chemists—of gas, used treacherously in despite of signed undertakings to the contrary; we, who were mechanics, of a self-propelled shield, from behind which we could direct an effective fire.

He knows how gas was countered, after the first surprise, by means of various air-filtering devices; but how the Tank gradually revolutionised warfare, because there was no particular specific or antidote to the Tank, which depended not so much upon surprise as on the simple factors of its enormous fire power, and its ability to surmount obstacles. For whether the troops attacked had fought against Tanks before or no, the Tank crushed down wire and smothered machine-gun fire just the same.

T

Marshal Foch is the first of our witnesses.

He sketches the evolution of the Tank, and describes the circumstances which called it into being, in his foreword to the English translation of his republished *Principles of War*. He has dealt with the old slowness of " digging in."

We translate his words literally:

> " The machine-gun and the barbed-wire entanglement have permitted defences to be organised with indisputable rapidity. These have endowed the trench, or natural obstacle, with a strength which has permitted offensive fronts to be extended over areas quite impracticable until this time. . . . The offensive for the time was powerless, new weapons were sought for, and, after a formidable artillery had been produced Tanks were invented—*i.e.*, machine-guns or guns protected by armour, and rendered mobile by petrol, capable, over all types of ground, to master the enemy's entanglements and his machine-guns. . . .
>
> " Thus it is the industrial power of nations that has alone permitted armies to attack, or the want of this power has reduced them to the defensive."

Monsieur Loucheur—in January 1919 French Minister of Munitions—was a strong advocate for Tanks in the French Army.

> " There are two kinds of infantry: men who have gone into action with Tanks, and men who have not; and the former never want to go into action without Tanks again."

Sir Douglas Haig's summing up in his Despatch, though necessarily conservative, is not therefore the less significant:

> " Since the opening of our offensive on *August* 8 Tanks have been employed in every battle, and the importance of the part played by them in breaking the resistance of the German infantry can scarcely be exaggerated. The whole scheme of the attack of *August* 8 was dependent upon Tanks, and ever since that date on numberless occasions the success of our infantry has been powerfully assisted or confirmed by their timely arrival. So great has been the effect produced upon the German infantry by the appearance of British Tanks that in more than one instance, when for various reasons real Tanks were not available in sufficient numbers, valuable results have been obtained by the use of dummy Tanks painted on frames of wood and canvas.

Epilogue

> "It is no disparagement of the courage of our infantry or of the skill and devotion of our artillery, to say that the achievements of those essential arms would have fallen short of the full measure of success achieved by our armies had it not been for the very gallant and devoted work of the Tank Corps, under the command of Major-General H. J. Elles."

Lastly, what is the opinion of the enemy?

Herr Maximilian Harden in a speech upon the causes of the German defeat, gave first place to the "physical shock of the Tank," at which "Ludendorff had laughed."

Speaking for the Minister of War in the Reichstag, General Wrisberg said:

> "The attack on August 8 between the Avre and the Ancre was not unexpected by our leaders. When, nevertheless, the English succeeded in achieving a great success the reasons are to be sought in the massed employment of Tanks and surprise under the protection of fog. . . .
>
> "The American Armies should not terrify us. . . . More momentous for us is the question of Tanks."

The G.O.C. of the 51st German Corps, in an Order dated July 23, 1918, remarks: "As soon as the Tanks are destroyed the whole attack fails."

On October 23 the German Wireless published the following statement by General Scheuch, Minister of War:

> "Germany will never need to make peace owing to a shortage of war material.
>
> "The superiority of the enemy at present is principally due to their use of Tanks.
>
> "We have been actively engaged for a long period in working at producing this weapon (which is recognised as important), in adequate numbers.
>
> "We shall thus have an additional means for the successful continuance of the war, if we are compelled to continue it."

The following passage occurred in a German Order issued on August 12, 1918:

> "It has been found that the enemy's attacks have been successful solely because the Tanks surprised our infantry, broke through our ranks, and the infantry thought itself outflanked."

The German Press was also very generally inclined to attribute the German failure to the Allied use of Tanks, and their attitude is well illustrated by the following paragraph which appeared early in October, a time when German journalists seem to have been most carefully instructed from official quarters. It was their task to prepare the German people for surrender.

"The successes which the Allies have gained since the First Battle of Cambrai do not rest on any superior strategy on the part of Foch or on superiority in numbers, although the latter has undoubtedly contributed to it. The real reason has been the massed use of Tanks. Whereas the artillery can only cut wire and blot out trenches with an enormous expenditure of ammunition, the Tank takes all these obstacles with the greatest of ease, and will make broad paths in which the advancing infantry can follow. They are the most dangerous foe to hostile machine-guns. They can approach machine-gun nests and destroy them at close range. The great danger of the Tank is obvious when one considers that the defence of the front battle zone chiefly relies on the defensive value of the machine-guns, and that the armour of the Tank renders it invulnerable to rifle fire, and that only seldom and in exceptional cases is machine-gun fire effective. The infantry is therefore opposed to an enemy to whom it can do little or no harm."

II

The question of the place of Tanks in the next war has been answered with the greatest emphasis by some enthusisatic advocates of this arm.

The possession of a superior weapon, they say, ensures victory to the army which possesses it. In war, any army, even if led by a mediocre General, can safely meet an army of the previous century, though the old force be led by the greatest military genius of his age.

* "Napoleon was an infinitely greater general than Lord Raglan, yet Lord Raglan would, in 1855, have beaten any army Napoleon could have brought against him, because Lord Raglan's men were armed with the Minié rifle.

"Eleven years after Inkerman Moltke would have beaten Lord Raglan's army hollow, not because he was a greater soldier than Lord Raglan, but because his men were armed with the needle gun.

* *W.T.N.*

Epilogue

> "Had Napoleon, at Waterloo, possessed a company of Vickers machine-guns, he would have beaten Wellington, Blücher, and Schwartzenburg combined, as completely as Lord Kitchener beat the Soudanese at Omdurman. It would have been another 'massacre of the innocents.'"

In every case, they say, the superior weapon would have defeated the great tactician before he had had time to show his mettle. To repeat the words of the German journalist: "Their infantry would be opposed to an enemy to whom it could do little or no harm."

We shall not discuss here the materialistic argument, except to say that if it were entirely true, savages and badly-equipped Tribesmen would never have completely beaten well-armed civilised troops. Yet they have done so on frequent occasions. Witness the First Afghan War, the Zulu Wars, the American-Indian Wars, and a host of minor actions. Material only wins hands down when the *moral* of the side possessing it is at least fairly comparable with that of its opponents. Otherwise Byzantium with its "Greek Fire" would have ruled the world.

According to this "material" school of thought, we have in Tanks our superior weapon. They will be developed upon more than one line, and we shall have cross-country equivalents for all arms and services except heavy artillery, the Navy and the Air Force.

Mr. Hugh Pollard, writing in the *English Review* of January 1919 states the case of the mechanical warfare and Tank enthusiasts with great vigour and ingenuity.

> "Even at present there is no effective answer to Tanks but possibly other Tanks, and in the Tank we have rediscovered a modern application of a very old principle. The Tank is the most economical method of using man-power in war, and it also affords the highest possible percentage of invulnerability to the soldiers engaged.
>
> "The armament problems of the future will be limited to three fleets of armoured machines, in which a very limited highly specialised number of men operate the largest possible number of weapons in the most effective way. Armoured fleets at sea, armoured aeroplanes, and armoured landships, or Tanks—these will be our forces for war."

Tanks of various speeds and carrying various weapons, will replace both infantry and cavalry, for one full-size modern heavy Tank holding eight men has the aggressive power of a hundred infantry with rifles, bayonets, bombs and Lewis guns. The Whippet has about the same speed and radius as cavalry, and one Whippet holding two men " could withstand the onslaught of a cavalry regiment and kill it off to the last man and the last horse without being exposed to the least danger or inconvenience." We shall soon regard the heroic tale of how men once exposed their defenceless bodies to machine-gun fire and shells, and depended for the élan of their assault upon the weight of human limbs and the endurance of human muscles, as almost legendary.

> "Most people think of a Tank as a rather ludicrous but effective engine of war. They look upon it as a mechanical novelty, and are content to assume that the Tank of to-day is not much of an improvement upon the earliest Tanks of the Somme battle, and that it is a war implement of indifferent importance. The real facts are entirely different, for the Tank of to-day is simply an infant, a lusty two-year-old, and there is no mechanical limit to its future. This may seem the remark of a fanatic, but it is perfectly true. . . .
>
> "The Tank of to-day is a little thing compared with the obvious developments which will result in the Tank of the future, but even as it stands to-day it is the most economical fighting-machine yet devised. A Tank uses petrol instead of muscle, and it extracts the highest possible fighting or killing value out of the men inside it; they can give their blows without being exposed to injury in return, and, above all things, they can fight while moving—a thing outside the powers of the infantry or guns of the land forces."

The arguments of those who maintain that the Tank must always be dependent upon the older arms are nearly all based upon the assumption that the Tank is already limited. " It is pointed out that they cannot cross rivers, that they are not proof against shell-fire, against mines, against special forms of attack. The answer is that the Tank of to-day may be subject to casualties, but all the skill and resources of the German nation have failed to produce an effective answer to Tanks, that river after river has been crossed, that line after line of 'impregnable' defences have fallen, that deeply écheloned artillery particularly arranged to fight Tanks has failed before Tank and aeroplane attack. We come to a war of sea, air, and land fleets acting in co-operation. Anti-Tank artillery is vulnerable to armoured planes. The big commercial freight-carrying planes of the future might even fly light Tanks into the heart of hostile territory. The unprotected men and arms of the present day must disappear."

And here another question is suggested—a question upon which the civilian ought to satisfy himself. Let us for the moment assume that it is superiority in weapons, not better generalship, not a more stubborn " will to win," that decides the fate of war.

What reason have we to suppose that it will be superiority in Tanks and not in some other weapon, in aeroplanes for example, that will decide the next conflict?

At present, when we try to imagine war upon a foreign army waged on one side by air alone, we encounter a dozen mechanical difficulties even in our attempted picture of the first stages: the enormous paraphernalia of bases, the ground-staff, fuel, weather conditions, difficulties of landing, and finally, what is perhaps the fundamental difficulty.

The aeroplane alone, like the big gun, is not an engine by whose means it is possible to come into decisive contact with an enemy who chooses to remain on the ground. The rabbits can always go to earth when they see the gliding shadow of the hawk.

Till both sides are equipped solely for air combat, Tanks or infantry will still be needed to play the part of ferret.

But these difficulties will almost certainly some day be overcome.

When they have been solved, then the day of the comparatively cumbersome Tank, with its dependence upon shipping and rail transport, will be over. But that will not be in our time, we are assured. To us, therefore, " War in the Air " remains of a somewhat academic interest. We have got to see to it that we survive the present.

For can the most optimistic of us truthfully declare, as he casts his eye over the world, as he looks from Middle Europe to the Far East, from Russia to Mexico, from the Balkans to Egypt, or from Asia Minor to the confines of India, that we need not even consider the possibility of a war within his own generation? Alas, no!

Now having for the moment dismissed the purely air war from our calculations, we can be pretty certain that a war between civilised countries fought within that period would not differ utterly from the war which is just over, and that a war between a civilised and an uncivilised country would differ from it only along well-known lines.

We have heard a good deal of evidence which makes it appear certain that, every other factor having cancelled out, the fact that the French and British possessed Tanks and the Germans did not, was just enough to win the last war for the

Allies. Let us then sedulously cultivate the grub of the present that we may survive to see the more glorious butterfly of the future—perhaps the aerial Tank. Shall we neglect the Tank because it seems likely that in this (as please Heaven in most other affairs) our sons will go one better?

The British and French led, and in 1919 still lead, absolutely with Tanks.

If we like to carry on, we have such a start both in design and manufacturing experience, that we could easily make it impossible for any other nation to draw abreast of us during the period after which we are assuming the "Tank Age" in military evolution may conceivably be over.

It is, of course, impossible to be too discreet as to the new machines which have already been made and tested, or as to the new projects which exist.

Perhaps the position can be best indicated by saying that progress has been so rapid of late that those who know would probably be delighted to sell any number of Mark V. Tanks to a prospective enemy.

III

The present writers are ignorant whether we have determined to keep our lead or no. Shall we have the foresight, when it comes to the remodelling of the Army, to give to Tanks the place they ought to hold in it? Shall we be willing to spend money on experiments, money which we must spend if we want to keep that lead? Will the Tanks be given the facilities for both mechanical and tactical training that they ought to have? We may so easily slide back into our old groove. It is always hard to turn to new ways, and to give a preponderating place in the "New Model" to Tanks, would certainly be to effect a very radical change. There does seem to be a certain fear that the Army and the public may feel that the Tanks are all right for War, but hardly the thing for soldiering.

And yet how well the requirements of a strong force of Tanks would in reality fit the kind of framework which the wisest minds seem agreed should be our Army of the future. We ought to have, they say, a small and highly specialised Standing Army, and behind that a vast Citizen Army on the basis of the Territorial system. What weapon could be more suitably added to the gun and the aeroplane than the Tank in the Regular Army? Our Standing Army would thus consist of a nucleus of mechanical experts.

Nor need the question of finance ever rise spectre-like between us and the idea of a strong force of Tanks, for the Tank is an absurdly cheap weapon compared with its co-efficient of infantry.

But there is another direction in which, if it claim any considerable place in our Standing Army, the Tank must make good. That Army may at any moment be called upon to undertake police work in any part of the world.

The Tank, even the old Mark I., is, as we saw at Gaza, suitable for desert warfare. The Mark V. and Whippets with General Denikin's force in Russia have been prodigiously successful, and there are probably few species of campaign against a semi-civilised enemy in which the newer "Medium" Tanks would not do admirably.

Another point is that "minor wars" are fought by us with as much avoidance of bloodshed as is compatible with the bringing of our opponents to reason.

A weapon which admittedly affected the *moral* even of admirably disciplined troops like the Germans to a phenomenal degree, is particularly well adapted to this purpose.

It is infinitely more humane to appal a rioter or a savage by showing him a Tank than to shoot him down with an inoffensive-looking machine-gun.*

There is yet one final consideration.

The reader may still very properly object: "Though the Tank may, as it rather begins to appear, have been the decisive factor in the last War, and though it might be very convenient to use it again, before we put our money on it, literally and metaphorically, for the future, are we sure that it is a weapon which suits the British soldier? Time was when at the direction of Military Experts we spent a great deal of money upon the building of forts at home and abroad which were never of the slightest use to any one, because they did not suit our style of fighting. What reason have we to suppose that we shall like the Tank as a permanent addition on a large scale to the equipment of our Army?" The present authors consider this line of criticism a very proper one. They differ from the "hard shell" advocates of the superior weapon in considering it of the greatest importance that the balance and poise of the broadsword should suit the hand that is to wield it. But they believe that the Tank, like the ship and the aeroplane, is a weapon peculiarly suited to the British temperament, and that fundamentally it was for that reason that we, and not some other nation, first evolved it. For good or ill, our Commanders both on land and sea have certain peculiarities. Our men dislike standing on the defensive. They hate digging,

* Tradition relates that had General Swinton had his way, the Tanks for Palestine would have had hideous faces and minatory texts from the Koran painted upon them.

and in the present War were beaten by the Germans every time at this particularly unpopular form of activity. Also, almost worse than digging, do they hate carrying things on their backs, and we are noted among all nations as the least tolerant of burdens. All these peculiarities have filled the ranks of the Navy and of the Cavalry, and all these peculiarities are suited by the aeroplanes and the Land Ships. Our Commanders, like their men, prefer to be the attackers, and like a war of movement. Almost the whole creed of Nelson, our most popular fighting-hero, was expressed in his assertion that the first and last duty of an Admiral was to find out the enemy's fleet and to attack it, and in his famous signal, "Engage the enemy more closely."

Further, our leaders particularly and temperamentally dislike a large butcher's bill. It was, indeed, their extreme reluctance to send unprotected men to meet the hail of bullets from German machine-guns, that lay behind most of the ostensible reasons for which the Tanks were first given a trial. It was a deciding factor. We may even perhaps say without seeming fantastic that it was their inhumanity which cost the Germans the War. They had no bowels of compassion, and were just as ready to send the "infantry equivalent" (say seventy unprotected men) over the top as they were to put in seven men enclosed in armour. To them it was the coldest question of military expediency. Purely upon military considerations they decided against the seven clad in armour. Our Commanders, though in theory they were inclined to agree with the German Higher Command, though they recognised the ultimate cruelty of the policy of "cheap war," and knew, with Nelson, that they had not come to the Western Front to preserve their lives, were yet tempted by the idea of using steel and petrol in place of flesh and blood. More than once in the course of the chequered career of the Tanks it was this consideration which saved the Corps from extinction.

But it is not, of course, enough that the Tank offers protection to those who fight in it. A trench or a hole in the ground will do the same. But the Tank is essentially a mobile weapon of *offence*. It is the weapon for the nation which does not fight willingly, but when it fights, fights to win, and to win quickly with as little bloodshed as possible. It is the weapon for men who, if they must fight, like to fight like intelligent beings still subjecting the material world to their will, and who are most unwillingly reduced to the rôles of mere marching automata, bearers of burdens and diggers of the soil, rôles from which the patient German did not seem averse.

IV

The creed of the present writers can be very briefly summarised. A considerable amount of evidence points to the conclusion that in the phase at which military science has arrived, and at which it will probably remain for at least a generation, a superior force of Tanks can always tip the scales of the military balance of power.

Within the period of a generation, a time may again come when we shall have to defend our lives and our liberties. We lead the world in the design and manufacture of Tanks. Let us not abandon that lead in the production and use of a vital weapon.

We know too well the tragic cost of one day of war, and it has been said that had we been visibly prepared the Germans would not have attacked.

Obviously we cannot be going to fall again so quickly into an old error. We certainly intend to be armed, but who can say that through sheer absence of mind it will not be with arquebuses? Surely not for the sake of Army precedent, for the sake of emphasising our pacific intentions, for the sake of saving a little money, or even—dearest of all—for the luxury of " not bothering " about our Army, must we lose our present unparalleled position of advantage. This advantage is not only a material one. The Tanks are accustomed to win. Do not let us throw away a fine tradition of victory.

Of all that in our agony of striving we gained by the way, let us lose nothing.

INDEX

AMERICAN Tanks, 122, 141, 145; in the Second Battle of Cambrai, 250, 251, 252; in the Battle of the Selle, 262, 263, 264
Amiens, the Battle of, 191–215
Arras, the Battle of, 48–62
Australians, the, and the Tanks, 60, 179–183, 197–199, 207, 208, 209, 210
Australian co-operation with the French, 185
Aveluy driving school, 168

Ballon d'Essai, the, 179
Bapaume, the Battle of, 224–227
Battalion, Brigade and Unit Histories, quotations from, 85, 91, 111, 164, 167, 170, 171, 174, 180, 181, 197, 198, 200, 201, 206, 208, 227, 229, 235, 236, 239, 240, 241, 246, 247, 269, 270
" Bridge of Tanks," the, 245
Buchan, Colonel, quotations from his *History of the War*, 32, 73, 74, 75, 146, 161

Cambrai, the First Battle of, 100–117; the German counter-attack, 117–120; the Second Battle of, 243–256

Drocourt-Quéant Line, breaking the, 228–238
Duel between Tanks, the First, 173
Dummy Tanks, 63

Epehy, the Battle of, 239–242
Exploits of individual Tanks, 28, 55, 58, 85, 86, 87, 163, 188, 199, 200, 201–206, 233, 247

Fifth Army Headquarters, the adverse report of, 89, 90
Fighting Side, the, 16, 121
Foch, Marshal, on the Tanks, 274
French Tank Corps, the, 135–141

Gaza, the Second and Third Battles of, 145–152
German Press, the, and the Tanks, 276
German Tanks, fights with, 172, 173, 259, 260

Germans, the, and the Tanks, 22, 23, 29, 60, 68, 216–222

Haig, Sir Douglas, the Despatches of, 13, 30, 76, 88, 99, 111, 118, 119, 176, 211, 212, 216, 238, 243, 249, 254, 262, 265, 269, 274
Harden, Herr Maximilian, on the Tanks, 275
" Hush " Operation, the proposed, on the Belgian coast, 69, 70, 71, 72

" Instructions for the training of the Tank Corps in France," 129–133

Le Cateau, the Second Battle of, 257, 261
Lewis Gun Detachments, 165
Littledale, Sergeant, his account of Tank Training at Bermicourt, 39, 40, 41
Losses of the Tank Corps, 177
Loucheur, M., on the Tanks, 274
Ludendorff, General, and the Tanks, 213, 217
" Lusitania " Tank, the exploit of the, 55, 56, 57, 58

Machine Gun Corps, Heavy Section of the, 19; Heavy Branch of the, 41
March 1918, the British Retreat of, 159–173
Messines, the Battle of, 63–68
Moreuil, the Battle of, 185, 190
Moroccans and Tanks, 175
" Musical Box " Tank, the adventures of, 201–206

Palestine, Tanks in, 145–152
Persons Mentioned in the Course of the Narrative :—
Allenby, General, 149; Archbold, Corporal S., D.C.M., 165; Arnim, General von, 75; Arnold, Lieutenant C. B., 201–206
Bacon, Admiral, 8, 9, 70; Baker-Carr, Colonel, 62, 92, 112; Bayliss, Second Lieutenant, 166; Bingham, Captain, M.C., 165; Birly, Captain Oswald, 245; Bourgon, General, 189; Bradley, Colonel, 16, 25; Broome, General, 92; Brough,

Colonel, 25; Brown, Captain F.C., M.C., 172; Bryce, Lieut.-Colonel, 198, 199; Byng, General Sir Julian, 100, 115

Capper, General, 46; Carney, Driver, 201–206; Carter, Colonel, 178, 193; Carter, Second Lieutenant, 166; Cassell, Second Lieutenant, 200; Ching, Second Lieutenant S. S., 58; Churchill, Mr., 8, 9, 10, 12; Courage, Brigadier-General, 118, 185, 186, 187

Dalton, Captain, 188; Dawson, Second Lieutenant, 166; Debeney, General, 186, 189; Denikin, General, 281; Denny, Colonel, M.C., M.P., 210, 250, 251; Diplock, Mr., 6, 8

Eade, Lieutenant Percy, 199; Edwards, Second Lieutenant, 182; Elles, General, 41, 44, 83, 95, 100, 107, 108, 109, 110, 112, 117, 144, 145, 154, 169, 173, 186, 275; Estienne, General, 135–141

Forsyth-Major, Major, 146; Fuller, Lieut.-Colonel, 103

Gould, Second Lieutenant, 200; Groves, Captain, 175

Haldane, Lieut.-General Aylmer, 62; Hankey, Brigadier-General, 194; Hankey, Colonel Sir Maurice, 8; Hardress-Lloyd, Brigadier-General, 213; Hatton-Hall, Captain, 252, 258, 263; Hedges, Second Lieutenant W. R., 240; Henriques, Captain, 20, 26; Hetherington, Captain, 6, 9; Hickson, Second Lieutenant, 226; Hotblack, Major, D.S.O., M.C., 37, 41, 70, 194, 195, 253, 254

Johnson, Lieut.-Colonel Philip, 70; Jones, Second Lieutenant, 175

Latham, Sergeant F., M.M., 57, 58; Le Maistre, General, 177; Lipsett, Major-General, 194; Luck, Second Lieutenant C. W., 247; Lyon, Private W., M.M., 165

Macavity, Major, 245; McFee, Mr., 8; McLagan, Major-General E. G. S., 215; Martell, Lieutenant, 260; Marwitz, General von der, 117; Maxse, General, 92; Mecredy, Second Lieutenant C., 189; Mitchell, Lieutenant, 172, 173; Monash, General, 194, 210; Murray, General, 147

Naedale, Lieutenant T. C., 252, 263; Noel, Sergeant J., D.C.M., 61; Norton, Major, 168; Nutt, Major, 146

O'Kelly, Colonel, 164

Pankhurst, Mrs., 10; Pitt, Lieutenant, 164; Ponsonby, General John, 112 Rawlinson, General Sir Henry, 214, 215; Rees-Williams, Lieutenant O. L., 233; Renouf, Major, 16, 17; Ribbans, Gunner, 201–206; Riddle, Second Lieutenant, 247; Robertson, Captain, V.C., 96, 97; Rowe, Captain, 259

Saunders, Lieutenant, 236; Sasse, Major, D.S.O., 259; Sewell, Lieutenant C. H., V.C., 233; Skeggs, Major, 247; Smallwood, Second Lieutenant G. F., 240; Smith, Captain G. A., 235; Smith, Second Lieutenant Henderson, M.C., 195; Stern, Sir Albert, 10, 14, 44, 46; Stewart, Ian, 169; Storm, Second Lieutenant, 164; Strachan, Captain, C. H., 236; Swinton, General E. D., 6, 7, 8, 10, 11, 16, 17, 19, 21

Tennyson-d'Eyncourt, Sir Eustace, 9, 46; Tritton, Mr., 9; Tulloch, Major, 6, 7, 8

Uzielli, Lieutenant C. F., 235

Van Zeller, Second Lieutenant T. E., M.C., 163

Weber, Second Lieutenant, 55; West, Captain Richard Annesley, D.S.O., 226; West, Lieut.-Colonel R. A., D.S.O., M.C., 236; Whatley, Sergeant, 247; Whyte, Second Lieutenant, M.C., 164; Wilkes, Major G. L., D.S.O., 98; Williams, Major-General, 62; Wilson, Lieutenant, 175; Wilson, Major, 9; Worsap, Second Lieutenant, 259

"Pill-boxes," 75, 91, 92, 93
Poelcapelle Road, the disaster on the, 97, 98
Pollard, Mr. Hugh, on the future of Tanks, 277, 278

Reconnaissance Branch, the, 4
Reconnaissance Officer, the narrative of a, 168
Reconnaissance Service, the, 41, 79, 80

St. Julien, the Tanks' success at, 82, 83
"Savage Rabbits," 154
Scheuch, General, on the Tanks, 275
Selle, the Battle of the, 262–265
Soldier's treachery, a, 77
Somme, the Battle of the, 24–29
Spectator, the, on the Battle of Gaza, 151

Tactics, the New, 161
Tanks, *the Inception and Progress of the* :—
 The inception of the, 1; different types of the, 2; the uses of, 3, 4; the training of the crews of, 4; pre-1914 designs for, 6; the first

Index 287

steps in the designing of. 7, 8; the War Office and the, 8-11; the Admiralty and the, 8-12; further steps in the progress of the, 12-23; 150 sanctioned, 21; production, the problem of, 42, 43; Mechanical War Supply Department, 14, 43, 44; Tank Committees, the, 46; Mark I. Tanks, 12, 15, 18, 27, 48, 65; Mark II. Tanks, 65; Mark IV. Tanks, 64, 65, 68, 123; Mark V. Tanks, the uses of, 2, 3, 4, 123, 177; Mark VI. Tanks, 123; Whippets, 123; Fascines, the manufacture of, 102, 103; Cribs, 177; Central Workshops, 124, 127, 177, 271

Tank actions, minor, 178
Tank Commanders, Maintenance Course, etc., for, 130, 133
'Tank Corps Intelligence Summary," 257, 260, 267, 268
Tank crew, the military history of the member of a, 127, 129
Tank Officers, narratives by, 34, 51, 52, 53, 112, 114, 187
Tank, the itinerary of a, 125, 127
Tanks : destroying the, 163; the future of the, 273, 283

Towns, Villages, etc., occurring in the Text :—

Acheux, 34; Achicourt, 52, 53; Achiet-le-Grand, 230, 231; Achiet-le-Petit, 225, 227; Adelpare Farm, 186, 188; Albert, 167, 168, 191, 228; Amiens, 172, 174, 176; Annoux, 248; Arival Wood, 246, 247; Arrachis Wood, 188; Auchonvillers, 35, 170; Auchy, 165; Avesnes, 271
Bailleul, 166; Bapaume, 167, 168, 233; Bavay, 271; Bayonvillers, 198, 199; Beaucamp Ridge, 246; Beaucourt, 35, 36, 200; Beaufort, 201, 209; Beaumont-Hamel, 23, 32, 34, 36, 170; Beaurevoir, 255; Bellenglise, 249, 254; Bellicourt, 244, 249, 250, 253, 254; Belloy, 178; Bermicourt, 39, 61, 63, 125, 128, 129, 177; Beugnâtre, 233; Bihucourt, 230; Blangy, 167; Bohain, 261, 262; Bois d'Abbé, 174; Bois d'Aquenne, 174; Bois de Harpon, 187, 188; Bony, 255; Bourlon Wood and Village, 101, 111, 115, 116, 117, 119, 244, 248; Bouzencourt, 170; Brancourt, 258, 259; Bray, 168, 169, 228, 232; Brie, 163; Bucquoy, 178, 224, 225; Bullecourt, 59, 60, 61, 159, 160; Bultiaux River, the, 269; Buvignies, 270

Cachy, 172; Caix, 164; Canal du Nord, the, 101, 244-248; Cantaing, 115; Cartigny, 162, 163; Cérisy Valley, 194, 198; Chipilly, 209; Chuignies, 230; Chuignolles, 206, 207, 228, 230; Cockcroft, the, 92, 93; Colincamps, 170; Contay, 178, 187; Courcelles, 226, 227, 230; Croisilles, 61, 232
Demilieue, 263; Desert Wood, 106; Domeny, 211; Dury Ridge, 237
Ecoust, 234; Epehy, 162, 239; Epinoy, 248; Erin, 69, 103, 125; Etinehem, 210
Fampoux, 233; Fanny's Farm, 66, 67; Faucourt, 206; Favreuil, 233; Fesny, 268; Flers, 28; Flesquières, 109, 111, 119, 244, 246, 247; Fleury Redoubt, 56; Fontaine-Notre-Dame, 115, 116, 119, 248; Framerville, 208; Frémicourt, 233; Fresnoy, 239, 241; Frezenberg, 87, 89, 94
Gauche Wood, 118; Ginchy, 27; Glencorse Wood, 87, 94, 95; Gomiécourt, 230; Gouzeaucourt, 117, 118, 244; Gonnelieu, 248; Graincourt, 111, 113, 244; Gueudecourt, 28, 33; Guillemont, 241, 250; Guise, 261
Hamelincourt, 230; Hamel Wood and Village, 180, 183; Hangard Wood, 173, 175; Happegarbes, 266; Happy Valley, 232; Harbonnières, 164, 198; Hargicourt, 240; Harpon Wood, 187, 188; Harp, the, 54; Haspres, 264; Hautmont, 271; Havrincourt, 101, 106, 111, 112, 117; Haynecourt, 248; Hazebrouck, 176; Hébuterne, 170; Hecq, 267; Hedecourt, 59, 60; Herleville Wood, 229; Hervilly Wood, 162; High Wood, 30; Hillock Farm, 92, 93
Ignaucourt Valley, 201; Inchy, 248; Inverness Copse, 94
Jerk House, 95; Jolimetz, 268; Juniper Cottage, 96
Kemmel, 166, 193; Knoll, the, 241, 244, 249, 250
La Fère, 160; Lagnicourt, 236; Lamotte, 198; Landrecies, 266, 267, 268; Langemarck, 91; La Signy Farm, 35; Lateau Wood, 110; La Vacquerie, 119; Le Quesneu, 200; Le Quesnoy, 207, 265, 266, 268; Les-Trois-Boqueleaux, 186, 188; Le Tréport, 128, 129; Lihons, 208, 211; Logeast Wood, 227; Longâtte, 234; Loop, the, 24-26; Luce River, the, 194
Mailly-Raineval, 186; Mailly-Maillet Wood, 170; Marcelcave, 198; Marcoing, 119; Marcourt, 164·

Maricourt, 167; Martinpuich, 27; Masnières, 110, 117: Masvillers, 164; Maubeuge, 191, 262, 272; Menin, 261; Mercatel, 228; Merlaincourt, 164; Merlincourt, 129; Merville, 168; Meteren, 166; Metz, 117; Molain, 263; Monchy, 59, 62, 233, 254; Mons, 272; Montbrehain, 255, 256; Mont des Cats, 166; Montdidier, 191; Mont du Hibou, 92, 93; Mont Rouge, 166; Morcourt, 194, 197; Mormal Forest, 264–269; Mory Copse, 232; Moyenneville, 224, 227

Neuve Eglise, 166; Neuville–Vitesse, 58, 59, 233; Neuvilly, 264; Niergnies, 259, 260; Nieppe Forest, 168

Oisy, 266; Oosthoek Wood, 77, 78; Oosttaverne, 66, 67

Passchendaele, 87, 97, 99; Pear-shaped Trench, 180; Peizière, 162; Péronne, 194; Poelcapelle, 96, 97, 98; Pozières, 27; Prémont, 258; Premy Chapel, 246, 247; Preux, 267; Proyart, 206, 207, 210, 211

Quadrilateral, the, 27, 239, 241; Quennemont Farm and Ridge, 241, 244, 249, 250, 253, 254

Ravenel, 178; Reutelbeek, the, 96, 97; Ribecourt, 246; Riencourt, 59, 60; Riquerval Wood, 262; Rœuse, 60; Ronssoy, 239, 240; Rosières, 208; Rossignol, 170; Rumilly, 110

St. Julien, 87, 91, 98; St. Legér, 61; St. Martin's Wood, 229; St. Pol, 176, 193; St. Quentin, 159; St. Quentin Canal, the, 249–251; St. Quentin Wood, 241; St. Ribert Wood, 186; St. Souplet, 263; Sambre and Oise Canal, 262; Sambre, the River, 266; Sauchy-Lestrée, 248; Sauvillers, 186, 188; Schelde, the, 264; Selency, 239, 241; Sensée Valley, 234, 236; Serain, 258; Seranvillers, 110; Solesmes, 264; Staden, 87; Steenbeek, the, 80, 82, 87

Thetford, 17; Thiepval, 32, 33; Tournai, 272; Triangle Farm, 92, 93, 95

Vaire Wood, 180, 183; Valenciennes, 264, 266, 268; Vaulx-Vraucourt, 235; Vauvillers, 208; Vaux, 185; Vendhuille, 249; Villeret, 239; Villers Bretonneux, 164, 172, 173, 174, 179, 195; Villers Guislain, 118, 119, 248; Vimy, 55

Wailly, 61, 129; Wanbeke, 67; Warfusée, 164, 198; Warvillers, 201, 209; Westhoek, 87; Wool, 120, 127, 128, 133, 155; Wytschaete, 66, 67, 76

Zonnebeke, 94

Tunnelling Company (184th), the work of the, 78

"Unditching Beam," the, 78

Vimy, the Canadians at, 55

Wailly, the training ground at, 61
Watson, Major, on the Battle of Bullecourt, 60
Weekly Tank Notes, quotations from, 21, 22, 74, 81, 92, 116, 171, 181, 183, 193, 201–206, 221, 261, 276
Wig, the comedy of a, 110, 111
Wrisberg, General, on the Tanks, 275

Ypres Salient, the sand model of the, 80
Ypres, the Third Battle of, 73–99
Yvrench, the training centre at, 24

www.ingramcontent.com/pod-product-compliance
Lightning Source LLC
Chambersburg PA
CBHW050334230426
43663CB00010B/1860